CRIMINALISAT
ADVANCED MAR

Critically exploring the work of
Loïc Wacquant

Edited by Peter Squires and John Lea

First published in Great Britain in 2013 by

Policy Press
University of Bristol
6th Floor
Howard House
Queen's Avenue
Bristol BS8 1SD
UK
Tel +44 (0)117 331 5020
Fax +44 (0)117 331 5367
e-mail pp-info@bristol.ac.uk
www.policypress.co.uk

North American office:
Policy Press
c/o The University of Chicago Press
1427 East 60th Street
Chicago, IL 60637, USA
t: +1 773 702 7700
f: +1 773-702-9756
e:sales@press.uchicago.edu
www.press.uchicago.edu

Reprinted 2014

British Library Cataloguing in Publication Data
A catalogue record for this book is available from the British Library.

Library of Congress Cataloging-in-Publication Data
A catalog record for this book has been requested.

ISBN 978 1 44730 000 7 paperback

Cover design by Policy Press
Front cover: image kindly supplied by www.istockphoto.com
Printed and bound in Great Britain by CMP, Poole

Contents

Response

Acknowledgements

The editors would like to thank all the organisers, contributors and participants who assisted with or took part in the Symposium on Advanced Marginality at the University of Brighton in September 2009, at which versions of most of these chapters were first presented.

Notes on contributors

Simon Hallsworth is Professor of Social Research and Director of the Centre for Social and Evaluation Research in the Department of Applied Social Science, London Metropolitan University.

Lynn Hancock is Lecturer in Sociology and Criminology in the Department of Sociology and Social Policy, University of Liverpool.

John Lea is Visiting Professor of Criminology in the School of Applied Social Science, University of Brighton.

Denise Martin is Senior Lecturer in Criminology in the School of Applied Social Science, University of Brighton.

Lynda Measor is Reader in Sociology in the School of Applied Social Science, University of Brighton.

Gerry Mooney is Senior Lecturer in Social Policy and Criminology and Staff Tutor in Social Sciences, for the Open University in Scotland.

Markus–Michael Müller is Postdoctoral Researcher at the Centre for Area Studies at the Universität Leipzig, researching policing, violence and state formation in Latin America.

John Pitts is the Vauxhall Professor of Socio-legal Studies, University of Bedfordshire.

John J. Rodger is Reader in Social Policy and Sociology and Associate Dean (Learning and Teaching) in the School of Social Sciences, University of the West of Scotland.

Vincenzo Ruggiero is Professor of Sociology in the Department of Health and Social Sciences, Middlesex University.

Peter Squires is Professor of Criminology and Public Policy in the School of Applied Social Science, University of Brighton.

Kevin Stenson is Professor of Criminology at London Metropolitan University and a Visiting Professor at the University of Kent.

Loïc Wacquant is Professor of Sociology and Research Associate at the Institute for Legal Research, Boalt Law School, University of California at Berkeley; he is also a researcher at the Centre européen de sociologie et de science politique in Paris.

Paula Wilcox is Principal Lecturer in Criminology in the School of Applied Social Science, University of Brighton.

ONE

Introduction: reading Loïc Wacquant – opening questions and overview

Peter Squires and John Lea

Most of the chapters in this collection originated from a conference on the recent work of Loïc Wacquant organised by the University of Brighton Criminology Group in September 2010.The decision to hold this conference arose from a reading of his recent book, *Punishing the poor* (Wacquant, 2009a), which, together with his earlier *Urban outcasts* (Wacquant, 2007), provide one of the most systematic and detailed accounts available in sociology of the impact of neoliberalism on the welfare state and the penal system in the US and Western Europe.

By now it is absolutely clear that earlier characterisations of neoliberalism as simply the 'retreat of the state' were wide of the mark.Although selective reductions in state spending and privatisation in various forms have been an important feature, of much more significance have been changes in the role of the state, in particular the emergence of new strategies of control and coercion. From the standpoint of a criminology and sociology of welfare, which have spent well over a decade focused on various forms of decentralisation and privatisation,Wacquant's return to a focus on the state as the key institution of surveillance and coercion is most welcome as is his focus on neoliberalism as involving not the retreat of the state but the development of new techniques of coercion and social control. In this light neoliberalism can be seen as a fundamentally coercive strategy aimed at demolishing many of the social rights of the welfare state and weakening the ability of the working class to defend itself against wage cuts and unemployment. These are seen by the defenders of neoliberalism as necessary 'medicine' to regain economic competitiveness under conditions of globalisation. One consequence has been the creation of a 'precariat' (see Standing, 2011), characterised by extremes of 'advanced' social and economic marginality and whose life is spent in and out of insecure, temporary, low-wage labour and unemployment. Variously termed the 'underclass' or the 'socially excluded', the precariat is typically the major focus of penal and social policy. For Wacquant, as for most of the contributors to this collection, the management of the precariat is 'the' or at least 'a' major component of penal and social policy.

It is for this reason that Wacquant sees the neoliberal state as at its core a 'penal state', managing the precariat through a mixture of prisonfare and workfare. Prisonfare is the turning away of the penal system from older welfarist themes of rehabilitation and reintegration into secure employment and towards a process fundamentally concerned with 'warehousing' the permanently unemployed sections of the precariat: the penalisation of poverty. There are continuities with Feeley and Simon (1992) here, and, of course, Jonathan Simon's more recent (2007) account of 'governing through crime'. Those sections of the precariat not in prison face workfare, the transformation of welfare citizenship as protection and insurance rights to conditionality on job seeking at low wages.

Wacquant is attentive to the symbolic and ideological dimensions – the role of 'race', the media portrayals of welfare dependency and a *penal pornography* of criminal offenders – of this coercive management of the poor. Part of this ideological onslaught is a campaign to persuade the poor to accept responsibility for their own plight, to reconcile themselves to the growing social and urban inequality and the life chances of the precariat. Another aspect is the attempt to persuade the middle classes and the powerful elites that neoliberal policy is in their interest and enhances their security. In this latter respect Wacquant characterises the neoliberal penal state as a 'centaur state', the mythical animal whose upper half was human and lower half was beast. The analogy was first used by Machiavelli (and subsequently by Gramsci) to refer to the diversity of strategies of rule deployed by the successful state towards various social classes combining a judicious mixture of coercion and consent. In Wacquant's usage the analogy refers to a neoliberal state that deploys coercion against the precariat and the marginalised poor while continuing to retain liberal strategies of consent towards the middle and upper classes.

Some emerging questions

Wacquant's work has been prolific, challenging and very wide-ranging and, in a short overview such as this, it is not possible to address all of the commentary, critique, engagement, application, development or elaboration of his ideas.

In this book we offer a series of commentaries that explore Wacquant's work and its implications in a variety of different ways. Chapters focus on the theorising of neoliberal governance and the role of the state; they discuss the politics of punitiveness and the de-civilising character of neoliberalism; the condition of urban marginality and social insecurity; and they dissect the 'pornographic' discourses of poverty and indolence which feed into the euphemistic double-speak deployed by governmental strategies for welfare 'reform'. Yet they also discuss some of the less thoroughly developed areas of Wacquant's writing regarding the gendered character of social disciplining and also the question of resistance. Finally, following in the tracks of this 'Americanised' neoliberalism as it makes its way into the 'global south', we explore some aspects of the politics and practices of law, order and penalisation in Latin America.

The scope of the work with which we engage is framed by Wacquant's two major studies, *Urban outcasts* and *Punishing the poor*. This is important because the existing English language commentaries emerging within criminology have thus far focused either primarily on the 'penal studies' aspects of *Punishing the poor* and *Prisons of poverty*, for example, in a special issue of *Criminology and Criminal Justice* (volume 10, number 4) and Nicola Lacey's analysis of comparative penal trends in the *British Journal of Sociology* (Lacey, 2010), or alternatively, they have arisen as responses to and commentaries on Wacquant's 'Theoretical coda' to *Punishing the poor*, published in the journal *Theoretical Criminology* (volume 10, number 1, 2010). The fact that we have tried to take on a wider canvas of Wacquant's work has raised further questions given the very different character of the two books. This has raised both theoretical and methodological issues, not to mention a broader series of substantive concerns.

But first, and briefly, it is worth reviewing just what the existing commentaries have had to say. The series of articles in the special editions of *Criminology and Criminal Justice* and *Theoretical Criminology* raised several questions but emphasised overall that they saw themselves, above all, as contributing to the Wacquantian project of resisting the further disciplinary turn in welfare, critiquing the penalisation of poverty and contesting the neoliberal myths of the 'new law-and-order reason' currently being disseminated (Cheliotis, 2010, p 327). This is a project that we fundamentally share and support.

First, David Nelken (2010) has sought to challenge Wacquant's account of the global dissemination of 'Americanised' law-and-order orthodoxies into Europe and Latin America. His particular case, like the argument of Campbell (2010) (discussed later), is that Wacquant has rather oversimplified the account of 'policy transfer' and that the penalisation agenda may have less overall application in Europe where the policing and moral behaviourism agendas are probably uppermost. Latin America may well be a different story again (see Müller [Chapter Ten] and Squires [Chapter Eleven], this volume), but for Europe, at least, while welfarist traditions were always far more established than in the US, they have provided, on the whole, some bulwarks against rampant penalisation and the associated punitive discourses, even if we should be wary of perpetuating rather over-romanticised myths of 'the welfare state'. Recent commentaries under the 'criminalisation of social policy' label (Rodger, 2008), drawing attention to the disciplinary and/or exclusionary functions of public welfare, offer an important corrective here.

Lacey (2010) and Newburn's (2010) arguments pose some similar questions of Wacquant's analysis, particularly in the light of the substantial variations in the rates of 'mass incarceration' across the US's 50 states (Newburn, 2010, pp 346-9). In effect there may be several different versions of the 'penal state' while 'neoliberalism' might produce differing outcomes when established in different global contexts – detailed comparative analysis may be a necessary complement to Wacquant's more general theory. Finally, they each argue the theory also needs complementing by a politics: it is not enough to read European changes as a creeping 'Americanisation' of law and order without showing how these influences work politically and institutionally (Lacey, 2010, p 780). As Newburn argues in respect of the advocacy for a US-style 'zero tolerance' policing agenda in the UK, while there may indeed have been some adoption of 'zero tolerance' rhetoric, there was rather less adoption of the practice. He attributes this to the historical, political, cultural and institutional factors working within UK policing, producing 'a consensus among senior police professionals ... which doubted the efficacy of an aggressive and narrowly enforcement-oriented approach to policing' (Newburn, 2010, p 344).

There are certainly parallels here with Pratt's commentary on Wacquant's account of the global dissemination of neoliberal penality (Pratt, 2011). Pratt contrasts Wacquant's analysis with that of Whitman (2003) and, arguing instead the case for a US punitive *exceptionalism*, attributes this to 'longer term historical trends, rather than the sudden ascendancy of neoliberalism' (Pratt, 2011, p 118). The historical evolution of state and federal relations in the US has rendered the penal system more 'vulnerable to populist intervention in the form of plebiscites, referenda and ... and prey to the agendas of vengeful victims' rights activists and other extra-governmental forces' (Pratt,

2011, p 118). In turn (and despite Wacquant's view that US capital punishment is 'structurally marginal and functionally superfluous'), Garland has also drawn on such a political and 'institutional relations' analysis to help explain the retention of the death penalty in many US states (Garland, 2005, p 363), an argument that also has some bearing on contemporary gun politics in the US, especially regarding the 40-plus states which license private citizens to carry concealed self-defence firearms (Squires, 2000).

In their contribution to the *Criminology and Criminal Justice* debate, Cheliotis and Xenakis (2010) specifically attempt to test the applicability of Wacquant's thesis to the case of Greece, a society they describe as 'semi-peripheral in the world economy' experiencing 'a different trajectory of capitalist development compared to core Western states' (2010, p 354). In a number of respects, Greece might bear some comparison with a number of Latin American countries, in that a virulent anti-communism, a civil war, the military coup and dictatorship have brought their own influences to bear on Greek penal history. So although Greece might now be said to share in the new 'Washington Consensus' of welfare retrenchment and punitive expansion as described by Wacquant, it has also known 'intense periods of punitiveness within living memory' and therefore 'punitive trends anticipated the recent advent of neoliberal policy making in the country' (2010, pp 354-5). Accordingly the authors argue that neoliberalism is somewhat insufficient as a full explanation of punitiveness in Greece. The broader point is that the analysis of neoliberal influences on punitiveness and penal expansion has to be reconciled with localised histories, struggles, the 'culpability of local elites' and the structural context of the national economy. Neoliberalism is neither a force of nature nor a global inevitability. In any event, as Piven asserts, Wacquant may not really be 'explaining neoliberalism as a whole'; he is really talking mainly about 'a predatory logic of neoliberalism in the United States' (Piven, 2010, p 112), a point endorsed by Mayer (2010, p 96).

Loraine Gelsthorpe's commentary (2010) seeks to extend Wacquant's account to the experience of women. Wacquant's penal state is primarily comprised of young men whereas rather less is attention is paid to the (largely) female clients of the disciplinary assistantial or workfare regimes which typically complement the penal. In Wacquant's own words, 'the misery of American welfare and the grandeur of American prisonfare at century's turn are the two sides of the same political coin' (2009a, p 292). Yet less attention is paid to the unfortunate female inhabitants of the US carceral archipelago, an oversight all the more surprising given the rapid acceleration, 'outstripping male increases for most of the past decade' (Chesney-Lind, 2006, p 17) even during the hyper-incarceration phases of male mass imprisonment. And, as Chesney-Lind adds, the trend is also entirely unrelated to changes in female-recorded crime rates. Alongside this observation, Gelsthorpe's central argument is that 'the penal treatment of women is often indistinguishable from "welfare" treatment' (Gelsthorpe, 2010, p 380). Furthermore, in an argument that takes us back to more Foucauldian themes, she adds that 'the concepts of "welfare" and punishment ... have *always* been two sides of the same coin as far as women are concerned [and] regulatory powers go well beyond "welfare" and "punishment"' (2010, p 382, emphasis added; see also Garland, 1985; Squires, 1990). As Piven acknowledges, in any event, 'American maternal and nurturing policies for the poor have always been underdeveloped' (Piven, 2010, p 112), and often subject to the dictates of market discipline (Mayer, 2010).

Developing some of these lines of analysis, John Campbell seeks a sympathetic extension of Wacquant's ideas even beyond 'welfare' and 'punishment' and the control of poverty and criminal marginality. He takes as his starting point an expansion of Wacquant's definition of the neoliberal imperative so as to include four features: (i) economic deregulation; (ii) welfare retraction and recomposition; (iii) an expanded and intrusive penal apparatus; and (iv) 'the development of the cultural trope of individual responsibility' (Campbell, 2010, p 60). It is this selective 'rolling back' of the state that establishes, for Wacquant, the Janus-faced or *centaur state*, supposedly liberal and permissive at the head for the middle and upper classes, but disciplining and controlling for the poorest (Mayer, 2010, p 94). By contrast, Campbell wants to insert his conception of 'the *debtor state*, another appendage of the neoliberal state but one that [Wacquant] overlooks even though it has had a dramatic impact on middle class behaviour' (2010, p 59, emphasis in original). Furthermore, paralleling the perverse consequences of the penal state (costly and self-defeating mass incarceration), increasing indebtedness and widespread home foreclosure and business failure are associated with the rising neoliberal *debtor state* (2010, p 68). The debtor state has not served the middle class anywhere near as well as it has the rich, but beyond crude 'fraudulent consciousness' arguments ('we're all in it together', and 'spending more than we earn') to account for why these middle-class victims appear to vote contrary to their economic interests, there is little by way of an ideological account of *debtor state* functioning. Cohen directly addresses these ideological questions.

Stan Cohen's (2010) short commentary on Wacquant serves to question the ideological origins of the ideas that underpin the newly invented 'punitive common sense'. He seems less convinced of Wacquant's suggestion that the think-tanks and policy advisers of the 'Washington consensus' are responsible for the dissemination of an ideology of 'new moral behaviourism' to which the subjects of the new mass incarceration are now exposed. He evokes the gloomy prospect of a 'post-moral' age, and expresses a certain scepticism that prisoners today – or the poor and excluded in general – are encountering any consistent or coherent new discipline which might guide a process of rehabilitation or reform. On the contrary, in the prison, warehousing of offenders is simply that, warehousing.

Similar ideological questions are uppermost in Peck's polemical take on Wacquant's 'zombie neoliberalism' of the 'ambidextrous state' (Peck, 2010, pp 104-10). This concept of the 'ambidextrous state' derives in part from the double imperative of the capitalist state (referred to later) of securing the conditions for capital accumulation and profitability and political legitimation. To deliver on this potentially contradictory mission, states deployed a hard economic right hand and a potentially softer, although sometimes still quite controlling, left hand. Peck suggests that Wacquant has borrowed this 'ambidextrous state' idea from Bourdieu's seeming realisation in the 1990s that 'the left hand of the state has the sense that the right hand no longer knows, or worse, no longer really wants to know what the left hand does' (Bourdieu, 1998, cited in Peck, 2010, p 104). Furthermore, in contemporary 'sullied, shop-worn, and profoundly discredited' neoliberalism, the relationship between the left and right hands is most usefully seen as a kind of 'symbiotic practical statecraft' rather than as an institutional–ideological unity (2010, p 105). For Peck, contemporary 'neoliberalism [is] a flexible creed', not primarily an ideological enterprise but rooted in a '*practice* of neoliberal statecraft [which] is inescapably, and profoundly, marked by compromise, calculation, and contradiction. There is no blueprint. There is not even a map' (2010, p 106, emphasis in original). Like the missing ideology alleged by Cohen, for Peck, 'the right and left hands of the neoliberal state may have an increasingly tight grip around the fraught regulatory problems of flex-labour and social marginality, but this should not be mistaken for an effective grasp' (p 107). This, he asserts, is the zombie phase of neoliberalism: 'the brain has apparently long since ceased functioning, but the limbs are still moving, and many of the defensive reflexes seem to be working too. The living dead of the free-market revolution continue to walk the earth, though with each resurrection their decidedly uncoordinated gait becomes even more erratic' (Peck, 2010, p 109). Dead labour, or capital, still preying on the living.

Frances Fox Piven (2010) largely seems to agree with both Peck and Cohen – mass incarceration is as ideologically irrational as neoliberalism is structurally chaotic. Yet for her, Wacquant's least convincing argument is that 'massive incarceration is driven by the logic of neoliberalism, indeed [that] it is part of what constitutes neoliberalism' (Piven, 2010, p 115). She questions how the evidence drawn from the circumstances of 'advanced marginality' and the street lives of the poorest ('broke and hustling, jiving, stealing, rapping, balling; and fighting') offers any understandable account of the purposes of punitive mass incarceration. Thus the 'vast budgets commanded by the penal system could … be directed to arguably more successful training programs' and play a more creative role for neoliberal labour markets – and this is to say nothing of the moral issues pertaining to the wasted lives and 'wasted people' cast off by the neoliberal economic system (p 115). Mayer (2010, p 100) further adds that 'governmental legitimacy deficits and discontent among marginalized groups may have been mitigated and … by the [kinds of social] inclusion and activation programs mentioned above'.

Turning to the very people cast adrift by neoliberalism or excluded to its penal margins, Piven poses her second key issue, concerning agency, politics and resistance: 'what about the people who were the objects of penal control. Were they merely the witless objects of social control, or were they also actors in the drama?' (Piven, 2010, p 114). As Mayer (2010, p 95) argues, we should avoid lumping together the 'precarious population', as it is typically a far from homogeneous grouping and is often animated and possessed by a multiplicity of grades and distinctions that only a view from below could discern.

Yet, for Wacquant, for the dispossessed of the 'outcast areas' and 'tainted districts', 'struggles do not seem to exist … these groups do not appear as actors, even though Wacquant repeatedly refers to them as "disruptive" and "recalcitrant": in his poverty areas, *collective* action does not seem to be possible' (Mayer, 2010, p 100), only the dog eat dog violence of a pre-political state of nature. As Mayer notes, Wacquant's other major text, *Urban outcasts* (2008), does posit some elements of potential resistance to the 'violence from above', but it still lacks a broad political alternative that does not simply 'reproduce all the well-known problems of the crisis of the Keynesian welfare state and Fordist wage labour'; furthermore, 'no agency or actors are discernible' by which to advance a progressive alternative (Mayer, 2010, p 100).

Harcourt's sketch towards a genealogy of 'neoliberal penality', on the other hand (2010), goes some way to try to account for the chaotic irrationality of neoliberal punitiveness. He does so by exploring the origins, in the philosophical writings of 18th-century economists, who counterposed a socially constructed and mythical 'natural order of the free market' with a distinct sphere of neoliberal penality, the supposed proper terrain of state action. Hence, the penal state, arising on the ruins of the welfare state, is, according to Wacquant, '*the* integral constituent of the neoliberal state' (Mayer, 2010, p 98). According to Harcourt (2010, p 84), this philosophical distinction between 'state' and '(civil) society' masks the substantial and foundational role of the state within the market, while, in the best traditions of social contract theory, it establishes a monopoly of democratic and legitimate coercion or violence within the social sphere where it translates economic injustices and predicaments (slavery, poverty, inequality, exploitation, unemployment and social exclusion) into social problems amenable to police action and penal treatment. And in this way, it specifically 'facilitates the growth of the carceral sphere' (2010, p 77). Here, perhaps, we might find another sense to Anderson's critique of Wacquant, specifically his notion of 'the most economically distressed and drug and crime ridden pockets of the city ... where the influence of the police ends' (Anderson, 2002, pp 1546-7). Where the influence of the police ends and the state ceases to rule would ordinarily – and certainly according to the theory – be the sphere of market relations, but in this case it is the sphere of the most vital social relationships of safety and personal protection (see Squires, Chapter Eleven, this volume). Might this suggest that the categories of neoliberalism are indeed flawed?

Perhaps it goes without saying but, in tracing the roots of neoliberalism to 18th-century changes in social and economic discourse (and not least, new forms of production and governance), Harcourt gives contemporary conceptions of 'neoliberal penal commonsense' a substantially longer and more complex pre-history than envisaged by Wacquant. He also, perhaps implicitly, raises an issue that, to some extent, extends beyond the aspirations of the present volume. Much of Wacquant's work and certainly many of the chapters in this book are concerned, above all, with what we might call the *consequences* of neoliberalism; the analysis of neoliberalism in and of itself may be another matter. For Wacquant, of course, a defining feature of contemporary neoliberalism has been the extent to which it has become centred on punitive capacity. In the longer term, a searching historical excavation of the development of a coercive statutory power over people and things (as demonstrated in Peter Linebaugh's excellent and incredibly detailed study of *The London hanged*, 2005), including the selective potential for violence, although always 'as allowed by law' and veiled by social contract mythology, would be the perfect complement to Wacquant's contemporary analysis.

Martin Jones (2010) draws together a number of the historical and political themes running through the contributions to the debate in *Criminology and Criminal Justice*: the need for proper historical focus; the need to properly situate the political struggles and contests surrounding policy change at the national and local level; the need to grasp more of the complexity and diversity of criminal justice policy change; and the contrasting practical experiences of criminal justice systems. These corrections are offered in response to Wacquant's famous expression of 'deadly symbiosis' (Wacquant, 2001), exposing the *'functional equivalency, structural homology,* and *cultural fusion'* tying the prison to the ghetto and sustained over three epochs of racialised disciplining: slavery, the Jim Crow laws and mass incarceration (Wacquant, 2001, p 95, emphasis in original). Instead of such sweeping generalisation, Jones seeks a deeper interrogation of causes and explanation and instead of a simple reliance on Bourdieu's conception of the 'bureaucratic field' (1994), suggests the need for a more sustained analysis of politics, state formation and transformation (Jones, 2010, p 400). For Mayer, as for a range of our other commentators, this raises a key issue for Wacquant, concerning 'the contradictions and disjunctures in this seemingly well-functioning regime of penal regulation of poverty' (Mayer, 2010, p 100).

Valverde (2010) poses an essentially similar point in her critical commentary on Wacquant in the *Theoretical Criminology* symposium. She argues that the analyses developed by Wacquant do indeed expose structural relationships, but 'they do not necessarily prove that there is a unified strategy or a single collective actor, a strategist...' orchestrating them all (Valverde, 2010, p 118). Sketching just such a more politicised analysis, Jones argues that the state needs to be approached and understood as a political terrain across which a series of competing tensions – including economic growth, political legitimacy and public order – have to be fought over and resolved. He calls this state form the *impedimenta state,* where 'state policy making constantly switches economic problems into concerns of state rationality' (2010, p 401), an analysis that recalls Marxist and post-Marxist analyses of rationality, legitimacy and the capitalist state (O'Connor, 1973; Held, 1984; Jessop, 2007). Similarly, for Valverde, while it might always be possible to attribute 'method' to 'any governmental madness', be it 'Americanisation', 'globalisation' or 'neoliberalism', political analysis must do much more than apply labels. The real political imperative is to be able to identify 'the very important differences that distinguish one battle from another, one state of the USA from another, one level of government from another, one political conjuncture from another' (Valverde, 2010, p 119). And as Campbell (among others) has noted, 'we should be careful about painting with too broad a theoretical brush when talking about neoliberalism in different countries' (Campbell, 2010, p 70).

Picking up on this political challenge, a final contribution to the *Criminology and Criminal Justice* debate came from Ian Loader and Richard Sparks and sought to engage with Wacquant's 'civic sociology of neoliberal penality' (2009b) from the perspective of their concerns with the development of a 'public criminology' (Loader and Sparks, 2010). Both perspectives, they argue, relate closely to the 'organised scepticism' that characterises a critical social science and, ultimately, they claim Wacquant as an ally in the challenge to expose the ideological blinkers, evidential weaknesses and fraudulent politics of the new punitive, penal reason.

Chapters in this volume

Most, although by no means all, the chapters in this collection share Wacquant's general orientation outlined earlier, albeit schematically, while engaging with many of the themes of these emerging commentaries. That said, the chapters are also searching and critical in locating the inevitable silences, weaknesses and one-sidedness inevitably to be found as well as suggesting useful ways in which Wacquant's work can be seen as complementary to that of other social theorists. The latter theme is taken up by John Rodger (in Chapter Five), who argues that Wacquant's concept of 'advanced marginality' can be situated as a complement to Norbert Elias's well-known discussion of 'civilising processes'. Rodger argues that a weakness in Elias's social theory is in understanding situations, including the present, in which 'de-civilising processes' arrest and reverse the historical tendencies to liberal democracy and the decline of violence in Western societies and how states respond. The argument is that Wacquant's concept of the advanced marginality and the penal state can fill some important gaps in Elias's argument.

Probably the most important single theme in critical responses to Wacquant has been that of his perceived over-emphasis on the prison system as the core coercive agency. Even with rising incarceration rates in most countries, the proportion of the poor and the precariat actually under penal supervision is a minority. Partly the response is extending Wacquant's perspective to embrace other agencies. Thus Markus-Michael Müller, in Chapter Ten, analyses the control of the precariat in Latin America. He emphasises the role of informal practices by state agencies of control – police and prison authorities – and in particular the role of the police in clearing out the poor and marginalised to make way for urban development. In this task the formal agencies are assisted by a variety of non-state actors including vigilante groups, death squads and other varieties of militia.

These latter varieties of non-state actors are mercifully still largely absent from the Western European scenario, but the issue of the over-emphasis on the penal system at the expense of both other criminal justice agencies such as the police and a wider range of non-penal agencies from welfare, housing, education and urban planning is an important theme in responses to Wacquant (see, for example, Mayer 2010). This usually combines with the argument that in laying the foundations of the theory of the penal state Wacquant has been over-reliant on the US.

Several of the chapters in this book elaborate on various aspects of this theme. In Chapter Six Lynn Hancock and Gerry Mooney seek to redress the balance by elaborating further the concept of advanced marginality and how it is controlled in the UK context. They extend Wacquant's term 'penal pornography' to embrace 'poverty porn' – the media portrayal of the feral and feckless poor as the source of social breakdown. They also argue that the idea of the poor as a problem self-generated by pathological culture pre-dates the emergence of the present conditions of advanced marginality, and indeed reinforces it. The effect is to emphasise the much greater role of welfare by contrast with penalisation. This theme is also echoed by Denise Martin and Paula Wilcox in Chapter Eight, who argue that in the UK welfare rather than penalisation has been the main site for neoliberalism's attempt to make the poor take responsibility for their own plight, and that this emphasis was key to the New Labour government. They also raise the question of the specific experience of women as victims of neoliberalism and the need for a distinct gender perspective, something also taken up by Lynda Measor in Chapter Seven.

In Chapter Nine Vincenzo Ruggiero also questions the clarity of Wacquant's account of the symbolic function of punishment and, echoing some aspects of Martin and Wilcox, argues that what is feared and punished about the poor is 'less the criminal capacity of these groups than their indolence'. In other words, it is not primarily a question of the criminality of the poor that leads to their criminalisation but their implicit challenge – just by being there – to the work ethic and exposure of the failure of capitalism to produce secure employment for all. Ruggiero refers to the tradition of urban social theory – Walter

Benjamin and Henri Lefebvre on the design of the city to render invisible the 'socially useless'. He also mentions the role of disorder and resistance in the structuring of the city.

This brings us to another critical focus that is the relative lack, in Wacquant's work, of a sustained focus on resistance. The precariat and the marginalised poor remain largely as the objects of the penal state and its consequent victims. In Chapter Eleven, Peter Squires, like Hancock and Mooney, also emphasises a longer and more subtle evolution of welfare as 'workfare' in the UK but also, like Ruggiero, introduces the key theme of resistance and disorder: on the one hand, the Hobbesian 'war of all against all', but also the violence that obstructs development and the violence of the state which often *provokes* resistance. Wacquant tends to under-estimate resistance. In this respect Squires refers to Frances Fox Piven's earlier critique of Wacquant's relative sidelining of the role of, for example, gangs as collective actors – forms of governance from below (Hagedorn, 2008).

Wacquant's relative lack of focus on resistance on the part of the precariat, including women members, is also the main theme of Lynda Measor's discussion. She argues that although sympathetic to the theme, Wacquant has actually little to say concerning the view from below and resistance as the 'second life' of the precariat, something she attempts to give voice to by reference to an ongoing study of teenage mothers. For Kevin Stenson (in Chapter Three) resistance is also a key theme which he elaborates from the perspective of what he sees as 'realist governmentality theory' that yields a more general view of the neoliberal state (by comparison with that of Wacquant) as composed of 'varied ... rationalities of liberal governance' of which 'governance from below' is a key ingredient. Stenson echoes the contributors who focus on resistance when he argues that the precariat must be seen not just as the victims of advanced marginality and penalisation but also as actors, with racial and ethnic identities, globally mobile, whose 'governance from below' is a challenge to 'elite state-craft'.

This restrictiveness of Wacquant's characterisation of the neoliberal state as a *penal state* is also the theme of the opening chapter by John Lea and Simon Hallsworth. They argue that Wacquant's notion of the 'centaur state', whose coercive gaze frowns on the poor and the precariat while it smiles on the middle and upper classes, fails to grasp a key dynamic of neoliberalism as the reconstruction of all social relations on the model of the entrepreneur responsible for her own fate, something which is coming to affect the middle classes as much as the poor. They see the coercive aspects of the penal state as one aspect of a wider *security state* whose increasing surveillance capacities and compromises on civil liberties have effects throughout society. As part of this process they see the growing role of private agencies as part of the process of expansion rather than displacement of the state.

Finally, in Chapter Four John Pitts reminds us that the argument of Wacquant and similar accounts of the emergence of the penal or security states rests, in the last analysis, on empirical data. While there might be room for considerable discussion about precisely what kinds of empirical data would constitute corroborations or challenges to Wacquant's argument, Pitts focuses on one area, recent developments in youth justice in England and Wales. Wacquant, Pitts argues, while identifying some significant developments, ultimately fails in developing a general model of the development of the Western penal system, and 'ignores crucial historical, political and cultural differences' between countries.

All the chapters in this collection relate to wider ongoing debates around the critique and extension of the recent work of Löic Wacquant and on those grounds alone the collection is, we feel, a very useful introduction to this important area of debate. But what marks out this collection as especially useful is the opportunity offered to Wacquant himself to write a response. The fact that Löic Wacquant himself tracked down the details of the Brighton conference on the internet, contacted us and offered to write a response to the papers is both one of the wonders of modern global electronic communications and, we think, an added attraction to this collection.

During his responding chapter Löic Wacquant asks: 'Why have researchers of criminal justice, on the one hand, and welfare policy, on the other, paid no attention to each other's work?' While accepting that there is a certain truth in this criticism, we would argue that this is not necessarily so accurate of those commentators (as reflected in this volume) writing in the 'critical policy studies' tradition.[1] So, perhaps above all, we offer this volume as a contribution towards the furthering of an analysis of disciplinary welfare and the penalisation of insecurity.

Note
[1] See, for example, Squires (1990, 2008) and Rodger (2008).

References

Anderson, E. (2002) 'The ideologically drawn critique', *American Journal of Sociology*, vol 107, pp 1546-7.

Bourdieu, P. (1994) 'Rethinking the state: on the genesis and structure of the bureaucratic field', *Sociological Theory*, vol 12, pp 1-19.

Campbell, J.L. (2010) 'Neoliberalism's penal and debtor states: a rejoinder to Loïc Wacquant', *Theoretical Criminology*, vol 14, no 1, pp 59-73.

Cheliotis, L.K. (2010) 'Preface to the special issue: Neoliberalism and penality: reflections on the work of Loic Wacquant', *Criminology and Criminal Justice*, vol 10, no 4, pp 327-30.

Cheliotis, L.K. and Xenakis, S. (2010) 'What's neoliberalism got to do with it? A political economy of punishment in Greece', *Criminology and Criminal Justice*, vol 10, no 4, pp 353-73.

Chesney-Lind, M. (2006) 'Patriarchy, crime, and justice: feminist criminology in an era of backlash', *Feminist Criminology*, vol 1, pp 6-26.

Cohen, S. (2010) 'Ideology? What ideology?', *Criminology and Criminal Justice*, vol 10, no 4, pp 387-91.

Feeley, M and Simon, J. (1992) 'The new penology: notes on the emerging strategy of corrections and its implications', *Criminology*, vol 30, no 4, pp 452-74.

Garland, D. (1985) *Punishment and welfare*, Aldershot: Gower.

Garland, D. (2005) 'Capital punishment and American culture', *Punishment and Society*, vol 7, no 4, pp 347-76.

Gelsthorpe, L. (2010) 'Women, crime and control', *Criminology and Criminal Justice*, vol 10, no 4, pp 353–73.

Hagedorn, J. (2008) *A world of gangs: Armed young men and 'gangsta' culture*, Minneapolis, MN: University of Minneapolis.

Harcourt, B. (2010) 'Neoliberal penality: a brief genealogy', *Theoretical Criminology*, vol 14, no 1, pp 74-92.

Held, D. (1984) 'Power and legitimacy in contemporary Britain', in G. Mclennan, D. Held and S. Hall (eds) *State and society in contemporary Britain*, Cambridge: Polity Press, pp 299-369.

Jessop, B. (2007) *State power*, Cambridge: Polity Press.

Jones, M. (2010) '"Impedimenta state": anatomies of neoliberal penality', *Criminology and Criminal Justice*, vol 10, no 4, pp 393-404.

Lacey, N. (2010) 'Differentiating among penal states', *British Journal of Sociology*, vol 61, no 4, pp 778-94.

Linebaugh, P. (2006) *The London hanged: Crime and civil society in the eighteenth century* (2nd edn), London: Verso.

Loader, I. and Sparks, R. (2010) *Public criminology?*, London: Routledge.

Mayer, M. (2010) 'Punishing the poor, a debate: some questions on Wacquant's theorizing the neoliberal state', *Theoretical Criminology*, vol 14, no 1, pp 93-103.

Nelken, D. (2010) 'Denouncing the penal state', *Criminology and Criminal Justice*, vol 10, no 4, pp 331-40.

Newburn, T. (2010) 'Diffusion, differentiation and resistance in comparative penality', *Criminology and Criminal Justice*, vol 10, no 4, pp 341-52.

O'Connor, J. (1973) *The fiscal crisis of the state*, New York: St Martin's Press.

Peck, J. (2010) 'Zombie neoliberalism and the ambidextrous state', *Theoretical Criminology*, vol 14, no 1, pp 104-10.

Piven, F.F. (2010) 'A response to Wacquant', *Theoretical Criminology*, vol 14, no 1, pp 111–16.

Pratt, J. (2011) 'The international diffusion of punitive penality: or penal exceptionalism in the United States? Wacquant v Whitman', *Australian & New Zealand Journal of Criminology*, vol 44, no 1, pp 116-28.

Rodger, J. (2008) *Criminalising social policy: Anti-social behaviour and welfare in a de-civilised society*, Cullompton: Willan Publishing.

Simon, J. (2007) *Governing through crime*, Oxford: Oxford University Press.

Squires, P. (1990) *Anti-social policy: Welfare ideology and the disciplinary state*, Hemel Hempstead: Harvester/Wheatsheaf.

Squires, P. (2000) *Gun culture or gun control: Firearms, violence and society*, London: Routledge.

Squires, P. (ed) (2008) *ASBO nation: The criminalisation of nuisance*, Bristol: The Policy Press.

Standing, G. (2011) *The precariat: The new dangerous class,* London: Bloomsbury Academic.

Valverde, M. (2010) 'Comment on Wacquant's "Theoretical coda" to *Punishing the poor*', *Theoretical Criminology*, vol 14, no 1, pp 117-20.

Wacquant, L. (2001) 'Deadly symbiosis: where ghetto and prison meet and mesh', in D. Garland (ed) *Mass imprisonment in the United States*, London: Sage Publications, pp 82-121.

Wacquant, L. (2007) *Urban outcasts: A comparative sociology of advanced marginality*, Cambridge: Polity Press.

Wacquant, L. (2009a) *Punishing the poor: The neoliberal government of social insecurity*, Durham, NC: Duke University Press.

Wacquant, L. (2009b) *Prisons of poverty* (expanded edn), Minneapolis, MN: University of Minnesota Press.

Whitman, J.Q. (2003) *Harsh justice: Criminal punishment and the widening divide between America and Europe*, New York: Oxford University Press.

Section 1
Theory and politics

TWO

Bringing the state back in: understanding neoliberal security

John Lea and Simon Hallsworth

The new 'great transformation'

By now the broad contours of the 'great transformation' through which we are living are reasonably clear. The combined forces of economy and state are rewriting the scripts governing social structure, class relations and politics in the advanced industrial countries of the global north. In particular the interventionist state is an essential part of the engine of transformation today as it was in the coming of industrial capitalism itself. The 'great transformation' of the early 19th century was one in which free market capitalism, the regime of '*laisser-faire* itself was enforced by ... an enormous increase in the administrative functions of the state' (Polanyi, 1957, p 139). Exactly the same has been happening over the last few decades in which 'the globalisation era was not one of *de-regulation* but of *re-regulation* in which more regulations were introduced than in any comparable period of history' (Standing, 2011a, p 26). The neoliberal state can indeed be seen as 'a transnational political project aiming to remake the nexus of market, state, and citizenship from above' (Wacquant, 2010, p 213).

The 'long boom' of the 1960s and 1970s of almost uninterrupted expansion of the industrialised Western economies provided a context in which many commentators assumed that most economic and social problems could be overcome by correct policy interventions by a benevolent state. The Keynesian welfare state pursued an economic policy oriented, at least in theory, to full employment, while social policy aimed, again in theory, at social cohesion through education, social mobility and welfare citizenship. Politics was dominated by the process of institutionalised class compromise between capital and labour. Finally, the residue of criminal offenders and socially excluded were to be, as far as possible, subject to rehabilitation and re-integration.

That world is now virtually dead and buried. Long-term falling profit rates from investment in the major capitalist economies over the last 40 years (Harman, 2009) put increasing pressure on capital to renege on the class compromise with labour. Globalisation and mobility enabled capital to both move to new sources of cheap labour and at the same time deploy new technology and work organisation to establish a regime of low-wage, deskilled, insecure, short-term and temporary employment and high rates of structural unemployment (Castells, 1999). This 'precariat' (Standing, 2011a), whose condition can also be characterised as 'advanced marginality' (Wacquant, 1996, 1999, 2007), has become a growing proportion of the working class. This class recomposition has been accompanied by intensification of social and regional inequality (for the UK see Dorling et al, 2007, 2008; Lansley 2009) and the virtual cessation of social mobility.

For many social scientists the retreat of the state from Keynesian economic management and large areas of social policy such as public housing led to a confusion of the changing role of the state with its retreat or even demise (Osborne and Gaebler, 1992; Strange, 1996). In the social sciences many were inspired by Foucault's dismissal of 'the excessive value attributed to the problem of the state' (Foucault, 1991, p 103) to abandon discussion of the state in favour of a focus on processes of 'governance' which can inhabit a variety of sites and be undertaken by a variety of actors, of which the state is only one alongside a plethora of market relations and private non-state actors. The impact of globalisation itself led many others to imagine that the state in a debordering world had become irrelevant. Meanwhile the language of 'markets' and 'actors' displaced any analysis of the dynamics of capital accumulation and the interests of social classes.

But events have forced a refocus. In political economy the financial crisis of 2008 reaffirmed the centrality of the state as the only institution capable of rapid and massive transfer of wealth from ordinary taxpayers to bankers and speculators, while rising rates of incarceration, dramatic increases in surveillance and police powers, the inauguration of a coercive regime of 'workfare' (social benefits contingent not on need but on adoption of job seeking in low-wage labour markets), have confirmed the state as the core agency of control over the poor. Far from being a peripheral actor the state has played a major role in the changes outlined above.

The Keynesian welfare state aimed at economic 'management' to secure growth combined and a social policy designed, especially in the UK, to integrate all classes into a welfare citizenship built around protection from risks defined famously by Beveridge as the 'five giants' of squalor, ignorance, want, idleness and disease. By contrast, the neoliberal state leaves economic growth to the working of the market but intervenes strongly to make labour attractive to mobile global capital and create cities and regions as 'business-friendly' environments. It has assisted capital by intervening massively to weaken the bargaining power of labour through restrictions on trades union rights and dismantling the old structures of political compromise, meanwhile deploying a battery of measures to reconcile the working class, and growing sections of the middle class, to the conditions of precarious employment. In the field of social policy the neoliberal state increasingly redefines Beveridge's risks as matters of personal responsibility and insurance while concentrating on security from another set of risks presented by the poor and the structurally unemployed to the middle classes and securely employed working class.

This strategy is not without its tensions and contradictions. On the one hand, much concern with security is about 'public protection', that is, the protection of the middle classes and the employed from 'risks' (of crime and disorder) posed by an 'underclass' drawn from the precariat and permanently unemployed. The middle class may resent taxation to fund social security benefits for a precariat with whom they no longer identify as fellow 'welfare citizens' with legitimate needs. On the other hand, there is also pressure to enforce the conditions of precarious labour on sections of the middle class who themselves now face what Sennett (2006) calls 'the spectre of uselessness'. Furthermore, in a country like the UK, with a strong tradition of welfare universalism, many sections of the middle class resent and oppose the privatisation of the old welfare state such as healthcare and public education. In a similar way, strategy towards the poor and unemployed may have to compromise between, on the one hand, varieties of 'warehousing' to minimise their perceived risks to the middle classes and each other and, on the other hand, the need to secure their integration into the precarious labour market so as to compete effectively and thereby exercise a downward pressure on wage levels. These contradictions may play themselves out in various policy or political conflicts between governments or political factions who share the broad outlines of the neoliberal agenda.

Warehousing and rehabilitation

The prison is the logical place to begin. Imprisonment is the most extreme form of state coercion in a modern liberal democracy. In the US critical commentators saw the resurgence in incarceration since the

1970s as largely a matter of warehousing the poor (Feeley and Simon, 1992; Parenti, 2000; Simon, 2007; Wacquant, 2009; Alexander, 2010). Loïc Wacquant, who is to be congratulated for returning criminology to a focus on the neoliberal state and in particular to the centrality of its punitive arm, argues that the concern with discipline and the production of 'docile and productive bodies' analysed by Foucault (1977) as characteristic of the 19th and early 20th century prison was in terminal decline as it became peripheral to the habituation of labour. Its resurgence (together with expanding parole and probation supervision) since the 1970s is that of an institution 'geared toward brute neutralisation, rote retribution and simple warehousing – by default if not by design' (Wacquant, 2009, p 296).

In Europe, however, although similar tendencies of increasing prison populations can be observed (Bell, 2011), the proportions are much lower than the US and sufficient to challenge any exhaustive characterisation of European neoliberal states as 'penal states'. Indeed, current UK government policy appears to support reductions in prison populations in favour of (outsourced) probation supervision (Ministry of Justice, 2010). While it is difficult to imagine the US 'supermax' prison as anything other than a warehouse, in the UK there are, despite a long-term decline in the status of rehabilitation (see Cavadino and Dignan, 2007), at least residual elements of rehabilitation both in prison and more importantly for the growing population under probation and parole supervision. The same applies even more so across Europe. It is clear in probation that what has changed is rather the meaning of rehabilitation. For example, the decline of rehabilitation *as a result of* the discipline of work (where the probation officer finds the ex-offender a job) tends to be replaced by risk management strategies including cognitive therapy and 'criminogenic needs' management programmes aimed at educating the client in 'correct choices'. On the one hand, this aims to inculcate *work-seeking* attitudes – acceptance of low-wage precarious labour – which may then attract employers, but by default, where jobs are not forthcoming, it becomes a variety of 'self-warehousing' through encouraging passivity and self-blame (Hannah-Moffat, 2005; Fitzgibbon, 2007; Fitzgibbon and Lea, 2010). It is thus entirely possible to see warehousing and rehabilitation as different sides of the same coin. This is entirely consistent with the notion that the unemployed, under penal or workfare supervision or neither, should be made to operate as a 'reserve army of labour', potentially competing with those already in precarious employment as a further downward pressure on already low wages.

Thus it is correct to see the penal and workfare systems as linked. Wacquant expresses this through the idea that 'welfare revamped as workfare and the prison stripped of its rehabilitative pretension now form a single organizational mesh flung at the same clientele mired in the fissures and ditches of the dualizing metropolis' (Wacquant, 2010, p 199). Rather, in the UK context at least, it is because both have blurred and contain punitive warehousing (including 'self-warehousing') elements alongside attempts at rehabilitation as willingness to submit to low-wage precarious labour. The transition from welfare as supplementary social wage based on need to benefit conditionality on work-seeking behaviour with penal sanctions for failure to comply also combines elements of both. This has been developing for some time in the UK (Jessop, 1994; Larkin, 2011). However, linking welfare too closely to the prison as a 'single organizational mesh' tends to sideline other developments in welfare and social policy which may in fact be more important than the penal system in the government of the precariat (see Hörnqvist, 2010; Mayer, 2010). The link-up between schools, urban and community 'renewal' and policing may be of considerably greater importance than any direct link with the prison system.

The interpenetration of warehousing and habituation to precarious low-wage labour is clear if we move to a key example of the extension of the penal system. Alessandro De Giorgi has studied the extension of the prison as warehouse to the internment camps for illegal migrants and failed asylum seekers. De Giorgi echoes the warehousing argument in claiming that we are witnessing 'the sunset of a disciplinary power whose ambition was to produce useful and docile subjects ... and the dawn of a power of control which supervises whole populations whose collective status justifies their *banishment*' (De Giorgi, 2006, p 85). Throughout the European Union (EU) such camps and other forms of legal restraint cover substantial immigrant populations (see Webber, 2006). The incarceration of migrants is simply one aspect of what De Giorgi calls their 'ontological criminalisation' – criminalisation by virtue of status as migrant and consequent subjection to a regime of regulation and loss of employment and social security rights based on the crossing of territorial state borders. Frontiers have become less to do with the boundaries between territories than 'flexible instruments for the reproduction of a hierarchical division between "deserving" and "undeserving" populations, "wanted" and "unwanted' others"' (De Giorgi, 2006, p 113; see also De Giorgi, 2010).

Such processes of de-citizenisation and ontological criminalisation provides new sites for panoptic surveillance and new discourses of nationality and citizenship (Bosworth and Guild, 2008). These play a key role in securing migrants as part of the low-wage precariat. Guy Standing points out that in the UK during the current recession and generally rising unemployment, the employment of migrants actually increased (Standing, 2011a, p 102). He characterises migrants as 'the light infantry of global capitalism', involving the 'de-citizenisation' of labour as a method to secure compliance to low wages and precarious employment (Standing, 2011a, p 113). De-citizenisation carries the constant threat of incarceration and deportation. It functions as an amalgam of the prison and workfare to secure compliance and passivity on the part of the excluded while also constructing as 'suitable enemies' the populations the neoliberal state claims to defend the socially included from.

The new panopticon

Populations in and out of incarceration and caught up in the criminalising process of crossing state borders are, although substantial and growing, still located at the margins of modern industrial capitalist societies. We have noted the impact of neoliberalism in polarising society into very rich and very poor, with a 'decline in the employment opportunities open to those on middle and lower earnings' (Lansley, 2009, p 4). It is perhaps easy therefore to retain a focus on the marginalised population which is in and out of prison and thereby characterised the neoliberal state as essentially a *penal* state (Wacquant, 2009) with the character of a *centaur*, which is 'liberal at the top and paternalistic at the bottom, which presents ... a comely and caring visage toward the middle and upper classes, and a fearsome and frowning mug toward the lower class' (Wacquant, 2010, p 217). This involves, in turn, a second dimension of the rejection of Foucault as outdated. Just as the prison regime as the exemplar of disciplinary power has passed into mere warehousing, so it is necessary to reject Foucault's well-known claim that the *panopticon* as the inspiration for the new model prisons, asylums, factories and schools emerging during the 19th century presaged a 'carceral archipelago' of institutions that transported the disciplinary techniques characteristic of the prison 'to the entire social body' (Foucault, 1977, p 298).

This perspective might suffice as a starting point but not, however, as an account of dynamics. Neoliberalism aims not just at warehousing the very poor or forcing them into low-wage labour but more widely at the breaking up of all forms of class, community or political organisation or spontaneous appropriations of space which might interfere with capital and which are to be redefined as threats to *security*. It is therefore important not to see the state *only* acting on the lower stratum, as *simply* a penal state for the containment of those in prison and on workfare benefits. To the very rich the state is indeed a grovelling servant but, acting in the interests of capital, it is anything but sentimental about the middle classes, who are ultimately just employees like any others. It is therefore necessary to see how the principles and techniques march from the periphery to the centre, to spread from the marginal populations to wider sections of society, and to see how the *penal* state merges into a wider *security* state as it develops new technologies and sites of rule (Hallsworth and Lea, 2011). Among the latter are certainly to be found new forms of recognisably panoptic power and, indeed, new forms of disciplinary power adapted to new ends.

Foucault's account of the role of panoptic power in the production of 'docile and productive bodies' is not entirely dead. But, as implied in the earlier discussion of probation, the focus is no longer about learning the disciplines of coordinated labour as such. As Antonio Gramsci observed, once modern factory workers internalised the techniques of disciplined labour as automatic then they were freed to think critically about the labour process along lines that were 'far from conformist' (Gramsci, 1971a, p 310). Because of his focus on the prison rather than the factory, Foucault did not stress that if one outcome of discipline was the productive worker, the other was the labour movement. It is this latter that neoliberalism is concerned to destroy in order to re-subordinate the worker entirely, mentally and physically, to the violence of the market. The new panopticon is not about training and habituation to the techniques of the labour process; it is about a frontal assault on workers' rights and replacing collective solidarity with organisational fragmentation, a 'docile mind' of unquestioning loyalty to the employer, no thoughts of union membership, acceptance of performance targets and precarious low-wage intensive labour, and driven, above all, by fear of, and self-blame for, unemployment.

The panopticon has certainly begun to embed itself in schools in poor areas where students are destined for unemployment and the precariat. In the US Jonathan Simon (2000, 2007) has described how issues such as equal opportunities and educational failure have been displaced by drug testing, metal detectors and curfews (see also Monahan and Torres, 2009). Wacquant describes the system of allocation of police officers to schools in France, replacing the nurse or social worker (Wacquant, 2008, p 26). In the UK a similar process of the 'securitisation' of the school began in fact as a fortification of the school against intruders from outside and then shifted as pupils themselves and their everyday lives became, under the impact of 'gang culture', sexual abuse of young women and fears concerning gun and knife crime, reconstructed as the object of a security programme. This was then used to justify the use of crime control technologies and practices previously unthinkable in a school setting. This involved the discursive reconstruction of *school space* as *crime space*, and the reclassification of the pupils into the binary categories of perpetrator and victim. It was then a simple move to install metal detectors at school gates and invite police and drug sniffer dogs to search students on entry and exit. Even more innovatory has been the incorporation of CCTV and audio surveillance into classrooms, ostensibly to aid teacher training. Indeed both teachers and students may be the objects of surveillance aimed at producing conformity that is now defined by the UK's Coalition government as an absence of 'extremist views' coupled, we might add, with an unquestioned acceptance of the market. In one recent incident in England students walked out of school in protest after discovering that cameras and microphones had been installed overnight. The leader of the walkout 'says his main objection to the "four tinted domes hanging from the classroom ceiling and the huge monitor staring right at us" is that it inhibits students and teachers from freely expressing their ideas' (Shepherd, 2009). And the school in question was hardly a warehouse for marginalised unemployables – the articulate, protesting students were headed for university entrance the following year.

Similar dynamics are increasingly securitising larger urban spaces. A major aim of urban policy, emerging over the last two decades, has been the development of 'community cohesion', social capital and 'capacity building', which is usually polite terminology for developing a labour force willing to turn out smartly and enthusiastically for work at low wages in precarious employment. If prison remains a primary institution disciplining migrant labour and those on workfare, this function is also mediated in even more important ways through new strategies of policing by an ever-expanding policing family which now includes, for example, social housing managers. The perennial popularity of the Wilson–Kelling argument (1982) – or variants of it – to show how a police crackdown on low-level street crime and disorder enables law-abiding citizens to retain, or retake, possession of the streets. Safe streets are then seen as providing a secure locale for business premises (Coleman, 2004; Coleman et al, 2005) while enabling young people to go to college and acquire relevant skills and work attitudes that advertise the existence of a compliant workforce (see Fitzgibbon and Lea, 2010). Ideologically the whole discourse of safety and security enables the shortage of actual employment opportunities to be hidden behind a smokescreen of issues concerning young people's ability to demonstrate 'their employability and marketability ... in an increasingly competitive labour market' (Fahmy, 2008, p 285).

The securitisation of the city involves a combination of warehousing and habituation or 'rehabilitation' to precarious low-wage labour combined with a more general extension of surveillance justified in the name of security. The recruitment of criminal justice agencies to the tasks of urban renewal, first graphically portrayed by Mike Davis (1990) in the US at the beginning of the 1990s, involves a whole new apparatus – an 'extended police family' of police, local authorities, social housing managements with legal powers to impose good behaviour contracts, curfews, dispersals and Anti-Social Behaviour Orders (ASBOs) (Squires and Stephen, 2005; Squires, 2008). These devices can be characterised as 'anticipatory criminalisation' (Lea, 2002), 'pre-emptive criminalisation' (Fitzgibbon, 2004) or 'pre-crime' (Zedner, 2007). Those who cannot be passively assimilated to the precariat will be both penalised by the benefit system and moved, through exclusion orders, loss of tenancies and other means, to 'social landfill sites', where they will not disturb the process of urban renewal. These areas, typically subject to permanent recession and high levels of interpersonal violence, are themselves intensively policed and subject to pervasive surveillance – in effect the prisonification of the ghetto. Further down the line many of its inhabitants also end up being warehoused in prison. The end result is a 'criminalisation of social policy' which becomes 'less about socially integrating those who live at the margins of society and more about guarding the boundaries between the established and the outsiders' (Rodger, 2008, p 165).

This new behaviour control may begin with a focus on the poor and socially deprived but it extends to institutions concerned with wider society (see Crawford, 2006), and as an apparatus it deploys forms of regulation which 'are being used to circumvent and erode established criminal justice principles, notably those of due process, proportionality and special protections traditionally afforded to young people' (Crawford, 2009, p 210). Such legal principles appear as a hindrance when agencies are less concerned with the conviction of individual offenders than the management of groups of (mainly young) people defined as risks to community cohesion and renewal, by keeping them out of areas or preventing them engaging in annoying but sub-criminal behaviour. The integration of policing into the business of urban renewal exemplifies what Simon (2007) calls 'governing through crime'. This is probably more important in the European context than the prison system (Hinds, 2005) as a mechanism of social control. It is a process accompanied by a high level of public hysteria and media moral panic about crime (Fitzgibbon, 2011) which, as Wacquant (2009) observes, Foucault's idea of the 'spectacle of punishment' exemplified in the public execution now returns in the form of *penal pornography*.

A relentless concern with urban security has legitimated the development of new surveillance systems, new public/private police hybrids and heavily fortified environments. Collectively these have reconstructed the city as a high tech urban panopticon – the punitive city of late modernity. While scholars differ on the transferability of Foucault's (and Bentham's) concept of the panopticon to such areas as urban space (see Wood, 2003), the essential dynamics of the panopticon – conforming behaviour produced by the fact that it is impossible to know whether or not one is under surveillance – is retained. The CCTV camera in the high street replaces the mirror in the central tower of the panopticon. Like inmates, the urbanite does not know whether they are being watched: 'Accordingly, in urban space unverifiability is characteristic to the function of surveillance. The consequence of increasing surveillance is that in everyday urban life people are more visible to invisible watchers than ever before' (Koskela, 2003, p 298). The 'extended police family' avails itself of a 'proliferation of "capable" eyes now surveying the streets of the UK including cameras, street wardens and business funded street cleansing initiatives' (Coleman, 2007, p 171). The private sector (business interests, police, local authority, security and surveillance firms) is heavily involved in new coalitions for extending state surveillance – funding CCTV, sponsorship money for the police (Coleman and Sim, 2000; Coleman, 2004) – all aimed at making city centres 'safe for business' by keeping out the 'social litter' and all who will not behave as rational consumers or take responsibility for themselves in the way that neoliberalism requires: the orientation to consumption and shopping in the city centre and docile precarious labour.

Part of making the area safe for business is that the technology is focused on a concept of crime and disorder which 'reinforces the gaze down the social and political hierarchy at the expense of scrutinising upwards upon the harms generated through entrepreneurialisation itself' (Coleman et al, 2005, p 2512). Business is constructed as the most important victim of crime while other forms of actions in public space, including political demonstrations or strike picket lines, are assimilated de facto to the concept of anti-social behaviour and disturbance. Even general political demonstrations and marches, citizens exercising fundamental democratic rights through the appropriation of public space, become seen as 'disturbances' and potential security threats and are policed accordingly.

The orientation of most of this surveillance is towards securitisation in the interests of capital against the poor and the unemployed. But there are important tensions. In Wacquant's picturesque terminology, the state certainly looks down with a 'fearsome and frowning mug' on the poor and the precariat but it is less clear that it looks upwards with an unambiguously 'comely and caring visage toward the middle and upper classes' (Wacquant, 2010, p 217). As far as the industrial and financial elites are concerned, this is certainly true. However, it is important to remember that neoliberalism is a project for the whole of society – a profound reconstruction of all social relations on the model of the entrepreneur in the service of capital. Indeed, the preoccupation of the middle classes with security is intensified by the fact that capital seeks to generalise the conditions of the precariat to wide sectors of employment including what are currently defined as highly paid middle-class occupations. The changing employment situation for many middle-class people in the private sector includes the rise of short-term and 'freelance' contracts, unpaid internships, a decline in job security and increasing risk of the obsolescence of hard-earned skills (Sennett, 1998, 2006; Hacker, 2006; Harris, 2007; Standing, 2011a).

While employers themselves carried through most of these changes, since it is a question of groups already in employment, the neoliberal state, as Standing observes, has played a major role in the dismantling and re-regulation of the powers of trades unions and professional associations to facilitate these changes (see Standing, 2011a, p 39 et seq). The conditions of the service sector of the middle class have also deteriorated. Those who helped build and sustain the edifice of the welfare state in the era of social capitalism have been under sustained attack by the political right who have consistently questioned their necessity. In the name of 'rolling back the state' and cutting the fiscal deficit jobs have been cut, while many functions once performed by the service class have been privatised into the hands of deskilling private providers.

Meanwhile, rising levels of debt, decline in pension security and, as welfare systems move from universalist to minimal safety-net and workfare, a decline in social benefits have all diminished the prospects of middle-class families. While large sections of the professional middle class are not facing warehousing, they are facing a sustained onslaught by capital and the neoliberal state in the areas of employment and life-course security. They are enjoined to become entrepreneurs or perish. These changes produce what Sennett (1998) called 'corrosion of character' – a decline in mutual trust, loyalty and commitment, which, coupled with a rise in paranoia and resentment, reinforces a willingness to see the security state as a necessary bulwark against not only the poor but also a society increasingly made up of unseen threats and untrusted others (Bauman, 1995; Young, 1999; Garland, 2001). As Hall et al (1978) noted, tendencies, which have their origin in the realm of the economic, have been effectively displaced in this process to the realm of ideology where they become reconstructed as a crisis of law and order. Such displacement itself reinforces the securitisation drift.

It is important to understand, therefore, that there are other important drivers for the security state which do not relate immediately to class fragmentation. In fact the dominant securitising discourses in recent years, particularly since '9/11', have included terrorism and international organised crime as much as concerns over the precariat and the unemployed 'underclass' in facilitating the move of the security state from the surveillance of marginalised populations towards a much more generalised surveillance of society as a whole. These of course are not unrelated to the global inequalities sustained and amplified by neoliberal capitalist expansion over the last three decades, but they are not related in an immediate sense to the control of the precariat. Middle-class insecurities link in with other security discourses derived from terrorism and organised crime. These then combine with and reinforce concerns about fragmented wage labour, immigration, the school and public urban space to create an environment conducive to the 'securitisation of the life-world' (Hallsworth and Lea, 2011; see also Monahan, 2010) in which wide areas of social life and the civil liberties associated with them are seen as potential trade-offs for security, as that which can be compromised or 'balanced' by the requirements of security 'without any idea of what lies in the scales, what tips them, and in whose interest' (Zedner, 2005, p 507).

They create a climate in which the further militarisation of urban security is both 'reasonable' and inevitable (Graham, 2010) through police acquisition of military surveillance technology (Hayes, 2009; Gallagher and Syal, 2011), increases in surveillance of electronic communications, uses of profiling and databanks. These technologies begin to permeate all areas of society. In the process all opposition becomes viewed as potential security risks. The security state marches to the core producing, as it does so, a 'securitisation of the lifeworld' in which social spaces and society itself become reconstituted as crime space. Normal social interactions are reconstructed as if in an airport departure zone in which passing through surveillance systems en route to boarding is not only tolerated but welcomed as a necessary security-enhancing device (see Lianos and Douglas, 2000). We come to accept a redefinition of civil liberties which ranges from acceptance of pre-emptive arrests or constraints on individuals suspected of 'connections' with terrorism, through climate change activism and public demonstrations to criminal record checks on your child minder. The sense of security that comes from knowing people is replaced by the security the defenceless feel having achieved a target-hardened environment which keeps outsiders out. The pervasiveness of the CCTV screen, the databank profile and the mobilisation of ordinary citizens as the 'eyes and ears' of the police and security services (see, for example, Travis, 2011) are sold as essential steps in the reduction of pervasive insecurity. This move in the direction of 'soft fascism' (Hallsworth and Lea, 2011) has precisely the opposite effect: the sense of *insecurity* is heightened.

The distributed state

There are limitations to Wacquant's account of the neoliberal state which stem from an insistence on seeing it as a *penal* state. This is rather one aspect of a wider series of neoliberal strategies that can better be described as a *security* state and which include the *political habituation* of the working class as a whole – and also large sections of the middle class – to the conditions of precarious labour and increasing self-responsibilisation for conditions such as ill health, old age and unemployment which were, under the old *welfare state*, dealt with in terms of rights flowing from welfare citizenship.

Wacquant's characterisation of the neoliberal state as a *centaur state* is used to imply that tendencies to authoritarianism are exclusively related to the control of the precariat. The analogy of the centaur used by Machiavelli and appropriated by Gramsci is used rather to contrast techniques of rule, 'the levels of force and of consent, authority and hegemony, violence and civilisation ...' (Gramsci, 1971b, p 170). While obviously force and coercion are likely to be deployed against the poor, there is no reason why strong elements of coercion should not, as we have suggested, be finding their way into neoliberal strategies that have an impact on the middle classes, resulting, in the UK at least, in a critique originating from the political right as much as the left, of loss of civil liberties from intrusive surveillance and other invasions of privacy (Porter, 2009; Raab, 2009).

These limitations, however, should not detract from the fact that Wacquant is overwhelmingly correct, first, in putting the state centre stage as the key vehicle of the neoliberal project and, second, in identifying its dynamic as a process of 'state-crafting' (Wacquant, 2010). The notion of state-crafting as a *dynamic process* is central in overcoming the essentialist view of the state as a set of essentially unchanging core institutions related to monopolies of legitimate coercion and taxation. As Bob Jessop, whose work follows that of Nikos Poulantzas (1978), put it: 'There is never a point when *the* state is finally built within a given territory and thereafter operates ... according to its own fixed and inevitable laws' (Jessop, 1990, p 9, emphasis in original). Rather it is the case that 'a given state form, a given form of regime, will be more accessible to some forces than others according to the strategies they adopt to gain state power' (Jessop, 1990, p 10). In other words 'the difference between state and society, politics and the economy does not function as a foundation or a borderline, but as an element and effect of specific governmental technologies' (Lemke, 2007, p 18). What is or is not part of the state is dependent on the dominant coalitions of interests involved, the ends to which core state powers such as the monopoly of legitimate force and taxation are being oriented and the technologies of rule being deployed. Thus, much of what appears as the privatisation or retreat of the state and the rise of governance by 'non-state actors' is in effect the emergence of new coalitions and technologies of state rule and state action (Lea and Stenson, 2007).

To take the example of the school discussed above, while schools have considerable autonomy in decisions to purchase security technology, such purchasing is increasing, and the security mentality increasingly dominates the orientation to school spaces. Meanwhile, the process is being driven forward with active support by government and relevant legislation and public funding subsidies. The police, a core state agency, are thus brought into close contact, influence and alliance with school officials and teachers. Rather than the emergence of some new form of non-state power, schools are being enrolled by the state as part of the wider securitisation project out of and through which the security state is itself being actualised. Similar considerations apply to the city centre security projects studied by Coleman and others and discussed earlier. The specific technologies of securitisation effect the ways and routes by which state power permeates increasingly larger segments of civil society. To put this another way, whereas the older 'orchestrated state' warehoused its violence in spaces like the garrison, the police station and prison, the contemporary distributed state distributes its violence into environments like the shopping mall, the airport, the train station and the urban estate.

Private capital, by playing an enhanced role in the provision of security, does not mean that the state loses its sovereign function, even when it appears to be privatising and rolling back the state. Rather what is occurring is the growth of mechanisms whereby the state delegates aspects of its core function to others. Such a process is by no means unique to the current neoliberal period. It is more generally a feature of any period of 'state-crafting' in which the state is being reconfigured to deal with new social processes. Indeed, as Charles Tilly (1985) showed, it characterised the very process whereby the modern state emerged. It was certainly a major characteristic of the adaption of the British and other European states to the techniques of colonial rule. The British and Dutch East India companies were both large private trading corporations and at the same time state-crafting bodies equipped with their own territorial administrative bureaucracies, the military, the police, courts and prisons (see Wilson, 2009).

For the British East India company substitute Blackwater and Halliburton today.

Destructive reproduction

Finally, how far is neoliberal state-crafting a viable project? There are, of course, highly visible contradictions in the form of policy dilemmas. The expansion of the security apparatus as a response to the emergence of the precariat runs up against the need to reduce state expenditure under conditions of recession together with the more general aims of reconstruction of a society of self-responsibilising entrepreneurs. As Wacquant (2009) notes, in the US penal expenditure is the one area of state spending whose legitimacy is assured in the context of a neoliberal inspired crusade against 'big government'. In the UK the current (2011) government's plans for massive reductions in state spending have not spared prisons and the police, albeit much of this will take the form of 'outsourcing' of probation supervision to private security agencies and is therefore a move to deskilling and wage reduction (Ministry of Justice, 2010; Fitzgibbon, 2011). Nevertheless, a state which attempts to secure legitimacy through security can only with difficulty sustain any large-scale reductions in such areas. Meanwhile, as already noted, strong historical traditions of both freedom from state surveillance and of welfare universalism in the UK have provoked middle-class reaction to the extension of surveillance and to privatisation and cuts in public education (including universities) and healthcare funding. The problems of political legitimation do not seem to be effectively countered by rhetoric such as the 'Big Society' celebrating the role of the voluntary and private sectors.

But more fundamentally, neoliberalism is oriented to the destruction of those forms of social solidarity characteristic of welfare state societies. These evolved, under pressure from the organised working class, to

---

counter precisely the insecurity, poverty and social inequality generated by a previous period of laissez-faire capitalism. Neoliberalism seeks to destroy these by turning them into commodities at the same time as the forms of working-class, and some middle-class, communities that they were designed to protect are themselves under assault from capital. The essence of the precariat experience is that it lacks both the state-funded welfare rights which ameliorated the worst ravages of the market and at the same time the solidarity from settled class-based communities and mutual support systems which were able to organise and defend those rights. In the short term this may drive many into the arms of the security state that is seen as the only source of protection. But it is a state which reproduces rather than ameliorates those very conditions of insecurity. It enjoins people to take responsibility for their own lives under conditions of the destruction of communities, trust and mutual support systems. As Richard Sennett observed, 'a regime which provides human beings no deep reasons to care about one another cannot long preserve its legitimacy' (Sennett, 1998, p 148). Karl Polanyi, with whose account of capitalist transformation we began, referred to the 'double movement' whereby the advance of laissez-faire capitalism during the 19th century called forth 'a reaction against a dislocation which attacked the fabric of society, and which would have destroyed the very organization of production that the market had called into being' (Polanyi, 1957, p 130). The Keynesian welfare state was the last such reaction. This is now being pillaged and destroyed by neoliberalism to facilitate the development of new forms of commodification to sustain capitalism's pressing need for new sources of profitable investment. There is no reason to suppose that there will not, eventually, be new forms of reaction against this new dislocation and its attack on the fabric of modern society. The question is what form it will take. Guy Standing, the economist who has recently done more than many to document the emergence of the precariat, recently pointed to the dangers that such reaction could take a right-wing form. 'Chronically insecure people easily lose their altruism, tolerance and respect for non-conformity. If they have no alternative on offer, they can be led to attribute their plight to strangers in their midst' (Standing, 2011b). The aim of a progressive politics is not just to prevent such an adaptation but to develop a project of social renewal that does not hinge on the self-destructive logic of a security state and unrestrained free market capitalism.

References

Alexander, M. (2010) *The new Jim Crow: Mass incarceration in the age of colorblindness* (1st edn), New York: The New Press.

Bauman, Z. (1995) *Life in fragments: Essays in postmodern morality*, Oxford: Blackwell.

Bell, E. (2011) *Criminal justice and neoliberalism*, Abingdon: Palgrave Macmillan.

Bosworth, M. and Guild, M. (2008) 'Governing through migration control: security and citizenship in Britain', *British Journal of Criminology*, vol 48, pp 703-19.

Castells, M. (1999) 'Flows, networks and identities', in M. Castells, R. Flecha, P. Freire, H. Giroux, D. Macedo and P. Willis (eds) *Critical education in the new information age*, Lanham, MD: Rowan & Littlefield, pp 37-65.

Cavadino, M. and Dignan, J. (2007) *The penal system: An introduction* (4th edn), London: Sage Publications.

Coleman, R. (2004) *Reclaiming the streets: Surveillance, social control and the city*, Cullompton: Willan.

Coleman, R. (2007) 'Whose right to the city? Surveillance and policing the working class in the regenerating city', in R. Roberts and W. McMahon (eds) *Social justice and criminal justice*, London: Centre for Crime and Justice Studies, pp 170-85.

Coleman, R. and Sim, J. (2000) '"You'll never walk alone": CCTV surveillance, order and neo-liberal rule in Liverpool City Centre', *British Journal of Sociology*, vol 51, no 4, pp 623-39.

Coleman, R., Tombs, S. and Whyte, D. (2005) 'Capital, crime control and statecraft in the entrepreneurial city', *Urban Studies*, vol 42, no 13, pp 2511-30.

Crawford, A. (2006) 'Networked governance and the post-regulatory state? Steering, rowing and anchoring the provision of policing and security', *Theoretical Criminology*, vol 10, no 4, pp 449-79.

Crawford, A. (2009) 'Governing through anti-social behaviour: regulatory challenges to criminal justice', *British Journal of Criminology*, vol 49, pp 810-31.

Davis, M. (1990) *City of quartz: Excavating the future in Los Angeles*, London: Verso.

De Giorgi, A. (2006) *Re-thinking the political economy of punishment: Perspectives on post-Fordism and penal politics*, Aldershot: Ashgate.

De Giorgi, A. (2010) 'Immigration control, post-Fordism, and less eligibility', *Punishment & Society*, vol 12, no 2, pp 147-67.

Dorling, D., Rigby, J. and Wheeler, B. (2007) *Poverty, wealth and place in Britain, 1968 to 2005*, Bristol: The Policy Press.

Dorling, D., Vickers, D., Thomas, B., Pritchard, J. and Ballas, D. (2008) *Changing UK: The way we live now*, Sheffield: Social and Spatial Inequalities (SASI) Group, Department of Geography, University of Sheffield.

Fahmy, E. (2008) 'Tackling youth exclusion in the UK: challenges for current policy and practice', *Social Work & Society*, vol 6, no 2, pp 279-88.

Feeley, M. and Simon, J. (1992) 'The new penology: notes on the emerging strategy of corrections and its implications', *Criminology*, vol 30, no 4, pp 449-74.

Fitzgibbon, W. (2004) *Pre-emptive criminalisation: Risk control and alternative futures*, London: NAPO.

Fitzgibbon, W. (2007) 'Risk analysis and the new practitioner: myth or reality?', *Punishment & Society*, vol 9, no 1, pp 87-97.

Fitzgibbon, W. (2011) *Probation and social work on trial: Violent offenders and child abusers*, Abingdon: Palgrave Macmillan.

Fitzgibbon, W. and Lea, J. (2010) 'Police, probation and the bifurcation of community', *Howard Journal of Criminal Justice*, vol 49, no 2, pp 215-30.

Foucault, M. (1977) *Discipline and punish: The birth of the prison*, London: Allen Lane.

Foucault, M. (1991) 'Governmentality', in G. Burchell, C. Gordon and P. Miller (eds) *The Foucault effect: Studies in governmentality*, Brighton: Harvester, pp 87-104.

Gallagher, R. and Syal, R. (2011) 'Police buy software to map suspects' digital movements', *The Guardian*, 11 May.

Garland, D. (2001) *The culture of control: Crime and social order in contemporary society*, Oxford: Oxford University Press.

Graham, S. (2010) *Cities under siege: The new military urbanism*, London: Verso Books.

Gramsci, A. (1971a) 'Americanism and Fordism', in Q. Hoare and G. Nowell Smith (eds) *Selections from the 'Prison Notebooks'*, London: Lawrence & Wishart, pp 277-316.

Gramsci, A. (1971b) 'The modern prince', in Q. Hoare and G. Nowell Smith (eds) *Selections from the 'Prison Notebooks'*, London: Lawrence & Wishart, pp 123-202.

Hacker, J.S. (2006) *The great risk shift: The assault on American jobs, families, health care, and retirement – And how you can fight back*, New York: Oxford University Press.

Hall, S., Critcher, C., Jefferson, T., Clarke, J. and Roberts, B. (1978) *Policing the crisis: Mugging, the state and law and order*, London: Macmillan.

Hallsworth, S. and Lea, J. (2011) 'Reconstructing Leviathan: emerging contours of the security state', *Theoretical Criminology*, vol 15, no 2, pp 141-57.

Hannah-Moffat, K. (2005) 'Criminogenic needs and the transformative risk subject: hybridisation of risk/need in penality', *Punishment & Society*, vol 7, no 1, pp 29-51.

Harman, C. (2009) *Zombie capitalism: Global crisis and the relevance of Marx*, London: Bookmarks.

Harris, J. (2007) 'The anxious affluent middle class insecurity and social democracy', *Renewal*, vol 14, no 4, pp 72-9.

Hayes, B. (2009) *NeoConOpticon: The EU security-industrial complex*, London: Statewatch.

Hinds, L. (2005) 'Crime control in Western countries 1970 to 2000', in J. Pratt, D. Brown, M. Brown, S. Hallsworth and W. Morrison (eds), *The new punitiveness: Trends, theories, perspectives*, Cullompton: Willan, pp 47-65.

Hörnqvist, M. (2010) 'Review symposium: "Punishing the poor: the neoliberal government of social insecurity" by Loïc Wacquant', *British Journal of Criminology*, vol 50, no 3, pp 599-603.

Jessop, B. (1990) *State theory: Putting the capitalist state in its place*, Cambridge: Polity Press.

Jessop, B. (1994) 'The transition to post-Fordism and the Schumpeterian workfare state', in R. Burrows and B. Loader (eds) *Towards a post-Fordist welfare state*, London: Routledge, pp 13-37.

Koskela, H. (2003) '"Cam Era" – the contemporary urban panopticon', *Surveillance & Society*, vol 1, no 3, pp 292-313.

Lansley, S. (2009) 'Unfair to middling: how middle income Britain's shrinking wages fuelled the crash and threaten recovery', Touchstone pamphlets, London: Trades Union Congress.

Larkin, P.M. (2011) 'Incapacity, the labour market and social security: coercion into "positive" citizenship', *The Modern Law Review*, vol 74, no 3, pp 385-409.

Lea, J. (2002) *Crime and modernity*, London: Sage Publications.

Lea, J. and Stenson, K. (2007) 'Security, sovereignty, and non-state governance "from below"', *Canadian Journal of Law and Society*, vol 22, no 2, pp 9-27.

Lemke, T. (2007) 'An indigestible meal? Foucault, governmentality and state theory', *Distinktion: Scandinavian Journal of Social Theory*, vol 8, no 2, pp 43-64.

Lianos, M. and Douglas, M. (2000) 'Dangerization and the end of deviance: the institutional environment', *British Journal of Criminology*, vol 40, pp 251-78.

Mayer, M. (2010) 'Punishing the poor – a debate: some questions on Wacquant's theorising the neoliberal state', *Theoretical Criminology*, vol 14, no 1, pp 93-103.

Ministry of Justice (2010) *Breaking the cycle: Effective punishment, rehabilitation and sentencing of offenders*, Cm 7972, London: The Stationery Office.

Monahan, T. (2010) *Surveillance in the time of insecurity*, Piscataway, NJ: Rutgers University Press.

Monahan, T. and Torres, R.D. (2009) *Schools under surveillance: Cultures of control in public education*, Piscataway, NJ: Rutgers University Press.

Osborne, D. and Gaebler, T. (1992) *Reinventing government: How the entrepreneurial spirit is transforming the public sector*, New York: Addison-Wesley.

Parenti, C. (2000) *Lockdown America: Police and prisons in the age of crisis*, New York: Verso.

Polanyi, K. (1957) *The Great Transformation: The political and economic origins of our time*, Boston, MA: Beacon Press.

Porter, H. (2009) 'We need to repeal 12 years of vile laws attacking our liberty', *The Observer*, 13 September.

Poulantzas, N. (1978) *State, power, socialism*, London: New Left Books.

Raab, D. (2009) *The assault on liberty: What went wrong with rights*, London: Fourth Estate (HarperCollins).

Rodger, J.R. (2008) *Criminalising social policy: Anti-social behaviour and welfare in a de-civilised society*, Cullompton: Willan.

Sennett, R. (1998) *The corrosion of character: The personal consequences of work in the new capitalism*, New York: W.W. Norton.

Sennett, R. (2006) *The culture of the new capitalism*, New Haven, CT: Yale University Press.

Shepherd, J. (2009) 'Someone to watch over you', *The Guardian*, 4 August.

Simon, J. (2000) 'Miami: governing the city through crime', in M. Polèse and R.E. Stren (eds) *The social sustainability of cities: Diversity and the management of change*, Toronto: University of Toronto Press, pp 98-122.

Simon, J. (2007) *Governing through crime*, Oxford: Oxford University Press.

Squires, P. (2008) *ASBO nation: The criminalisation of nuisance*, Bristol: The Policy Press.

Squires, P. and Stephen, D. (2005) *Rougher justice: Anti-social behaviour and young people*, Cullompton: Willan Publishing.

Standing, G. (2011a) *The precariat: The new dangerous class*, London: Bloomsbury Academic.

Standing, G. (2011b) 'Who will be a voice for the emerging precariat?', *The Guardian*, 1 June.

Strange, S. (1996) *The retreat of the state: The diffusion of power in the world economy*, Cambridge: Cambridge University Press.

Tilly, C. (1985) 'War making and state making as organized crime', in P. Evans, D. Rueschemeyer and T. Skocpol (eds) *Bringing the state back in*, Cambridge: Cambridge University Press, pp 169-91.

Travis, A. (2011) 'Doctors asked to identify potential terrorists under government plans', *The Guardian*, 6 June.

Wacquant, L. (1996) 'The rise of advanced marginality: notes on its nature and implications', *Acta Sociologica*, vol 39, no 2, pp 121-39.

Wacquant, L. (1999) 'Urban marginality in the coming millennium', *Urban Studies*, vol 36, no 10, pp 1639-47.

Wacquant, L. (2007) *Urban outcasts: A comparative sociology of advanced marginality*, Cambridge: Polity Press.

Wacquant, L. (2008) 'Ordering insecurity: social polarization and the punitive upsurge', *Radical Philosophy Review*, vol 11, no 1, pp 9-27.

Wacquant, L. (2009) *Punishing the poor: The neoliberal government of social insecurity*, Durham, NC: Duke University Press.

Wacquant, L. (2010) 'Crafting the neoliberal state: workfare, prisonfare, and social insecurity', *Sociological Forum*, vol 25, no 2, pp 197-220.

Webber, F. (2006) *Border wars and asylum crimes*, London: Statewatch.

Wilson, E. (2009) 'Deconstructing the shadows', in E. Wilson (ed) *Government of the shadows: Parapolitics and criminal sovereignty*, London: Pluto Press, pp 13-55.

Wilson, J.Q. and Kelling, G.F. (1982) 'Broken windows: the police and neighborhood safety', *Atlantic Monthly*, March, pp 29-38.

Wood, D. (2003) 'Foucault and panopticism revisited', *Surveillance & Society*, vol 1, no 3, pp 234-9.

Young, J. (1999) *The exclusive society: Social exclusion, crime and difference in late modernity*, London: Sage Publications.

Zedner, L. (2005) 'Securing liberty in the face of terror: reflections from criminal justice', *Journal of Law and Society*, vol 32, no 4, pp 507-33.

Zedner, L. (2007) 'Pre-crime and post-criminology?', *Theoretical Criminology*, vol 11, no 2, pp 261-81.

THREE

The state, sovereignty and advanced marginality in the city

Kevin Stenson

Introduction

This chapter sketches Loïc Wacquant's key arguments about the neoliberal state project and advanced marginality with particular reference to the impact of these processes on racial and minority ethnic groups and the neighbourhoods in which they are concentrated in advanced societies. It notes criticisms of this position, and while acknowledging strengths in Wacquant's attempts to bring together materialist Marxist and cultural, neo-Durkheimian perspectives, it is argued that in practice there is an over-reliance on materialist assumptions that depict social actors primarily as economic actors in the last instance. The chapter provides an alternative perspective, developed by this author in a series of publications, rooted in a revisionist interpretation of governmentality perspectives. This highlights a broadened conception of sovereignty, understood not as a structure but as a series of interrelated processes deployed to secure control and legitimation of nation-states. These range from coercive practices to the struggle for different forms of security – from food security to nation-building strategies and technologies. This perspective does not primarily view people as economic actors; indeed it views economic relations and practices as politically and culturally constructed. Hence sovereign nation-state practices in relation to minority groups are not always or primarily best understood in terms of notions of advanced economic marginality. They are also bound up with contested attempts to create and reproduce both ethnic and civic forms of national citizenship at different spatial scales, from local to national. This perspective also highlights that attempts to enact sovereign governance 'from above' always interact with forms of territorial governance by myriad groups and sites of governance 'from below'. These may include a range of religious, ethnic, racially or spatially defined and based groupings.

Wacquant's originality

Through a series of publications, Wacquant argues that we need to broaden our conception of neoliberalism from a narrow focus on economic policies promoting the virtues of lightly regulated markets over state activity, towards a more sociological conception (see, for example, Wacquant, 2008, 2009a, 2009b, 2011). This recognises that, given the painful, destabilising effects of the international agenda of neoliberal policies, there is a functional need for interdependent linkages between strategies of 'state-craft' – state-orchestrated economic and social controls. In addition to economic policies these include tough, punitive modes of policing, criminal justice and punishment, along with a shift away from state-funded welfare benefit safety-nets for the poor towards more conditional 'workfare' policies. These provide time-limited benefits linked with training and other measures – deploying both policy sticks and carrots – to channel people from welfare dependency into low skills labour markets. Yet, Wacquant was not the first to identify these changes brought about by the administrations of the New Right from the 1980s. Commentators from a range of ideological and theoretical positions noted the toughening of policies of control accompanying the neoliberal economic agenda. Because of the growing inequalities, job insecurity, social dislocation and public disorder associated with the policies of the New Right, from riots and chronically high levels of violent crime in US city ghettos, to the miners' strike and uprising by poor whites and minority ethnic groups in England, these usually involve the toughening of police and criminal justice policy. They also involved a fiscally tighter approach to welfare benefits and services for the poor and economically inactive (see, for example, Scraton and Chadwick, 1991; Gamble, 1994; Young, 1999; Garland, 2001; Dean, 2007; Simon, 2007; Parenti, 2008).

While ingredients of Wacquant's arguments may be familiar in other work, his originality lies in the way he recombines these ingredients in a new theoretical dish. There are two theoretical props to Wacquant's broadened sociological model of neoliberalism, one historically materialist/Marxist and the other philosophically idealist, culturally focused, and embodied in the Durkheimian sociological tradition. He tries to synthesise these, and in doing so he joins a long tradition of varied radical French theorising, including Sartre's attempts to synthesise Marxism with existentialist phenomenology (Sartre, 2006). This can be seen as a continuation of Wacquant's collaboration with his late colleague Pierre Bourdieu. The cultural dimension of this analysis emphasises the role of cultural (as well as economic) capital in reproducing class and power relations, the meaning and collective representations of policing, criminal justice, prisons and penality, the symbolic staging to the public of the state's sovereign power through propaganda and demonstrations of the overwhelming coercive powers available to the state to suppress dissent and conduct foreign wars, and the attempts to legitimate the new methods of state-craft linking policy streams that may have originally developed somewhat independently, to control the economically marginalised populations (Wacquant, 2009b, pp 304-14). There is symmetry in these shifts between a highly gendered division of labour in styles of disciplinary control: the harsh father combined with a more emollient, nurturing mother. In 'workfare states' new forms of control are less emollient and nurturing. There are masculine-toned, punitive, 'zero tolerant' developments in policing and criminal justice, aimed mainly at perceivably troublesome boys and men, and the shift away from maternal, feminine-toned, nurturing dimension of state-craft, once aimed also and perhaps mainly at managing and supporting poor women and children (Gelsthorpe, 2011).

The neoliberal move was from universal or general welfare programmes of support and rehabilitation for the poor, vulnerable or deviant, towards narrowly targeted and tougher policies of 'workfare', ironically introduced in the US by Democrat President Clinton in his 'tough love' welfare reforms of the 1990s, providing benchmarks for parallel policy shifts in the UK and elsewhere. Whether this signifies a move from soft femininity to hard-hearted masculinity is a moot point. It depends on how we define femininity. One is reminded of UK neoliberal, Conservative Prime Minister Margaret Thatcher's response, in an interview, to charges that she was unfeminine and lacking in compassion in her approach to the poor and vulnerable:

> 'It's really like a nurse mothering a patient with sympathy. A good nurse will say "Now come on, you've been very ill, but you've got to try to get up".... If a nurse just smothers a patient with sympathy and says "Oh you just stay in bed", instead of saying "Now come on make the effort, you can do it", which do you think produces the best human being?' (quoted in *Catholic Herald*, 5 December 1978)

For Wacquant there is a close link between the advanced marginalisation of populations and shifting racial politics. He insists that 'race' in its spatially segregated form is not a timeless, unchanging essence. The explanation of the economic, cultural and institutional construction of 'race' emphasises major political and economic changes, largely beyond the awareness of ordinary citizens and their ability to shape events. There have been, so the argument goes, significant shifts in the US between the period marked by slavery, followed by Jim Crow laws and institutions controlling freed slaves, including share-cropping, after the Civil War. This transformed during the 20th century, giving way to a period of the relatively well ordered black ghetto, with its complex hierarchies, internally protected markets and a degree of economic self-sufficiency. This changed after the civil rights movement's partial liberation of the educated black middle class from the late 1960s, creating the parlous state of the present hyper-ghetto, where many black people, unable to benefit from upward mobility to the suburbs, are excluded from the official economy.

With the flight of the black professional and entrepreneurial classes and their representative organisations, since the 1960s the new ghetto has become an increasingly impoverished and brutalised warehouse of the poor, subject to intense punitive disciplines and surveillance, and increasingly denuded of effective political advocates willing and able to speak up for those at the bottom of the barrel. While there is recognition of the legal and cultural constructions of 'race' involved in these changes, at root the emphasis is on the role of 'race' in the economy, and the different modes of exploitation – and more recently marginalisation or wholesale exclusion – of black labour (Wacquant, 2009b, pp 195-208).

One of the hallmark features of these changes is the symmetry in the last three decades between the warehousing in prisons of growing numbers of poor people, especially from minority ethnic groups, and the policies of containment of people in poor neighbourhoods, via surveillance, aggressive policing and other means (cf Stenson, 2007). In the new security state the boundaries between prison and ghetto become increasingly blurred. This may involve tolerance shown for the corralling in zones of poverty of illegal drugs markets and the associated violent conflict over turf that involves, and the huge industry of drug money laundering that implicates major banks and financial centres. These developments blur the boundaries between legal and illegal economic networks that are increasingly international in scope and operation (Vulliamy, 2010).

There are caveats in Wacquant's arguments about the differential unfolding of these developments in varying national and local contexts. For example, the poor city and suburban neighbourhoods with high proportions of racial and minority ethnic groups in France and other European countries, while marked by high levels of crime and unemployment and prone to periodic insurrection against the police, have a stronger legacy of welfare, assistantial support than in the US, are more porous, less isolated than US hyper-ghettos, and have more complex, diverse, shifting demographic profiles. Nevertheless, he is clear that with the growing urban inequalities, unemployment and other strains resulting from neoliberal globalisation, we can expect these US policy agendas or modes of state-craft to become incorporated across the advanced capitalist world via a process of policy transfer through exchanges by intellectuals, civil servants and policy makers (Wacquant, 1999; cf Stenson and Edwards, 2004; Jones and Newburn, 2007).

Criticisms of Wacquant

Some criticisms of Wacquant are by now familiar. There is, for example, the view that rather than an international benchmark, the US is an outlier among advanced countries in having harsher policing and higher levels of incarceration, more limited public services, and, despite the crime drop, as measured by official indices over the last decade, very high levels of crime in workless, poorer areas, much of which is probably not reported to little trusted officialdom. Moreover, there is perhaps too much reliance on the example of African American South Side Chicago, itself an outlier within the US, where most of the cities now – as in Europe – have more fluid, plural poor populations from very diverse immigrant origins (Putnam, 2007; Patillo, 2009). Since the complex riots and conflicts that exploded in US cities from the early 1990s it is clear that the old 'race' conflict model, depicting conflict vertically between a powerful white majority and powerless black minority, is no longer sufficient. With the new urban demography, including a growing Latino population, South East Asians and so on in an ethnic kaleidoscope, intergroup relations become more salient. New groups come into the city, are often involved in lateral, economic, political and cultural 'turf wars' with each and disturb the older African American hegemony in poorer neighbourhoods. These new groups may have little knowledge of or sympathy with age-old narratives of racial domination and exploitation within the US. Their places within this old narrative may be unclear and new power relations emerge at local levels (Miles, 1992; Abelman and Lie, 1995). Since the UK and US city riots in the 1980s and early 1990s it is clear that while black/white racial – intersecting with vertical class – tensions remain potent in some areas, rapidly increasing immigration into wealthy countries has made a significant difference. Older cleavages supplement and complicate tensions between varied, poor minority groups defined more by ethnic/religious cultural identities and struggling with each other to survive and prosper within cities (Waddington et al, 2004; Stenson and Waddington, 2007).

Furthermore, Wacquant's focus on synchronic linkages between structures and variables within a particular epoch downplay deeper continuities. Beneath the fast-changing events on the surface of history, institutional life changes more slowly. To what extent is neoliberalism old wine blended for modern conditions? Earlier generations in the 19th and 20th centuries were likely to refer to 'laissez-faire' capitalism, or Manchester Free Trade ideology. These are variants of the long tradition of Anglo-Scottish political economy, central to the movements between the 18th and 20th centuries for nation-states founded on democracy, the separation of governmental powers, liberal freedoms, the formation of markets governed by law rather than monarchical whim and cronyism, free trade and movements for ethnic self-determination. With these and other ingredients, rebellious English gentry forged the intellectual vision of the American Republic (Friedland, 1998). Moreover, the picture Wacquant paints of the awesome power of the US security state is unconvincing. Constitutional checks and balances on state and federal government powers have always frustrated centralising executive powers within the republic, whatever its foreign activities, especially by comparison with Europe, whose sovereign nation-states enjoy much greater powers over citizens and localities. This is why, in a diverse, turbulent society, imbued with the myths of independent, armed frontiersmen, there has always been a strong reliance on the sanctity and majesty of a tough rule of law (where it can be enforced) in order to provide the glue of solidarity (Gurr, 1989; Garland, 2007). Furthermore, workfare-style policies were familiar in US history, and the huge scale of costly current incarceration may prove to be unaffordable, counter-productive and dysfunctional rather than a functionally essential element of current state-craft (Piven, 2010).

More broadly, it is tempting for radical social scientists, in Marxist vein, to use the functionalist language of material 'forces', that are held to summon new approaches to economic and social regulation required by Western capitalism, in which new technologies have raced ahead and Fordist manufacturing has largely collapsed or been outsourced to developing economies. In this Marxist view, capitalism is conceived of as a material process, an economic system based on regimes to accumulate capital and exploit labour, which regularly creates explosive internal contradictions leading to major changes (Jessop, 2007). Political economic, materialist explanations try to discover laws which are supposed to govern economic relations, whether understood in terms of regimes of capital accumulation and class struggle or, in the political economic language of mainstream market economics, the operations of markets and the laws that supposedly govern them and enable us to model and predict economic behaviour. Those approaches focus on 'material' economic relations said to be, in the last instance, determinant of cultural processes – the realm of non-material 'ideas' and actions. In philosophical terms they echo Descartes' dualism of mind and body: the spiritual and the material and the Judaeo-Christian theological baggage that entails. For this author, the temptations of these explanations should be resisted. Mechanistic or organic metaphors in explanation, while at times having a poetic power, are, at best, shorthand for complex processes and can mislead. Let us turn to an alternative approach that rejects the basic categorical distinction between the material and the cultural: realist (as distinct from the more familiar discursive) governmentality theory.

Realist governmentality theory: a broader conception of sovereignty

Its focus is on sovereignty and the interaction between governance from above and below. Governmentality theory in its discursive form focuses not directly on institutions and practices but on the varied mentalities, or rationalities, of liberal governance. These theorists study reflections on, and ways of thinking about, how to govern. They downplay the role of the sovereign state and can even be agnostic about its very existence, focusing on myriad forms of governance beyond the state. They extend Foucault's examination of shifts in European liberal governance (Foucault, 1991; Rose et al, 2006; Valverde, 2010). By contrast, realist governmentality theory rejects the claim that you can differentiate the study of the mentalities of liberal governance from the ways that politicians, officials, professional agents and other citizens interpret and apply them in their everyday practices and the contexts in which they operate (Stenson, 1998, 2005, 2008a, 2008b; Lippert and Stenson, 2010).

This approach highlights the central role of an expanded understanding of sovereignty as the meeting point, in advanced democracies, for liberalism and (ethnic and civic) nationalism. In addition to the struggle to maintain physical security through force by the military, security and police agencies, sovereignty involves attempts to exercise fiscal and monetary controls and provide a guarantor of the value of state currencies that facilitate economic activity, a function that can be traced back to the states of ancient Greece. Sovereign technologies of government also involve nation-building, for example, myriad attempts to foster cultural solidarity among increasingly diverse and pluralistic populations (Stenson, 1993, 2007, 2008a, 2008b). Moreover, in the modern era of nation-states since the 17th century, the universalistic values of liberalism with their emphasis on equality, human rights and so on, emerged in close relationship with nationalist ideologies. These emphasise ethnic, religious and other values, identities, histories and solidarities *particular* to a given nation.

They developed within emerging nation-states in the 19th and 20th centuries and welfare states were the product of nation building, often linked to military agendas, combined with social liberalism as an internationally transferable, cosmopolitan discourse (Tilly, 2003). There are no known examples of states that govern in the name of liberal, social or capitalist principles and values that are not intrinsically intertwined with and legitimated by particular forms of ethnic, leavened somewhat with civic, nationalism (Smith, 2010). Furthermore, claims that nation-states are leaving the historical stage, and that banks and corporations are increasingly independent from them, are weak. Their ultimate protectors remain the citizens of the nation-state within which they are headquartered. The dependence by financial services companies on nation-state governments and national taxpayers bailing them out with loans during the 2008-09 global banking crisis and credit crunch supports this view. Even with globally interdependent markets, the nation-state remains the most significant unit of political authority and the powers of agencies of international governance like the United Nations (UN) or International Monetary Fund (IMF) are largely delegated from strong nation-states (Lea and Stenson, 2007). This becomes starkly apparent at times of war or financial collapse when international agencies of law and governance routinely falter in generating collective remedial action that can command general consent (Stenson, 2008a, 2010). Hence, in this theory, rather than seeing sovereign processes as part of the superstructure of the state, driven by material economic forces from below, the relationship is precisely the reverse. Modern sophisticated economic activity is made possible by the coercive and symbolic activities of nation-states. Social life is driven by political, symbolic and military drivers (Tilly, 2003).

Realist governmentality theory emphasises, in addition to sovereignty: the importance of the contexts, at different spatial scales, of the interaction between struggles by dominant state, commercial and non-governmental organisation (NGO) agencies of governance 'from above' with those emanating 'from below' to govern territory and manage risks. It also emphasises the need to employ a range of data sets, including both oral and textual discourses, and methodologies. The analysis of governance must recognise the interactions between the attempts 'from below' to conceptualise and manage risks and control territories by a range of ethnic, religious, criminal and other social networks and, on the other hand, attempts by state, commercial and NGO modes of governance, to manage risk and govern 'from above' (Stenson, 2005, 2010). Realist governmentality theory views politics, culture and active human agency as central. In challenging the dualistic distinction between materialist and cultural explanation, it views the differentiation between society and the market economy as a historically produced political and cultural creation; these divisions are not given in nature (Gordon, 1991).

Making a living and struggles over the allocation of wealth and income are indeed central to social life and should be for social science, but that does not mean we should see those processes as operating in a separate sphere from the rest of human existence, and subject to separate laws, whether of efficient, self-clearing markets or of capital accumulation. For example, rather than accepting dry assumptions about economic actors exercising rational choices, ethnographic description and analysis of the group dynamics, and volatile, emotive, gendered, motivations and behaviour patterns operating among market traders in the financial services industry can be crucial to understanding how markets are reproduced in myriad local settings (Tett, 2010). Hence, here, capitalism is seen not as a global *system* but as a *process*: intrinsically cultural, variable processes, politically shaped and rooted in particular values, beliefs and habits. These are interpreted and applied in varying settings (Chang, 2010; Stiglitz, 2010).

So, the changes associated with the rise of neoliberalism were only inevitable and functionally necessary with the wisdom of hindsight. But this is seen through a guttering light from the stern, not the bow, of history's galleon. These neoliberal policy developments involved considerable, artful political effort and coalition building (in overt and covert forms) over many years by an international intellectual and social/political movement inspired by Friedrich Hayek, Milton Friedman, Alan Greenspan and their acolytes (Harvey, 2005). If these intellectuals and politicians had the hand of history on their shoulders, they, as political agents, also put their own shoulders and creative energy to its wheel. This involved frequent meetings in Switzerland and other locations since the 1940s, and from the 1960s the ideology was championed in the economics and law departments of the University of Chicago and the major US business schools. It was disseminated by lobbyists possessing deep pockets, burrowing into Wall Street, the US government, the City of London and other centres of financial corporate, and political party power. At its core neoliberalism is a set of political economic beliefs enshrined in so-called positive, 'scientific' economics, accredited by state ministries, prestigious universities, and major business corporations. These beliefs posit the naturalness and self-regulatory efficiency of free markets. They also posit the pre-eminence of the principles of 'shareholder value' (although not the influence of shareholders) in corporate governance. These principles trump wider conceptions of the public interest, yet are held to provide the basis for liberal democracy and valued freedoms (Hutton, 2003).

Thus neoliberalism is an international political/social movement peddling a self-serving package of diagnoses and solutions, often termed the 'Washington Consensus'. These have been funded by business interests set to gain by the reordering, along business-friendly lines, and scaling down, of state activity, and the reduction of taxes on business and high earners. In effect its major goal has been to enhance the power of financial managers, and diminish the powers of shareholders in corporations (representing, for example, the pension savings of many millions of workers). And, notwithstanding rhetorical froth about extending liberty and democracy, it also aims to diminish the power of elected politicians in leading liberal nation-states and, hence, the masses of citizens they represent, to constrain and shape the operation of businesses and markets in ways that may reduce short-term profitability. This movement, at least in Western capitalist nations, has concentrated power in the hands of a super rich, mobile international elite with an increasingly homogeneous, high-end consumerist, and high security, lifestyle. These are people with doubtful patriotic loyalty to any one nation (Frank, 2008; Stiglitz, 2010).

Nevertheless, as the rising economic powers of the East, with their burgeoning sovereign wealth funds indicate, where there is strong political will it is possible for politicians to seize back the initiative from speculative bond traders and investment banks like Pimco and Goldman Sachs, and their lobbyists. At every stage the implementation of neoliberal policies has involved choices over political values and political strategies and complex coalition building to win popular support for these policies (Chang, 2010). After the financial collapse, bank bailouts and frauds on epic scale by New York hedge funder Bernie Madoff and others between 2007 and 2009, many senior economists and executives in the banks and finance regulatory agencies have accepted that the pretensions of neoliberal market economics to be an objective science capable of prediction are threadbare (Turner, 2009). On the contrary, this 'science' is an instrument of governance, working on behalf of sectional privileged interests, crime-generating on an industrial scale, for both upper and lower class offenders (Reiner, 2007), and it puts the stability of the global economy and economic security of billions of people at constant risk.

In the Cold War era it was politically useful for neoliberals to play down the differences between Western social democracy and Soviet state socialism – and indeed Fascist forms of collectivism – with their police state/bureaucratic tyrannies, and dysfunctional economic systems. In the neoliberal vision, social democracy was Stalinist socialism in diluted form. However, the major function of this social movement, both before its politicians formed government administrations and after their formation, was to provide a critique of and mobilisation against the variety of social democratic welfare states that had emerged in the 20th century, reaching their high point in the long economic boom following the Second World War and 1950s austerity. Moreover, while neoliberal and Marxist political economists from the right and left, respectively, group states under the broad heading of the Keynesian welfare state, this operates at a high level of abstraction. In practice, particular nation-states have diverse histories, demography, social and governance structures, including varying forms of policing, criminal justice and penality and welfare, from the Catholic corporatism of Italy and Spain to the secular rights-based public services of Sweden (Esping-Andersen, 1990; Cavadino and Dignan, 2005).

The liberal shield and non-punitive social control

Social liberal and Keynesian political rationalities created, in the advanced social democracies and more liberal US states, the political and bureaucratic space – relatively shielded from the rough play of democratic politics – for the development of new liberal professions adjunct to the law. These were armed with new social science-based expertise in pathological conduct, especially of young offenders deemed salvageable from a life of crime. This expertise, hence, provided warrant for publicly funded, crime prevention and rehabilitative alternatives to a more primeval, punitive retributive justice. These professions and alternative approaches to justice, dealing with the alleged deeper causes of crime, flourished where variants of Keynesian welfarism and support (especially among unionised public sector workers) for the parties of the Centre Left were greatest, for example, in Western Europe and, in the US, in states that had been solid Democrat territories, like Massachusetts (Simon, 2007).

Support for these progressive alternatives has tended to be greatest among the (numerically modest) senior members of the liberal political classes, senior civil servants and liberal, educated middle-class professionals, although now may be faltering amidst heightened middle-class insecurity (Garland, 2001). Moreover, the extent to which these measures command support among the mass of the working classes most likely to be victimised by routine volume crime and anti-social behaviour in their neighbourhoods remains a matter of controversy. There is evidence that public attitudes may soften when people are informed of the complex contexts of offending, yet this is unlikely to affect large numbers of citizens (Pratt et al, 2005; Roberts and Hough, 2011). It is difficult to find hard evidence of a golden age when there was truly mass working-class popular support for less punitive approaches to criminal justice and generous welfare benefits for the long-term poor and unemployed. It was always easy for the popular media to reflect and reinforce the common view that the recipients of welfare are workshy, devious or lazy and criminals are, mostly, morally culpable deviants deserving of penalty (Wilkins, 1991). This illustrates the point that, while mutually constitutive, liberalism, democracy and (communitarian-flavoured) nationalism are uneasy bedfellows. The good liberal wants democracy yet may fear that – as in the US in the long-term grip of the New Right – it brings in its train what is seen through a liberal lens as the spectre of mob justice, driven not by reason but by bigotry and demagoguery (Stenson, 2001).

Criminology, an instrument of governance

One of Wacquant's strengths is that given the cultural dimension of his theories, he draws our attention to the role of neoliberal intellectuals and their technical associates, and the think-tanks and other institutions that employ them, in driving these policies and in the creation and dissemination of the ideas that underpin and legitimate the punitive neoliberal agenda. This raises awkward questions for criminology. Can it tell truth to power? Or is it, like economics, inevitably drawn into the service of the state and big corporations as an instrument of governance? Whose side are we on? Who funds our teaching, research and publications, and do those who pay us academic pipers call the tunes we play? Wacquant is right to argue that it is not enough to characterise and typologise criminological perspectives in narrowly discursive terms (Loader and Sparks, 2010; Wacquant, 2011, p 444). We need a sociological, realist account of the production, reception and impact of knowledge. In the Durkheimian tradition sociological explanations differ from individualistic explanations of social behaviour in recognising that our motivations and behaviour are influenced not simply by processes within the body and individual mind, or emergent interactions between individuals, but also by the institutions that we forge and which help to shape our thinking and behaviour. It is dangerous to regard institutions in rigid reified form. They are usually, to a degree, fluid, messy, protean entities. Individuals reproduce institutions through their thoughts and actions; nevertheless they usually involve a measure of continuity in shared memory, ways of thinking and habituated patterns of action (Berger and Luckmann, 1967). Hence, social institutions, from the family to the international corporation, are more than the sum of the individuals that make them up. These are in part shaped by wider pressures, often beyond the awareness of citizens, which need to be uncovered by the social science expert: for example, how private troubles are shaped by public issues. It is hence important always to be alert to the interaction between the habitus – or actions and predispositions of individuals or groups as actors in the social drama – and the institutional field or networks within which they operate. They include, as Wacquant argues, for example, the bureaucratic field of state institutions, which have their own distinct modes of operation (Bourdieu, 1999). This reminds us that the tendency among post-modernist, post-structuralist and interpretivist social scientists to downplay the role of the nation-state as a unitary, well-resourced social actor has been greatly exaggerated (Lea and Stenson, 2007).

It is, hence, also important to try to analyse academic knowledge within the institutional contexts and networks in which criminologists work. This author argued similarly – and perhaps in complement to Wacquant's argument – in sketching a Foucauldian analysis of the production of criminological perspectives as complexes of power and knowledge within interdependent and interpenetrating circuits of power for the production of what counts as accredited 'truth' (Foucault, 1980; Stenson, 1991). This is an argument that requires updating and further development. We need to go beyond the analysis of mainstream and right-wing criminological ideas and related policies and also analyse the role of radical forms of criminology. Radicals can be just as prone to the taint of self or sectional interest, and selective myopia in creating knowledge and the will to power (Stenson and Waddington, 2007). Moreover, there has been considerable interplay between theories and policies on the fringes and in the mainstream. Radical ideas in critical criminology, such as restorative justice, anti-racist critiques of policing and criminal justice, mediation and harm reduction drug management policies, can move from radical periphery to the orthodox mainstream within a few years. But these initiatives, in official policy mode, sometimes take forms which the radical theorists may not have envisaged, nor approved (Stenson, 1991).

These overlapping and interpenetrating circuits of power/knowledge include, first, the varying financial and class settings within which criminologists work in universities, research institutes, government departments and so on. Second, these circuits involve the criminologist's conditions of life and work as an intellectual. That is the field of research, place in the academy, the disciplinary professional associations – like the British, European and American Societies of Criminology – and the political and economic demands to which he or she submits or against which he or she rebels in the university or other place of work. In the struggle for survival and dominance, criminologists (both mainstream, state-sponsored and radical, critical scholars), like other professional groups, tend to form tribe-like groupings and hierarchies, create quasi-sacred texts delineating school orthodoxies, and powerful gatekeepers of knowledge and professional access through, for example, the major, prestigious, 'high impact' learned journals, or leading critical, radical, peer-reviewed journals.

Third, criminologists operate in relation to the politics of what counts as truth in the wider society through, for example, the mainstream media, professions, industrial groups and their governing associations, and the more influential policy think-tanks with hotline access to senior politicians, and to formal democratic political institutions. To be taken seriously by the public and key policy makers, academic knowledge preferably adopts a mathematised, quantitative form, even if qualitative data and analysis can play a complementary role. Criminologists also need, for occupational survival, to adapt flexibly to prevailing policy currents and available sources of funding. For example, this may mean adjusting to the outsourcing of policing and probation practice to the private sector and a neoliberal contract regime of paying for results judged by reduction in reoffending rates (Fitzgibbon, 2011).

Hence, to have any chance of influence in the wider national or international settings it is important that criminologists work with the grain of what counts as the 'common sense' of the age, even as it tries to shift its centre of gravity (Stenson, 1991, pp 11-27). They may even achieve the status of 'public intellectual', with ready access to the media, ability to command broad public attention and articulate new directions for understanding crime and shifting crime control policy (Wacquant, 2011). This involves telling stories that render difficult issues intelligible to those beyond the worlds of expertise. Hence, in that sense, the true public intellectual is a story teller as much as a West African Griot, or a Siberian shaman; he or she performs a similar function, universal to human societies. In addition to scientific expertise, the public intellectual must also be an expert in rhetoric. This term is sometimes used pejoratively to denote preference for style over substance. Yet rhetoric, the art of persuasion, is crucial. It is not enough for an argument to be logical and coherent and well supported by evidence. It must also persuade the listener or reader, to move him or her emotionally, aesthetically or morally, often with metaphoric, figurative images and language that resonate with audiences (Stenson, 2008b).

Conclusion

By these measures Wacquant is emerging as a public intellectual. With panache, he has had an impact on the academic world at least and beyond into the media world, perhaps demonstrating the benefits of his voyage of personal discovery into the world of boxing. However, from the perspective of this author, his Achilles heel remains his attempt to bring together the discordant elements of Marxist, materialist political economy with his creative cultural analysis. One consequence is a tendency, despite recognising the shifting cultural constructions of racial identities, to view actors and groups at root as economic agents: the advanced marginal populations are seen primarily in relation to their marginalisation from labour markets and the troubles they cause for agents of the state. There is the danger, in this analysis, of under-emphasising the global and historical ubiquity of the use of racial and ethnic/tribal, biological and cultural markers of difference as a basis for individual and collective identity, social, economic and political organisation, and social competition (albeit in a host of different, evolving ways). These processes can operate in societies with varying economic arrangements. And ethnicity and religion can also interact with other sources and markers of collective identity such as shared sexual orientation, youth subcultural affiliation, and so on.

They are not simply a function of state-craft managed by elites from above, nor of macro, economic changes. Furthermore, in nation-states, there are always dominant ethnic groups, or alliances of dominant groups. At national level, the dominant groups or racial/ethnic alliances tend at any one time to monopolise power and access to social honour and resources, and shape the dominant culture in their images. This can also operate at neighbourhood level, sometimes reversing the intergroup power relations that operate in the upper reaches of society. These changes can happen while groups compete and manoeuvre to defend and advance their interests from below. Other upwardly mobile groups strive to penetrate or replace the hierarchy (Horowitz, 1985;

Lind, 1997; Smith, 2010). The socioeconomic position of cultural groups does not simply stem from the activities of state agencies and large corporations; it also involves cultural processes from below: how, for example, individuals and groups identify themselves, the nature of their lifestyles, mind sets, values and routine activities, the capacities and forms of capital they acquire and marshal, including the legacy of family and ethnic histories. These factors vary and can have considerable impact on how different groups interact with each other and on their life chances (Modood, 1998; Sen, 2007). These complex processes need to be factored into our explanations. We are not just passive playthings of material structural forces governing from above. Nor are we necessarily confined simply to resisting or adapting to agendas of governance emanating from above. Many groups at ground level, from street gangs to religious organisations, can set their own agendas.

Hence the familiar language of state-craft regulating the relations between majority and minority racial/class relations, retains some utility in the mainly white, rural and suburban heartlands of formerly 'indigenous' or long dominant populations (for example, in Europe, the US Mid-West and Australasian suburbia). However, this majority–minority language is less useful in hyper-diverse urban settings where it is unclear who is in the majority, where the previously dominant groups of whatever 'race' may now be in a minority and the power relations between new groups and old are changing (Stenson and Waddington, 2007). With rapidly growing and mobile global populations, this is likely to be increasingly characteristic of the modern Western city (Putnam, 2007). To explore and understand these new complexities and the emerging power relations involved, we need more than just critical, normatively based, social constructionist reflections on state-craft, and on the role of the media, police, criminal justice and other regulatory agencies (Lippert and Stenson, 2010). That is the easy bit and only scratches the surface of social life. We also need a programme of engaged, realist study of the fast-changing lives of the new populations in the city and their shifting relations of allegiance or otherwise with the nation-states in which they are situated. The insistence in realist governmentality theory on the cultural and political nature of social life, while breaking the umbilical cord with Marxist and bourgeois political economy, in no way blunts our critical edge as social scientists, nor evades attention to what are conventionally defined as economic relations. On the contrary, it can sharpen our critical edge, provide us with a larger conceptual tool box and firmly shoulder social actors high and low with moral responsibility for their policies and actions.

References

Abelman, N. and Lie, J. (eds) (1994) *The Los Angeles riots: Lessons for the urban future*, Boulder, CO: Westview Press.

Bourdieu, P. (1999) *The weight of the world: Social suffering and impoverishment in contemporary society*, Cambridge: Polity Press.

Berger, P.L. and Luckmann, T. (1967) *The social construction of reality*, London: Allen Lane.

Cavadino, M. and Dignan, J. (2005) *Penal systems: A comparative approach*, London: Sage Publications.

Chang, H.-J. (2010) *23 things they don't tell you about capitalism*, London: Allen Lane.

Dean, M. (2007) *Governing societies: Political perspectives on domestic and international rule*, Maidenhead: Open University Press.

Esping-Andersen, G. (1990) *The three worlds of welfare capitalism*, Cambridge: Polity Press.

Fitzgibbon, W. (2011) *Probation and social work on trial: Violent offenders and child abusers*, London: Palgrave.

Foucault, M. (1980) 'Truth and power', in C. Gordon (ed) *Michel Foucault: Power/knowledge – Selected interviews and other writings 1972–1977*, Brighton: Harvester.

Foucault, M. (1991) 'Governmentality', in G. Burchell, C. Gordon and P. Miller (eds) *The Foucault effect: Studies in governmentality*, Hemel Hempstead: Harvester Wheatsheaf.

Frank, R. (2008) *Richistan: A journey through the American wealth boom and the lives of the new rich*, New York: Three Rivers Press.

Friedland, J. (1998) *Bring home the revolution: The case for a British republic*, London: Fourth Estate.

Gamble, A. (1994) *The free economy and the strong state: The politics of Thatcherism*, London: Palgrave Macmillan.

Garland, D. (2001) *The culture of control: Crime and social order in contemporary society*, Oxford: Oxford University Press.

Garland, D. (2007) 'Death, denial, discourse: on the forms and functions of American capital punishment', in D. Downes, P. Rock, C. Chinkin and C. Gearty (eds) *Crime, social control and human rights: From moral panics to states of denial, Essays in honour of Stanley Cohen*, Cullompton: Willan, pp 136-56.

Gelsthorpe, L. (2010) 'Women, crime and control', *Criminology and Criminal Justice*, vol 10, no 4, pp 375-86.

Gordon, C. (1991) 'Governmental rationality: an introduction', in G. Burchell, C. Gordon and P. Miller (eds) *The Foucault effect: Studies in governmentality*, Hemel Hempstead: Harvester Wheatsheaf, pp 1-52.

Gurr, T.R. (1989) *Violence in America: The history of crime, vol 1 (Violence, cooperation, peace)*, London: Sage Publications.

Harvey, D. (2005) *A brief history of neoliberalism*, Oxford: Oxford University Press.

Horowitz, D.H. (1985) *Ethnic groups in conflict*, Berkeley, CA: University of California Press.

Hutton, W. (2003) *The world we're in*, London: Abacus.

Jessop, B. (2007) *State power*, Cambridge: Polity Press.

Jones T. and Newburn, T. (2007) *Policy transfer and criminal justice*, Maidenhead: Open University Press.

Lea, J. and Stenson, K. (2007) 'Security, sovereignty, and non-state governance "from below"', *Canadian Journal of Law and Society*, vol 22, no 2, pp 9-28.

Lind, M. (1997) *The next American nation: New nationalism and the fourth American revolution*, New York: Simon & Schuster.

Lippert, R. and Stenson, K. (2010) 'Advancing governmentality studies: lessons from social constructionism', *Theoretical Criminology*, vol 14, no 4, pp 473-94.

Loader, I. and Sparks, R. (2010) 'Wacquant and civic sociology: "formative intentions" and formative experiences', *Criminology and Criminal Justice*, vol 10, no 4, pp 405-15.

Miles, J. (1992) 'Blacks vs Browns: the struggle for the bottom rung', *The Atlantic Monthly*, October, pp 41-66.

Modood, T. (1998) *Ethnic minorities in Britain: Diversity and disadvantage – The Fourth National Survey of Ethnic Minorities (PSI report)*, London: Policy Studies Institute.

Parenti, C. (2008) *Lockdown America: Police and prisons in the age of crisis*, London: Verso Books.

Patillo, M. (2009) 'Revisiting Loïc Wacquant's *Urban outcasts*', *International Journal of Urban and Regional Research*, vol 33, no 3, pp 858-64.

Piven, F.F. (2010) 'A response to Wacquant', *Theoretical Criminology*, vol 14, no 1, pp 111-16.

Pratt, J., Brown, D., Brown, M., Hallsworth, S. and Morrison, W. (eds) (2005) *The new punitiveness: Trends, theories, perspectives*, Cullompton: Willan.

Putnam, R. (2007) 'E pluribus unum. Diversity and community in the twenty first century (The 2006 Johan Skytte Prize Lecture)', *Scandinavian Political Studies*, vol 30, no 2, pp 137-74.

Reiner, R. (2007) *Law and order: An honest citizen's guide to crime and control*, Cambridge: Polity Press.

Roberts, J.V. and Hough, M. (2011) 'Custody or community? Exploring the boundaries of public punitiveness in England and Wales', *Criminology and Criminal Justice*, vol 11, no 3, pp 181-97.

Rose, N., O'Malley, P. and Valverde, M. (2006) 'Governmentality', *Annual Review of Law and Social Science*, vol 2, pp 83-104.

Sartre, J.-P. (2006) *The critique of dialectical reason*, London: Verso.

Scraton, P. and Chadwick, K. (1991) 'The theoretical and political priorities of critical criminology', in K. Stenson and D. Cowell (eds) *The politics of crime control*, London: Sage Publications, pp 161-87.

Sen, A. (2007) *Identity and violence: The illusion of destiny*, London: Penguin.

Simon, J. (2007) *Governing through crime*, Oxford: Oxford University Press.

Smith, A. (2010) *Nationalism*, Cambridge: Polity Press.

Stenson, K. (1991) 'Making sense of crime control', in K. Stenson and D. Cowell (eds) *The politics of crime control*, London: Sage Publications, pp 1-31.

Stenson, K. (1993) 'Social work discourse and the social work interview', *Economy and Society*, vol 22, no 1, pp 42-76.

Stenson, K. (1998) 'Beyond histories of the present', *Economy and Society*, vol 27, no 4, pp 333-52.

Stenson, K. (2001) 'The new politics of crime control', in K. Stenson and R.R. Sullivan (eds) *Crime, risk and justice*, Cullompton: Willan, pp 15-28.

Stenson, K. (2005) 'Sovereignty, biopolitics and community safety in Britain', *Theoretical Criminology*, vol 9, no 3, pp 265-87.

Stenson, K. (2007) 'Framing the governance of urban space', in R. Atkinson and G. Helms (eds) *Securing an urban renaissance: Crime, community, and British urban policy*, Bristol: The Policy Press, pp 23-38.

Stenson, K. (2008a) 'Governing the local: sovereignty, social governance and community safety', *Social Work and Society* (online), vol 6, no 1 (www.socwork.net).

Stenson, K. (2008b) 'Surveillance and sovereignty', in M. Deflem (ed) *Surveillance and governance: Crime control and beyond, Sociology of crime, law and deviance, 10*, Bingley: Emerald, pp 279-304.

Stenson, K. (2010) 'Risk, crime and governance', in M. Herzog-Evans (ed) *Transnational criminology manual, Volume 1*, Nijmegen: Wolf Legal Publishers, pp 169-92.

Stenson, K. and Edwards, A. (2004) 'Policy transfer in local crime control: beyond naive emulation', in T. Newburn and R. Sparks (eds) *Criminal justice and political cultures: National and international dimensions of crime control*, Cullompton: Willan, pp 209-33.

Stenson, K. and Waddington, P.A.J. (2007) 'Macpherson, police stops and institutionalised racism', in M. Rowe (ed) *Policing beyond Macpherson: Issues in policing, race and society*, Cullompton: Willan, pp 128-47.

Stiglitz, J. (2010) *Freefall: America, free markets and the sinking of the world economy*, London: W.W. Norton & Co.

Tett, G. (2010) *Fool's gold: How unrestrained greed corrupted a dream, shattered global markets and unleashed a catastrophe*, London: Abacus.

Tilly, C. (2003) *The politics of collective violence*, Cambridge: Cambridge University Press.

Turner, A. (2009) *The Turner review: A regulatory response to the global banking crisis*, London: Financial Services Authority (www.fsa.gov. uk/pubs/other/turner_review.pdf).

Valverde, M. (2010) 'Comment on Loïc Wacquant's "Theoretical coda" to *Punishing the poor*', *Theoretical Criminology*, vol 14, no 1, pp 117-20.

Vulliamy, E. (2010) *Amexica: War along the borderline*, London: Bodley Head.

Wacquant, L. (1999) 'How penal sense comes to Europeans: notes on the transatlantic diffusion of the neo-liberal doxa', *European Societies*, vol 1, pp 319-52.

Wacquant, L. (2008) *Urban outcasts: A comparative sociology of advanced marginality*, Cambridge: Polity Press.

Wacquant, L. (2009a) *Prisons of poverty*, Minneapolis, MN: University of Minnesota Press.

Wacquant, L. (2009b) *Punishing the poor: The neoliberal government of social insecurity*, Durham, NC: Duke University Press.

Wacquant, L. (2011) 'From "public criminology" to the reflexive sociology of criminological production and consumption: a review of *Public Criminology?* by Ian Loader and Richard Sparks (London: Routledge, 2010)', *British Journal of Criminology*, vol 51, no 2, pp 438-48.

FOUR

The third time as farce: whatever happened to the penal state?

John Pitts

'There is and never has been, in my opinion, any direct correlation between spiralling growth in the prison population and a fall in crime. Crime fell throughout most of the western world in the 1990s. Crime fell in countries that had, and still have, far lower rates of imprisonment than ours.' (The Rt Hon Kenneth Clarke, Justice Secretary, The Mansion House, 13 July 2010)

'Labour introduced a ludicrous list of powers for tackling anti-social behaviour – the Iso, the Asbi, the Asbo and the Crasbo. Crack house closure orders, dog control orders, graffiti removal orders, litter and noise abatement orders, housing injunctions and parenting orders. These sanctions were too complex and bureaucratic. There were too many of them, they were too time consuming and expensive and they too often criminalised young people unnecessarily, acting as a conveyor belt to serious crime and prison.' (The Rt Hon Theresa May, Home Secretary, 11 August 2010)

Hegel remarks somewhere that all great world-historic facts and personages appear, so to speak, twice. He forgot to add: the first time as tragedy, the second time as farce. (Marx, 1852)

The penal state

In a recent lecture, Loïc Wacquant (2009) argued that the criminal justice and social policies of neoliberal states have, together, spawned what he describes as 'the third age of the great confinement'. In the process, Wacquant contends, the 'economic state' and the 'social state' are supplanted by the 'penal state' and, more contentiously, that a 'carceral catastrophe' is already upon 'us'. In an earlier paper on the same theme, he wrote (2001):

> This new "government" of social insecurity – to speak like Michel Foucault – rests on the discipline of the deskilled and deregulated labour market and on an intrusive and omnipresent penal apparatus. The invisible hand of the market and the iron fist of the state are complementary and combine to make the lower classes accept desocialised wage labour and the social instability it brings in its wake. After a long eclipse, the prison thus returns to the front line of institutions entrusted with maintaining social order. (p 81)

Wacquant's thesis contains three main propositions: (i) that the globalisation of neoliberal forms of economic organisation, the inevitable concomitant of which is chronic lower-class job insecurity, economic polarisation and burgeoning social marginality, represents a unique historical conjuncture that confronts Western governments with unprecedented, challenges; (ii) that governments will respond to these challenges by strengthening and extending the reach of what Louis Althusser (2005) once called the 'repressive state apparatus', in general and the prison in particular, as a means of instilling discipline in the urban poor and bolstering the government's political legitimacy in the face of mounting 'social anxiety'; and (iii) that governments will simultaneously relinquish responsibility for intervening in the economy, giving free rein to the vagaries of the market, while drastically reducing the size and scope of the 'welfare state'.

In this chapter the focus is largely on developments in youth policy, arguing that although the *penal state* thesis identifies significant developments in criminal justice and social policy in some Western states, Wacquant's attempt to synthesise these into a universal model of neoliberal penology (2008) ignores crucial historical, political and cultural differences between societies, which have resulted in quite different policy responses to neoliberalisation. Furthermore, as Wacquant himself acknowledges, the *penal state* thesis fails to consider the many instances where the trends he posits have been successfully resisted or failed to emerge at all. Crucially, because his thesis was developed when neoliberalism still appeared to be 'delivering the goods', it also fails to deal with the abrupt and radical policy shifts that followed the financial crisis that began in 2007.

Loïc Wacquant and the harbingers of doom

Although Wacquant endeavours to distance himself from other 'Marxist', 'post-Marxist', 'post-Foucauldian', 'post-traditional' (etc) theorists who, like him, foretell impending 'catastrophe', his arguments have strong echoes of what, for the sake of brevity, we might call their 'advanced liberal governance' thesis (Beck, 1992; Rose, 1996; Young, 1999; Simon, 2001; Garland, 2005; Pratt et al, 2005).

Deriving from Michel Foucault's work on governmentality (1991), the advanced liberal governance thesis contends that in 'late modernity' new forms of governance will emerge to enable the state to (re-)establish and sustain its political authority in a situation where its capacity to govern directly has been substantially eroded (Rose, 1996). Whereas, on the one hand, globalisation and a declining tax base have limited the capacity of the nation-state to intervene effectively in social and economic life, on the other, the waning of traditional social divisions has served to release individuals from the 'conscience collective' of class, family, 'race' and gender, requiring them to assume unprecedented authorship of their own lives. Thus, they must effect choices and assume responsibilities in the spheres of employment, education, personal relationships, location, leisure and lifestyle that, in a traditional society, were determined in large part by culture and social structure and serviced by an interventionist state.

Whereas in the heyday of the welfare state, it is argued, governments endeavoured to ameliorate the depredations of the capitalist market by direct intervention in the social and economic spheres, in 'post-traditional' (Giddens, 1999), 'advanced liberal' (Rose, 1999) 'late modern' (Garland, 2001) societies, spheres of activity previously administered by government – health, education, policing, public transport etc – are increasingly ceded to the market. Rose (1996) characterises this shift as the 'death of the social', a process in which the welfare state relinquishes its role as a universal safety-net for the citizen. Now, he argues, particular socially marginal 'communities', not 'society', become the focus of state intervention.

These new forms of governance become necessary, the argument runs, because the withdrawal of the state during a period of accelerated social transformation generates heightened social anxiety that threatens to undermine its political authority, thereby fostering dissent and social disorder. In these circumstances, it is argued, government must galvanise a constituency and devise forms of 'governance' that will allow it to re-establish the political authority it enjoyed when it was able to 'govern' directly. It achieves this by directing the anxieties generated by accelerating social, economic and cultural change, via a process of 'populist ventriloquism' (Matthews, 2005), towards certain categories of demonised 'other', against whom governments then act. Whatever else divides them, these critiques share a conviction that advanced capitalist societies pursuing neoliberal economic policies will inevitably become more punitive.

To achieve effective 'governance' the state must operate at both the discursive and institutional levels. On the one hand, it must forge links between the political, social and cultural constituencies and discourses necessary to create a new 'common sense', sufficiently plausible to allow its intended subjects to recognise themselves in these newly manufactured identities, and thence to become the vehicles for their reproduction (Pecheux, 1982). However, as Law (2010) has observed:

> Much of (this) sub-Gramscian approach to hegemony pictures the social world as being formed by a clash of distinct political ideologies, one of which becomes dominant and eventually makes its way through all levels of social life to ensconce itself deep into the heart and soul of individual subjects.

Like the structural functionalism of half a century ago, the advanced liberal governance thesis marries an 'over-socialised conception of man' with an 'over-integrated view of society' (Wrong, 1961). In reality, the forms of ideological domination suggested in the advanced liberal governance thesis are never as politically or culturally homogeneous as this gloomy picture would have us believe, nor are social structures so entirely closed. Instead, the social world is always characterised by 'antagonism, contingency and dislocation' (Laclau and Mouffe, 1985), aptly demonstrated on 9 August 2007, when the 'credit crunch' was triggered.

When it came to the crunch

In August 2007, neoliberalism's ideological ascendancy faltered, as financial markets in advanced capitalist societies plummeted. Far from the 'erasure' of the 'economic state' that Wacquant's thesis predicts, governments in Britain, the US and mainland Europe effectively nationalised major banks and large corporations (General Motors being the most noteworthy). In the US Barack Obama introduced measures to halt the repossession of the homes of the poor and began dismantling banks which were 'too big to fail'. Meanwhile, across the

Western world, national governments, led by the UK, embarked on a strategy of 'quantitative easing', in which billions of pounds, euros and dollars of government money were pumped into the financial system to forestall an impending recession. Politically, the financial crisis and the ensuing 'cuts' brought into sharp relief the fundamental tension in advanced capitalist societies, between the needs of the people and the demands of the market. As David Harvey (2009) observes:

> ... why are we empowering all the people who got us into this mess.... I think we are headed into a legitimation crisis. Over the past thirty years we have been told, to quote Margaret Thatcher, "there is no alternative" to a neo-liberal free market, privatised world, and that if we didn't succeed in that world it's our own fault. I think it's very difficult to say that when, faced with a foreclosure crisis, you support the banks but not the people who are being foreclosed upon.

Suddenly, the ideological trick which endeavours to pass off socially constructed and historically contingent economic regimes as natural and normal isn't working, and the idea that the market should be a tool for eliminating scarcity, rather than just a mechanism for consolidating the power and privilege of the few, has re-entered mainstream political discourse. What form any political backlash may take remains unclear but we can no longer assume an uncritical acceptance by governments and the public that untrammelled neoliberalism is the natural default setting of successful economies. Neither can we entertain the uncritical assumption, implicit in the dystopian commentaries discussed here, that the interests of 'the state' and the interests of 'capital' are necessarily synonymous. By suspending these postulates, we loosen the analytic straightjacket that has prevented us from seeing if not the 'big picture', then the complexities of the real picture.

'It's the state what done it'

Along with other Anglo-American commentators, Wacquant (2008) is primarily concerned with the way 'the state' conspires to 'demonise' the socially marginal, 'other' (see also Garland, 2001; Muncie and Hughes, 2002; Simon, 2007; Hallsworth and Young, 2010). While not in the same league as the 'faked US moon landings' myths of the 1970s, these are, nonetheless, conspiracy theories and, as such, share the same punch line: 'It's the state what done it'.

As Michel Foucault (1972) observes, changes in control systems are complex. New fields of knowledge, elaborated initially by power-seeking social actors within the 'carceral archipelago', will, over time, come to infuse popular discourses of crime and justice and, even though the state may endeavour to orchestrate the utterances of these actors to achieve its ends, the discourses remain relatively, and often wholly, autonomous from both developments in the 'economic base' and the imperatives of the 'state', not least because they contain both contradictory and oppositional strands. Thus Garland identifies the successful assault on 'penal modernism' by 'radical criminology' in the 1970s as a significant contributory factor to the emergence of a *culture of control* in Anglo-America in the 1980s. 'The real challenge for theorists', as Ignatieff (1981) has observed:

> ... is to find a model of historical explanation which accounts for institutional change without imputing conspiratorial rationality to a ruling class, without reducing institutional development to a formless ad hoc adjustment to contingent crisis, and without assuming a hyper-idealist, all-triumphant humanitarian crusade. (p 185)

This is a challenge to which the *penal state* thesis has not risen.

Altered states

Like his late mentor Pierre Bourdieu (1998), Loïc Wacquant, tends to conflate the global advance of neoliberalism with US economic imperialism. Clearly there is something to this, but in doing so he fails to distinguish between nation-states that have embraced Americanisation and those which have resisted it, ignoring their different cultural, civic and judicial traditions that explain, in part at least, why this should be the case.

In the US, it is not only ultra-Republicans who believe that the introduction of universal healthcare, free at the point of access, represents the thin end of the totalitarian wedge – this view is only slightly to the right of mainstream political opinion. However, this has very little to do with the economy and a great deal to do with the political culture of the US whose constitution is rooted in a profound suspicion of federal government and its alleged propensity to arrogate the freedom of the individual. For many Americans, the 'market' is the fullest expression, and the ultimate custodian, of 'freedom' (Fukuyama, 1992; Messner and Rosenfeld, 1994; Zizeck, 2009), and a bulwark against the 'un-American', totalitarian ambitions of 'dangerous left-wing politicians' like Barack Obama. This preoccupation with 'freedom' does not extend to the sphere of crime and justice, however.

Resistance to real or imagined totalitarianism takes markedly different forms in different nation-states. As Gøsta Esping-Andersen (1990) has observed, while social policy in 'liberal welfare states' is primarily concerned with the preservation of individual 'freedom' and the inculcation of 'responsibility', 'Bismarckian welfare states' are preoccupied with 'security', and social policy in Nordic welfare states emphasises 'equality'.

For example, from the 1950s, Finland attempted to distance itself from the Soviet bloc, with which it had previously been closely politically allied. In doing so, it deliberately constructed a national identity, akin to that of other social democratic Scandinavian and Nordic states, and very different from that of both the US and the USSR. This has led to the development of world-leading public health, welfare and educational provision, free at the point of access, radically redistributive fiscal policies and robust childcare and protection policies. However, an apparent paradox in Finnish social policy appears to vindicate those commentators who equate vigorous state intervention with totalitarian intent because, as a consequence of its robust childcare and protection policies, Finland removes more poor, socially disadvantaged children and young people from their own homes, pro rata, than the UK (Pitts et al, 2006). From Wacquant's Anglo-American perspective, this would appear to be evidence of the 'iron fist' of the *penal state* in action (Muncie and Hughes, 2001; Wacquant, 2001, 2010). When, however, we compare outcomes for young people in the UK care system, rooted as it is in an ideology of freedom, and the Finnish care system, which pursues 'equality', we find that a higher proportion of those in the Finnish system enter higher education than is the case in the general population, although this is itself very high by European standards. Interestingly, the evidence suggests that most Finns are proud of this achievement (Bateman and Randall, 2007). Meanwhile, the majority of young people the UK care system fail to achieve five A–C grade GCSEs, let alone move on to higher education. This indicates the importance ascribed by the Finnish government to the task of caring for neglected and abused children and young people, which finds expression in the quality of provision and high standards of professional practice. It also suggests that systems rooted in a positive conception of freedom, in which the achievement of social equality is the primary objective, may produce superior outcomes to those that are rooted in a negative conception of freedom.

Following the precept that *good social development policy is the best criminal justice policy* (Christie, 2000), Finland has pursued a 'minimalist' criminal justice strategy that has resulted in one of the lowest imprisonment rates in the world. Research suggests that the Finns are happy to support a low imprisonment rate and a high degree of state involvement in the lives of troubled and troublesome children and young people, because they see both aims as complementary, contributing to greater social equality and social cohesion and a low crime rate (Lappi-Seppala, 2001; Honkatukia and Kivivuori, 2003). Such optimism is explicable in part because, unlike Anglo-American political culture, in Finland the relationship between the state and the citizen is not couched in adversarial terms, a heroic struggle between Leviathan and the individual. Thus, while Nikolas Rose (1996) laments the *death of the social*, David Garland (2001) bemoans the demise of the *solidarity project* and Loïc Wacquant prophesies the coming of the *penal state* in Finland, an advanced capitalist society with one of the highest GDPs in the Western world, thanks to economic globalisation (think Nokia), robust social intervention and penal minimalism rule.

In developing his critique, Wacquant deploys the metaphor of the 'right hand' and the 'left hand' of the state, coined originally by Pierre Bourdieu (1998). In so doing, he suggests that the impetus for the development of the welfare state, which Bourdieu characterises as a 'product of working-class struggle', will necessarily come from the political left, while attacks on the welfare state will necessarily come from the political right. However, somewhat surprisingly, this betrays a singularly Anglo-American view of the origins and significance of the French welfare state.

As A.J.P. Taylor (1972) once observed, while Karl Marx took his philosophy from Germany and his economics from Britain, it was in France that he learned his politics. Whereas Anglo-American political culture is predicated on the pessimistic utilitarian assumption that other people represent a threat to our liberty, in post-revolutionary France, *fraternité* was presumed to be a prerequisite of *liberté* and *egalité*. Whether or not this characterisation corresponds with contemporary social and political reality, these cultural assumptions have left an indelible mark on the policies and practices of the two nations. It also explains why questions of *solidarité* and *inclusion* are so central to contemporary French political discourse (Cooper et al, 1995; Pitts, 2003).

In post-revolutionary France, the family has been viewed as the bedrock of the social and political structure. As Jean-Étienne-Marie Portalis (1746–1807), the influential French jurist and politician, has observed: 'The Family is the cradle of the state, for domestic virtues are of the same strain as the virtues of citizenship' (quoted in Commaille, 1994).

Present-day French social policy has its origins in the furore surrounding what came to be called the 'social question' in the late 19th century. This concerned the impact of industrialisation and rapid social change on the French family. Catholic employers were stung into action by the promulgation in 1891 of the papal encyclical *Rerum Novarum* by Pope Leo XIII, entitled *The rights and duties of capital and labour*, a radical document opposing socialism and asserting the moral duty of employers to improve the conditions of working-class families.

This resulted in the introduction of a system of supplementary wages, which was originally based on the voluntary participation of individual businesses, but became a statutory requirement on all businesses by 1932. Whereas in the UK the impetus for the development of the welfare state came primarily from Fabian socialists and the trades unions, in France the welfare state was the child of the Catholic Church and 'big business', supported by powerful, politically conservative, Catholic women's associations. Moreover, throughout the post-war period, progressive, pro-natalist, family policies were supported by the Gaullist right, largely because of an abiding concern about the high levels of male mortality in the First and Second World Wars. Post-war legislation extended and consolidated these benefits and by the mid-1990s France devoted 4 per cent of its GDP to supporting families, putting it among the top five nations in Europe. In comparing attitudes to the welfare state in the US and France, Wacquant (1996) wrote:

> Europeans have emphasised a language of class, labour and citizenship when considering urban hardship, while American discourse has been framed by a 'supply-side' view of poverty anchored in the vocabularies of family, race and individual (moral and behavioural) deficiency. ... (p 546)

Because the welfare state in France emerges from a national culture and a political tradition that is markedly different from that of either Britain or the US, the present struggle by the French government to 'reform public services' has a different political significance, and meets with far greater resistance from what, to Anglo-American eyes, are some unlikely quarters. Moreover, in the post-war period, the French political left has been and remains a more potent political force than is the case in Anglo-America. Whereas in the UK today, for example, strikes and industrial disputes are, of political necessity, confined to particular sectors of the economy, and more commonly to individual businesses, the political left in France is still able to orchestrate national strikes against government cuts. Thus, in his attempts to push through his mildly neoliberal public expenditure reforms, President Sarkozy must do battle with both the political left and the political right. These profound national political and cultural differences alert us to what Jamie Peck and Adam Tickell (2007) describe as the remarkable adaptability of neoliberalism and its capacity to produce quite different, 'local neoliberalisms' in different places.

Rolling back the state

In presenting the advent of the *penal state* as a singular, and apparently inevitable, effect of a unique, contemporary, social and economic transformation, Wacquant, along with other scholars, has failed to explain why, at different times in the same nation-state, 'neoliberal' governments have made markedly different policy choices in the spheres of criminal justice and social policy.

Wacquant argues that the UK has served as the 'Trojan horse', whereby neoliberalism/US economic imperialism has insinuated itself into Europe. Most commentators would pinpoint the advent of UK neoliberalism as October 1976. This was when the former Chancellor of the Exchequer Denis Healey was forced to negotiate a £2.3 billion bailout package with the International Monetary Fund (IMF).

If the *penal state* thesis is correct, we should have seen a concomitant intensification of penal intervention with juveniles and young adults, the social groups with the highest levels of structural unemployment, social exclusion and detected criminality (Rose, 1999; Garland, 2001; Muncie and Hughes, 2001; MacDonald, 2008). In fact, from the early 1980s, the UK witnessed an unprecedented decline in the numbers of children and young people entering the youth justice system. This was echoed in an equally dramatic fall in the numbers sentenced to security and custody (from almost 15,000 pa in 1980 to around 1,500 in 1991; see Pitts, 1988; Hagell, 2005) and those consigned to residential children's homes and 'special schools', most of which had been closed down by the early 1990s (see Table 4.1).

Nor is there any evidence that those who became embroiled in the system were treated any more harshly (Bottoms et al, 1990). This rolling back of the youth justice and residential childcare systems was paralleled by widespread closures of mental hospitals and swingeing cut-backs in mainstream education, the educational welfare service, home–school liaison, school counselling, social services departments,

Table 4.1: Annual changes in the numbers of children and young people held in residential institutions in England and Wales

	1977	1996/98
Children's homes	25,000	7,000[a]
Approved schools/ community homes (local authority young offenders provision)	7,000	1,000[b]
Young offender institutions (Home Office prison department provision)	8,500	6,500[c]
Residential special schools (local education authorities)	21,000	10,000[d]
Total	**61,500**	**24,500**

Sources:
[a] Berridge (1998)
[b] DHSS (1975, 1978); DH (1996)
[c] Home Office (1977); Millham (1978); NACRO (1998)
[d] DfEE (1998)

the Youth Service, voluntary sector youth and play provision and the closure of child and family guidance clinics.

It was not until 1993, in the wake of the murder of two-year-old James Bulger, that New Labour commenced its assault on the Tory 'law and order' record. This was 13 years after the election of the first neoliberal/monetarist Thatcher government and 17 years after the advent of neoliberalism. This suggests, as Wacquant (2001 has argued, that 'the penal state is not a destiny', but rather, a consequence of political choice). However, contrary to Wacquant's contention that a burgeoning *penal state* will supplant the *welfare state*, Margaret Thatcher took the axe to the criminal justice, educational *and* welfare systems.

The impetus for the state's withdrawal was in part fiscal – in the early 1980s, escalating unemployment and unemployment benefit paralleled a plunging tax yield (Scull, 1977; Pitts, 1988). However, during this period there was also a widespread perception, among government ministers, civil servants, the judiciary, justice system professionals and criminologists, that placing troublesome young people in closed institutions, because of institutional abuse, the attenuation of family relationships and abysmal re-conviction rates, merely compounded the problems it was supposed to solve (Pitts, 2003). And yet, contrary to Wacquant's predictions, despite 30 years of neoliberal ideology, Conservative government ministers still appear to believe this (see Clarke and May, quoted at the start of this chapter).

The unprecedented decarcerations of the Thatcher era stand in marked contrast with the escalation of youth incarceration under Ronald Reagan's neoliberal administration in the US (Krisberg and

Austin, 1993). This divergence suggests that, just as there is no obvious causal link between the introduction of a 'free market' and the flowering of democracy (Fukuyama, 1994), so there is no necessary link between the advent of neoliberalism and the emergence of a *penal state*. Crime control in advanced liberal societies may take a variety of forms, from the robustly interventionist (cf Reagan in the US) to the radically minimalist (cf Thatcher in the UK), and both 'welfarism' (Republic of Ireland; see O'Donnell and O'Sullivan, 2003) and informalism (New Zealand; see Braithwaite, 1989) may flourish. This would suggest that, while control systems may be shaped, to an extent, by economic exigencies and the changed modes of governance they precipitate, the direction of these changes cannot be 'read off' from them in any straightforward way.

Peck and Tickell (2007) contend that neoliberalism has passed through two distinct phases: a first phase of 'roll back' that took the form of 'destructive', deregulatory attacks on the state and the liberalisation of 'markets' that characterised the Thatcher and Reagan eras, and a second 'roll out', which, from the 1990s, served to consolidate the changed conditions for capital accumulation through pragmatic, pro-market, re-regulation. And as Drahokoupil (2004) has argued, this dualism, of anti-state deregulation and pro-market re-regulation, is not unique to neoliberalism but has characterised capitalism from its earliest days (Polanyi, 1944 [2002]).

Rolling out the third way

When, in 1996, Nikolas Rose (1996) announced 'the death of the social' and the 'dismantling, or phasing out, of welfare state institutions', he was, presumably, reflecting on the depredations wrought by Margaret Thatcher. Yet, many contemporary commentators who cite this seminal text appear not to have noticed that, from the early 1990s, this contraction in state services was, in fact, reversed (Fawcett et al, 2004). This *volte face* was due in no small part to the intervention of John Major, Thatcher's successor, who, being far less antagonistic to the public services, threw them a political lifeline by making funding contingent on forms of 'market testing' designed to demonstrate that they represented 'value for money'. This ushered in a new era of growth and diversification in the public sector (Fawcett et al, 2004).

Although Tony Blair was viewed by many on both the left and the right as Margaret Thatcher's natural successor, on being elected, New Labour embarked on an ambitious programme of social investment, facilitated by unprecedented levels of public spending, suggesting that

Wacquant's contention that the demolition of the welfare state is the inevitable corollary of neoliberalisation is simply wrong.

In the sphere of services to young people, New Labour set in train an apparently unending stream of policies concerned with their capacity to make a successful transition to a self-sufficient, law-abiding, adulthood (Coles, 2000; Mizen, 2003). Yet far from being unambiguously repressive, many of these policies echoed the concerns, and embodied the changes for which radical professionals and academics in the fields of youth work, youth justice, education, child welfare, policing and drug treatment had been campaigning for almost 30 years (Jeffs, 1979). This unprecedented investment was a response to governmental anxieties that, left unaddressed, the social consequences of the profound economic changes occurring in the UK in the preceding 20 years – structural, transgenerational, unemployment, family breakdown and widening social and economic polarisation, resulting in heightened levels of crime and disorder among the most disadvantaged – would lead to the erosion of social cohesion and the breakdown of social control (Social Exclusion Unit, 1998).

These policies and, the extra investment they generated, created a new, expanded, market in youth services, attracting many non-traditional, service providers into the sector. Unlike traditional youth work (Davies and Gibson, 1967; Firmstone, 1998; Jeffs and Smith, 2002; Crimmens et al, 2004), these services tended to be time-limited, 'problem-oriented' and 'target-driven', concerned, for example, with employability, youth crime prevention, substance abuse, sexual health, teenage pregnancy, youth homelessness, truancy and school exclusion (Crimmens et al, 2004). This changed emphasis was part of a broader reconfiguration of the welfare state in which social policy was supposed to 'buttress rather than burden the wealth producing economy' (Taylor-Gooby, 2003). In this shift from the 'welfare state' of old to a new 'social investment state' (Fawcett et al, 2004), the eradication of dependency and the promotion of future employability became a central rationale for state expenditure.

While these developments marked a further retreat from 'universalism', they can hardly be described as the 'death of the social' (Rose, 1996). Universalism lives on in the services and benefits, in the areas of healthcare, employment, disability, family allowances, secondary education, state pensions, etc, introduced by the Attlee government in the wake of the Second World War. The second wave of welfare state expansion occurring in the 1960s was specifically targeted at those who, because of 'ignorance' or 'psycho-social problems', were either 'unwilling' or 'unable' to take advantage of the opportunities made possible by educational reform, a welfare state, redistributive taxation and a booming economy (Longford, 1963; Pitts, 1988).

Yet the 'social investment' rationale informing contemporary interventions with young people has been evident in educational, welfare, employment and youth service policy throughout the post-war period. Similarly, the provision of services to troubled and troublesome young people has always been motivated as much by a concern about the threat they pose to the law-abiding as a desire to meet their needs or defend their rights (see, for example, Smith et al, 1979). This calls into question the distinctiveness of the concerns faced by Western governments in a neoliberal era, of which more later.

Meanwhile, of course, the Blair government was 'rolling out' its 'New Youth Justice' (Goldson, 2001; Pitts, 1999). For New Labour, wresting the mantle of 'law and order' from the Tories was designed to serve as a political hermetic which, by emphasising the threat posed by the criminal to the 'law-abiding majority', would hold together a new constituency of the centre, composed in no small part, of disenchanted Conservatives.

New Labour's legislative flagship, the Crime and Disorder Act 1998, drew a new population of younger children into the youth justice system, via measures that targeted their 'incivilities' and the inadequacies of their parents. Informalism was abandoned in favour of earlier, formal intervention by the police, via reprimands and final warnings. Diversion from custody into 'community alternatives' gave way to 'community penalties'. Meanwhile, an expanded range of semi-indeterminate custodial penalties was introduced, and the age at which they could be imposed was lowered from 15 to 12, and in some cases, 10. Unsurprisingly, these changes served to induct children and young people who offended into the youth justice system at an earlier stage in their criminal careers, and to accelerate their progress through it.

The numbers of children and young people aged 10-17 sentenced to security or custody in England and Wales between 1992 and 2002 rose by 85 per cent to a record 12,592 in 2002/03 (Youth Justice Board, 2004). Moreover, in the decade 1992–2002, the numbers of under-15s held in security or custody had increased by a remarkable 800 per cent (Bateman, 2003). These increases are accounted for in part by the larger numbers entering security and custody during the decade, but also by increases in sentence length. Between 1992 and 2002 the average custodial sentence for 15- to 17-year-old boys increased from 5.6 months to 10.3 months and for girls, from 5.5 months to 7.1 months (Pitts, 2003). These figures are more remarkable when we recognise that, during this period, crimes recorded as having been committed by children and young people fell by 20 per cent (Bateman, 2003).

What's new, Labour?

Wacquant argues that neoliberalism produces a unique set of social and economic effects, that he describes as 'advanced marginality', and that politicians in advanced capitalist societies will deal with this by expanding the criminal justice system and shrinking the welfare state. Yet whereas, under Margaret Thatcher, the welfare state and the justice system were savagely pruned, under Tony Blair, both expanded exponentially, just as they had twice before in the 20th century.

The ostensible concerns of contemporary criminal justice and social policy, the widening gap between the 'haves' and 'have-nots' (Tax Credits, Urban Regeneration) the capacity of the lower-class family to offer adequate parenting (Sure Start, Youth Inclusion and Support Panels [YISPs], Parenting Orders), the attitudinal, physical and technical preparedness of the young to enter education, training and employment (Education Action Zones, academies, Connexions, Offending Programmes), the threat to social order (The New Youth Justice, Community Safety Partnerships, ASBOs) and social and political cohesion (Active Communities, Citizenship Education, Restorative Justice) have been central to the major developments in family policy, education, youth work and youth justice in the 20th century. Moreover, as is the case today, these concerns and these developments have tended to emerge during periods of rapid social and economic change and heightened social anxiety (Hall et al, 1978; Pitts, 1988).

The economic recession in the final decade of the 19th century triggered political and media concern about the perceived 'crisis of control' in the industrial cities (Pearson, 1983) and the apparent ineffectiveness of the justice system and other agencies of control (Garland, 1985). This crisis was seen to be a product of the effects of economic recession on the capacity of the lower-class family to exert control over its children. Alongside this were related concerns about the academic and physical fitness of British youth for military service and their capacity to resist the blandishments of a newly ascendant Bolshevism, as well as religious and philanthropic concerns about the suffering of lower-class children and young people. These concerns triggered the proliferation of uniformed youth organisations and 'street' and club-based youth work (Kaufman, 2001), radical educational reform, in the shape of Balfour's Education Act 1902, which brought local education authorities into being, and the introduction of a new youth justice system by the Asquith administration in 1908 (Newburn, 1995).

From the late 1950s, concerns about growing social inequality (Abel-Smith and Townsend, 1965), rising crime and disorder, political disengagement among the young, the employability of low-achieving working-class children and a perceived decline in the quality of lower-class parenting, precipitated a national poverty programme (Community Development Projects), further expansion of 'street' and club-based youth work (Ministry of Education, 1960), radical welfare reform (the Children and Young Persons Act 1963), and educational reform culminating in the advent of comprehensive education and a raised school-leaving age (Newsom Report, *Half our future,* 1961), and the introduction of a new youth justice system by the Wilson administration (the *Children in trouble* White Paper and the Children and Young Persons Act 1969).

Then, as now, it was 'modernising' governments that triggered this intensification of intervention with lower-class children and young people and then, as now, these governments argued that their new measures were 'evidence-based', being informed by the new sciences of paediatrics, child psychology, social administration, sociology, criminology and penology. Then, as now, they attracted the enthusiastic legitimation of academics and then, as now, this intensification of intervention with lower-class children and young people led to the simultaneous expansion of youth provision and youth justice, generating both heightened levels of 'social education' (Davies and Gibson, 1967), and greater incarceration and community surveillance (Garland, 1985; Pitts, 1988; Newburn, 1995).

This would appear to cast doubt on Wacquant's claim that the concerns of neoliberal governments are exceptional, rather than perennial, and that these concerns trigger unique policy responses.

Whatever happened to the penal state?

As Robert MacDonald (2008) has argued, in the UK, what Wacquant (2008) refers to as 'advanced marginality' is primarily a condition afflicting poor, lower-class, young people. Between 1984 and 1997 the numbers of 16- to 24-year-olds in the labour market shrank by nearly 40 per cent. In January 2010, one in five White and one in two Black and minority ethnic 16- to 24-year-olds was unemployed (IPPR, 2010). During this period, 10- to 20-year-olds were responsible for almost one third of all recorded crime and 50 per cent of all recorded violent crime (Smith, 2003). This being so, we might expect a *penal state* to focus its attentions on the discipline and punishment of this population and for this to be evidenced by the numbers entering the youth justice system and the 'secure estate'. In fact, as Table 4.2 indicates, entrants to the youth justice system peaked in 2006/07, around the time of the 'credit crunch', and have been falling steadily since.

Table 4.2

2003/04	2004/05	2005/06	2006/07	2007/08	2008/09
185,084	195,483	212,242	216,011	210,670	184,850

In 2008, the widely criticised and 'resource-intensive' 'sanction detection' Key Performance Indicator (KPI), imposed on the police by government earlier in the decade, was abandoned and replaced by a KPI concerned with reducing the number of first-time entrants to the youth justice system (Nacro, 2008). This pragmatic rediscovery of 'diversion' had a marked effect on the numbers of children and young people entering the system per se and on the number of first-time entrants in particular, which fell from a peak of 104,361 in 2006/07 to 74,003 in 2008/09 (Ministry of Justice, 2010). Anti-Social Behaviour Orders (ASBOs), which had in the past served to swell the numbers entering the penal system, having peaked at 4,122 in 2005, fell steadily to 2,027 in 2008. In 2010, Home Secretary Theresa May announced that they would be phased out. As Tables 4.3 and 4.4 indicate, one of the results of reducing the numbers of young people entering the 'front end' of the youth justice system has been a decline in the numbers being incarcerated in the 'secure estate' at the 'back end' (Youth Justice Board, 2010; *Youth Justice*, 2010).

This swing of the penal pendulum (Bernard, 1992), back towards non-intervention and decarceration, is occurring in both the UK and

Table 4.3: Offenders aged 10–17 sentenced to immediate custody

Year	Number
1998	4,294
2001	5,440
2004	4,326
2006	4,209
2008	3,421

Source: Ministry of Justice (2010)

Table 4.4: Offenders aged 18–20 sentenced to immediate custody

Year	Number
1998	8,191
2001	9,391
2004	7,171
2006	6,560
2008	5,436

Source: Ministry of Justice (2010)

the US. In the case of the US, this regression to the norm follows a three-decade-long carceral bonanza (Blumstein and Beck, 1999; Pitts, 2010). Although this shift is supported by evidence that most first-time entrants to youth justice systems would have desisted from crime of their own accord and that incarceration tends to compound nascent criminal careers, it is almost certainly prompted by dwindling policing and youth justice budgets.

Ultimately, the importance governments assign to any particular policy area is signified by the resources they are prepared to dedicate to it. In 2009/10 four secure children's homes were closed (falling from 30 to nine in the past decade), as was one young offenders institution (Ministry of Justice, 2010). In 2010, the Coalition government withdrew its tender for a new 'super' young offenders institution in East Anglia (Ministry of Justice, 2010). Meanwhile, in the adult system, the proposed New Labour prison building programme has juddered to a halt and the closure of several older prisons, including Dartmoor, now seems likely (Ministry of Justice, 2010). The proposed cut of £2 billion from the Ministry of Justice's £9 billion annual budget in 2010/11 could see the loss of 15,000 of the department's 80,000 staff, many of whom are 'front-line' operatives: prison officers, probation officers, court ushers, etc (Ministry of Justice, 2010). Moreover, substantial cuts in police funding will further limit the capacity of the criminal justice system.

New Labour was born into an era of economic expansion, not a propitious time in which to challenge an incumbent government, but it also faced the bigger problem of 'reinventing' an ostensibly defunct political party and building, and then holding together a political constituency that would elect it. In trying to resolve this conundrum New Labour strategists turned to the US, where Bill Clinton and his team had achieved considerable 'political traction' for an apparently moribund Democratic Party by outflanking the Republicans on 'law and order'. Clinton's promise to contain the threat posed by socially and economically marginal African American and Latino 'ghetto youth' to those in the social and economic 'mainstream', made in the wake of the Los Angeles riots of 1992, had helped him secure the presidency, and New Labour saw this as a template for electoral success. This electoral strategy was made more attractive by the fact that, under the Thatcher governments, recorded crime rose further and faster than at any time since records began, from around 3.5 million recorded offences in 1982 to almost 6 million in 1992 (Home Office, 1993).

However, in 2010 in the UK, the economy is teetering on the brink of meltdown, and recorded crime in general, and youth crime in particular, had been falling steadily for nearly two decades. Furthermore, penal reform was one of a number of 'lines in the sand' drawn by the Liberal Democrats in their post-election Coalition negotiations with David Cameron's Conservatives in May 2010. This was not a sticking point for the Conservative 'modernisers' on the Tory front bench, however, who were more than happy to distance themselves from the 'Old Tory' 'hangers and floggers' in their own party. Moreover, it is a tried and trusted truism that, when they need to, Conservative governments are able to achieve far more radical penal reforms than their Labour counterparts because, in the popular imagination and the tabloid press, they remain the 'natural party of law and order'. Besides, as New Labour belatedly discovered, law and order crusades cost a great deal of money, and the Coalition hasn't got any.

Loïc Wacquant argues that, far from being inevitable, the *penal state* is brought into being by the conscious policy choices of governments. The Coalition's decision to put 'law and order' on the 'back burner' is also a freely chosen decision. But as Karl Marx (1877) observes, 'Freedom is the consciousness of necessity', and today necessity dictates that a *penal state* is neither ideologically necessary nor economically viable.

References

Abel-Smith, B. and Townsend, P. (1965) *The poor and the poorest*, London: G. Bell & Sons.

Althusser, L. (2005) *For Marx*, Cambridge: Verso.

Bateman, T. and Randall, V. (2005) 'The attitudes of English and Finnish child care professionals to residential and custodial disposals for children and young people', Unpublished, Luton: University of Bedfordshire.

Beck, U. (1992) *The risk society: Towards a new modernity*, London: Sage Publications.

Bernard, T. (1992) *The cycle of juvenile justice*, Oxford: Oxford University Press.

Berridge, D. (1998) *Children's homes revisited*, London: Jessica Kingsley Publishers.

Blumstein, A. and Brown, A. (1999) 'Population growth in US prisons 1980-1996', *Crime & Justice*, vol 26, pp 17-61.

Bottoms, A., Brown, P., McWilliams, B., McWilliams, W. and Nellis, M. (1990) *Intermediate treatment and juvenile justice: Key findings and implications from a national survey of intermediate treatment*, London: Home Office.

Bourdieu, P. (1998) *Acts of resistance*, Cambridge: Polity Press.

Braithwaite, J. (1989) *Reintegrative shaming*, Cambridge: Cambridge University Press.

Christie, N. (2000) *Crime control as industry: Towards Gulags, Western style?* (3rd edition) London: Routledge.

Coles, B. (2000) 'Slouching towards Bethlehem: youth policy and the work of the Social Exclusion Unit', in H. Dean, R. Sykes and R. Woods (eds) *Social Policy Review 12*, London: Social Policy Association.

Commaille, J. (1994) 'France: from a family policy to policies towards the family', in W. Dumon (ed) *Changing family policies in member states of the European Union*, Brussels: European Union.

Cooper, A., Hetherington, R., Baistow, K., Pitts, J. and Spriggs, A. (1995) *Positive child protection: A view from abroad*, Lyme Regis: Russell House Publishing.

Crimmens, D., Factor, F., Jeffs, T., Pitts, J., Spence, J., Pugh, C. and Turner, P. (2004) *Reaching socially excluded young people: A national study of street-based youth work*, Leicester/York: National Youth Agency/Joseph Rowntree Foundation.

Davies, B. and Gibson, A. (1967) *The social education of the adolescent*, London: University of London Press.

DfEE (Department for Education and Employment) (1998) *Response to enquiry made of Statistics Section* (June), London: HMSO.

DH (Department of Health) (1996) *Annual return*, London: DH.

DHSS (Department of Health and Social Security) (1975) 'Young offenders in care', Preliminary report, Unpublished.

DHSS (1978) 'Preliminary report on Care Order Survey', Unpublished.

Drahokoupil, J. (2004) 'Re-inventing Karl Polanyi: on the contradictory interpretations of social protectionism', *Socialogicky casopis, Sociological Review*, vol 40, no 6, pp 835-49.

Esping-Andersen, G. (1990) *The three worlds of welfare capitalism*, Princeton, NJ: Princeton University Press.

Factor, F. and Pitts, J. (2001) 'From emancipation to correctionalism: UK youth work and the politics of the third way', in V. Puuronen, *Youth on the threshold of the third millennium*, Joensuu, Finland: Joensuu University Press.

Fawcett, B., Featherstone, B. and Goddard, J. (2004) *Contemporary child care policy and practice*, Basingstoke: Palgrave.

Foucault, M. (1972) *Power/knowledge*, London: The Harvester Press.

Foucault, M. (1991) 'Governmentality', in G. Burchell, C. Gordon and P. Miller (eds) *The Foucault effect: Studies in governmentality*, London: Harvester Wheatsheaf, pp 87-104.

Firmstone, V. (1998) *An evaluation of the Wesley Castle Information and Coffee Shop for Young People and the Three Estates Youth Information Shop and Detached Project*, Birmingham: Southern Birmingham Community Health NHS Trust/Westhill College of Higher Education.

Fukuyama, F. (1992) *The end of history and the last man*, New York: Aron.

Garland, D. (1985) *Punishment and welfare: A history of penal strategies*, London: Gower.

Garland, D. (2001) *The culture of control: Crime and social order in contemporary society*, Oxford: Oxford University Press.

Garland, D. (2005) 'Capital punishment and American culture', *Punishment & Society*, vol 7, no 4, pp 347-76.

Giddens, A. (1999) *The third way: The renewal of social democracy*, Cambridge: Polity Press.

Goldson, B. (ed) (2001) *The new youth justice*, Lyme Regis: Russell House Publishing.

Hagell, A. (2005) 'The use of custody for children and young people', in T. Bateman and J. Pitts (eds) *The Russell House companion to youth justice*, Lyme Regis: Russell House Publishing, pp 151-7.

Hall, S., Critcher, C., Jefferson, T., Clarke, J. and Roberts, B. (1978) *Policing the crisis: Mugging, the state and law and order*, London: Macmillan.

Hallsworth, S. and Young, T. (2008) 'Gang talk and gang talkers: a critique', *Crime, Media and Culture*, vol 4, no 2, pp 175-95.

Harvey, D. (2009) 'Is this really the end of neoliberalism?', 13-15 March (www.counterpunch.org/harvey03132009html).

Home Office (1977) *Prison statistics*, London: HMSO.

Home Office (1993) *Criminal statistics for England and Wales*, London: Home Office.

Honkatukia, P. and Kivivuori, J (eds) (2003) *Nuorisorikollisuus*, Helsinki: The Finnish National Research Institute of Legal Policy.

Ignatieff, M. (1981) 'State, civil society, and total institutions: a critique of recent social histories of punishment', *Crime and Justice*, vol 3, pp 153-92.

IPPR (Institute for Public Policy Research) (2010) *Youth tracker: Reporting on challenges and solutions for young people in the UK during recession and recovery*, London: IPPR.

Jeffs, T. (1979) *Young people and the Youth Service*, London: Routledge & Kegan Paul.

Jeffs, T. and Smith, M. (2002) 'Individualisation and youth work', *Youth and Policy*, vol 76, pp 39-65.

Kaufman, S. (2001) 'Detached youth work', in F. Factor, V. Chauhan and J. Pitts (eds) *The Russell House companion to working with young people*, Lyme Regis: Russell House Publishing.

Krisberg, B. and Austin, J.F. (1993) *Reinventing juvenile justice*, London: Sage Publications.

Laclau, E. and Mouffe, C. (1985) *Hegemony and socialist strategy*, London: Verso.

Lappi-Seppala, T. (2001) 'Sentencing and punishment in Finland', in M.Tonry and R. Frase (eds) *Sentencing and sanctions in western countries*, Oxford: Oxford University Press, pp 92-150.

Law, A. (2010) '"The callous credit nexus": ideology and compulsion in the crisis of neoliberalism', *Sociological Research Online*, vol 14, no 4, p 5.

Longford, L. (1964) *Crime: A challenge to us all*, Report of a Labour Party Study Group, London: The Labour Party.

MacDonald, R. (2008) 'Disconnected youth? Social exclusion, the "underclass" and economic marginality', *Social Work & Society*, vol 6, no 2, pp 236-48.

Marx, K. (1852) *The 18th Brumaire of Louis Bonaparte*.

Marx, K. (1877) *Economic and philosophical manuscripts*.

Matthews, R. (2005) 'The myth of punitiveness', *Theoretical Criminology*, vol 9, no 2, pp 177-203.

Merquoir, J. (1985) *Foucault*, London: Fontana Press.

Messner, S. and Rosenfeld, R. (1994) *Crime and the American dream*, Belmont, CA: Wadsworth.

Millham, S. et al (1978) *Locking up children*, Farnborough: Saxon House.

Ministry of Education (1960) *On the youth service in England and Wales* (Albemarle Report), London: HMSO.

Ministry of Justice (2010) *Visions for the estate*, London: Ministry of Justice, July.

Mizen, P. (2003) 'Tomorrow's future or signs of a misspent youth', *Youth and Policy*, vol 79, pp 1-19.

Muncie, J. and Hughes, G. (2002) 'Modes of youth governance, political rationalities, criminalisation and resistance', in J. Muncie and G. Hughes, *Youth justice: Critical readings*, London: Sage Publications, pp 1-18.

Nacro (1998) *Response to enquiry made of Youth Justice Section* (June) London: NACRO.

Newburn, T. (1995) *Crime and criminal justice policy*, London: Longman.

O'Donnell, I. and O'Sullivan, E. (2003) 'The politics of intolerance: Irish style', *British Journal of Criminology*, vol 43, no 1, pp 41-62.

Pearson, G. (1983) *Hooligan: A history of respectable fears*, Basingstoke: Macmillan.

Pecheux, M. (1982) (translated by H. Nagpal) *Language, semantics and ideology: Stating the obvious*, London: Macmillan.

Peck, J. and Tickell, A. (2007) 'Conceptualising neo-liberalism, thinking Thatcherism', in H. Leitner, J. Peck and E. Sheppard (eds) *Contesting neo-liberalism: Urban frontiers*, New York: The Guilford Press, pp 26-50.

Pierson, J. (2002) *Tackling social exclusion*, London and New York: Routledge.

Pitts, J. (1988) *The politics of juvenile crime*, London: Sage Publications.

Pitts, J. (2003) *The new politics of youth crime: Discipline or solidarity*, Lyme Regis: Russell House Publishing.

Pitts, J. (2006) (with T. Kuula and M. Marttunen) 'Nuoret Laitoksissa Suomessa Ja Englanissa' ['Incarceration of juveniles: Finland compared with England and Wales'], in P. Honkatukia and J. Kivivuori (eds) *Nuorisorikollisuus*, Helsinki: The Finnish National Research Institute of Legal Policy, p 17.

Pitts, J. (2010) 'Bringing the boys back home', *Safer Communities*, vol 9, no 1, pp 27-9.

Polanyi, K. (1944 [2002]) *The great transformation: The political and economic origins of our time*, Boston, MD: Beacon Press.

Pratt, J., Brown, D., Brown, M., Hallsworth, S. and Morrison, W. (2005) *The new punitiveness: Trends, theories, perspectives*, Cullompton: Willan Publishing.

Rose, N. (1996) 'The death of the social? Re-figuring the territory of government', *Economy and Society*, vol 25, no 3, pp 327-46.

Rose, N. (1999) *Powers of freedom: Reframing political thought*, Cambridge: Cambridge University Press.

Rusche, G. and Kirchheimer, O. (1939) *Punishment and social structure*, New York, NY: Columbia University Press.

Scull, A. (1977) *Decarceration*, New York: Vintage Books.

Simon, J. (2001) 'Entitlement to cruelty: neo-liberalism and the punitive mentality in the United States', in K. Stenson and R. Sullivan (eds) *Crime, risk and justice*, Cullompton: Willan Publishing.

Simon, J. (2007) *Governing through crime: How the war on crime transformed American democracy and created a culture of fear*, New York: Oxford University Press.

Smith, C. (2003) *Violent crime in England and Wales*, London: Home Office.

Smith, C., Farrant, M. and Marchant, H. (1979) *The Wincroft Youth Project*, London: Tavistock.

Social Exclusion Unit (1998) *Bringing Britain together: A national strategy for neighbourhood renewal: The report of Policy Action Team 12: Young people*, London: The Stationery Office.

Taylor, A.J.P. (1972) *An introduction to the Communist manifesto*, Harmondsworth: Penguin.

Taylor-Gooby, P. (2003) 'The genuinely liberal genuine welfare state', Paper presented at the Social Policy Association Conference, University of Teesside, 16 July.

Wacquant, L. (1996) 'The comparative structure and experience of urban exclusion: "race", class and space in Chicago and Paris', in K. McFate, R. Lawson and W.J. Wilson (eds) *Inequality and the future of social policy*, New York: Rand, pp 543-69.

Wacquant, L. (2001) 'The advent of the penal state is not a destiny', *Social Justice*, vol 28, no 3, Fall, pp 81-7.

Wacquant, L. (2008) *Urban outcasts: A comparative sociology of advanced marginality*, Cambridge: Polity Press.

Wacquant, L. (2009) 'The penal state', A public lecture at the London School of Economics and Political Science.

Wrong, D. (1961) 'The oversocialised conception of man in modern sociology', *American Sociological Review*, vol 26, April, pp 183-93.

Young, J. (1999) *The exclusive society*, London: Sage Publications.

Youth Justice Board (2004) *Annual return*, London: Youth Justice Board.

Youth Justice Board (2010) *Youth Justice*, vol 10, no 1.

Zizeck, S. (2009) *First as tragedy then as farce*, London: Verso.

Section 2
Welfare, agency and resistance

FIVE

Loïc Wacquant and Norbert Elias: advanced marginality and the theory of the de-civilising process

John J. Rodger

Introduction

Loïc Wacquant shares with Norbert Elias and Pierre Bourdieu an interest in the mechanisms through which political, socioeconomic and cultural change leads to the transformation of human *habitus* in the modern world. There are few existing social analysts who have done more than Wacquant to place the neglect and deprivation of life in the urban periphery on the policy and research agendas of the social sciences. In drawing attention to the violence and de-pacification of the 'hyper-ghetto' in the US, and the 'degraded ecology' of the *banlieues* and marginal communities of Western Europe, the research agenda that is wrapped up in his analysis of *advanced marginality* is complementary to Elias's historical sociology of the processes that create divisions between the *established* and the *outsiders* in the modern world (Elias, 1982; Elias and Scotson, 1965). There seem to be real synergies between the two theoretical perspectives that this chapter explores.

There is a sense in which the Eliasian thesis on the *civilising process* has been waiting for Wacquant's emerging analysis of *advanced marginality* to boost its contemporary relevance: to sketch out a framework for understanding the circumstances that lead to de-civilising tendencies in present-day societies governed by neoliberal market principles. While Elias's developmental theory of the civilising process describes the consequences for social relationships and mentalities resulting from the pacification of society, he did not consider to any significant extent the contradictions of that process, and the theory has continued to appear less than convincing in accounting for the conflict, violence and disorderly features of Western society, both historically and today. Indeed it has often appeared to be a theory exclusively about the socially integrative aspects of modernity, about the sensibilities of the *established* to the neglect of documenting the experience and emotions of the *outsiders*.

It has been obvious for some time that what Eliasian process-sociology needed to preserve its currency was a coherent theory of the de-civilising processes inherent in neoliberalism and global society. Eliasian sociology should be able to explain in a single theoretical structure the association between processes of pacification in contemporary Western societies with evidence of the deep-rooted disorder, violence and decay that disfigure marginal pockets of most large cities in the US and Europe today. Wacquant's analysis of advanced marginality, it is argued here, contributes to developing a rather neglected aspect of the civilising process. A key feature of advanced marginality is that it prefigures a future social figuration in which some *outsider* groups will remain on the periphery of economy and society, trapped in a spatial, cultural and economic form of exclusion 'functionally disconnected from macro-economic trends' with declining utility for society. In coming to terms with this phenomenon, particularly the social and human costs that it creates, we can glimpse at the productive synergies between the work of Wacquant and Elias – between the analyses of *advanced marginality* and *de-civilising processes*.

The outline of the argument presented here starts by discussing the fundamental principles driving Elias's thesis on the *civilising process* while highlighting its contradictions. This is followed by a description of Wacquant's analysis of the US ghetto which draws on Elias's rather embryonic use of the concept of the *de-civilising process*. Wacquant has constructed an analytical vocabulary for the sociological analysis of neoliberalism and its role in creating the conditions within which the *de-civilising* of some parts of Western society can flourish and, sadly, become an embedded characteristic of the modern city. While it is suggested here that Wacquant's focus on neoliberalism augments the Eliasian theory of the de-civilising process, the final section turns the argument more in favour of Elias by suggesting that his perspective draws our attention to the importance of understanding the visceral human reaction to changing social, economic and political changes wrought by neoliberalism. In the words of Sennett and Cobb, we are encouraged to consider the 'hidden injuries of class' and the attack on the sense of self-worth and self-identity that results from being consigned to the margins of society.

The civilising process and its contradictions

As one of the most prominent interpreters of Elias's work has observed, the civilising process 'is a very complex theory that has been subject to as much gross oversimplification as Marx's' (Mennell, 2009, p 98). The issue at the heart of this reflection is that the sociology developed by Elias insisted on maintaining a focus on constantly flowing and 'intertwining long-term processes' which, Stephen Mennell (2009) suggests,

> yields complicated and superficially contradictory predictions ... of simultaneous civilising and de-civilising spurts, of functional democratisation and de-democratisation, of increasing and decreasing foresight, of widening and narrow circles of mutual identification. (Mennell, 2009, p 98)

Elias did not assume that the long-term developmental processes that he describes at the heart of his civilising process theory, involving the connection between state formation and changing interpersonal behaviour, would inevitably, and for all time, lead to a transformation in *social habitus* characterised by peaceful and orderly relationships between people in their social, cultural and economic exchanges. While he insisted that history points to the dominance of 'a humanity-wide process of civilisation ... dominant in a continuous conflict with countervailing, de-civilising processes', he also acknowledged that 'there is no basis for assuming that it must remain dominant' (Elias, cited in Mennell, 2009, p 99). Violence, Elias maintained, was always behind the scenes and always, therefore, a potential that could surface and disfigure social order. It is precisely such a development in the marginal communities of the advanced societies that Wacquant is pointing to.

However, the status of de-civilising tendencies in Elias's work throws up a problem of interpretation: should we understand the possibility of de-civilising to be a sequential or a simultaneous phenomenon? Elias tended to suggest that de-civilising breaks through when the integrative forces of the civilising process are thrown into a state of disequilibrium, when the balance of power tilts towards those influences and forces that lead to regression and away from an orderly state of interdependency and solidarity. However, a number of interpreters of Elias have pointed to the ambivalence in the civilising process, particularly through focusing on government-sponsored 'civilising offensives' against problem populations (see Bruer, 1991; Burkitt, 1996; van Kriekan, 1999; Powell, 2007; Rohloff, 2008).

This aspect of the civilising process is shown in a particularly clear way by van Krieken (1999). He draws attention to the ambivalence inherent in the Australian government's policy of removing indigenous Aboriginal children from their families as part of a eugenics programme of social engineering between the early 1900s and the 1930s. His analysis points to the intrinsic 'barbarity' in the practices of a 'civilising offensive' designed to achieve what were ostensibly welfare objectives. The very idea of a 'civilising offensive' implies that *functional democratisation* is not solely an outgrowth of growing social interdependence but can also be coercively created by state power, sometimes in an integrative and inclusive way, but often in a marginalising and aggressive way that can disrupt social interdependency and undermine rather than build social solidarity. Indeed 'civilising offensives' are the normal way in which the civilising process operates in modern societies. They represent the withdrawal of violence from public view and its manifestation in bureaucratic, judicial and regulatory forms that are consistent with liberal-democratic sensibilities. Indeed it is this aspect of state action that Wacquant highlights in *Punishing the poor* (2009). We can interpret the processes surrounding the penalisation of poverty as part of a 'civilising offensive' designed to contain and discipline the *precariat* in a post-welfare era. Alvin Gouldner's (1981) précis of the *civilising process* since the 19th century captures this aspect of its changing forms. While his interpretation is clearly aimed at the explanation of genocide and holocaust in the modern era, if the words 'killed' and 'mutilated' are interpreted in a broad psychological and emotional sense, and not simply in terms of their literal physical and military meaning, then Gouldner's words describe the neoliberal drive of much contemporary public policy as much as the industrialisation of murder.

> ... there is more than one type of violence. What has happened since perhaps the nineteenth century is the diminution of only one kind of violence, ferocity – especially privately undertaken ferocity. This wanes with the emergence of the centralised state effectively claiming a monopoly of legitimate violence. Ferocity comes to be succeeded by other forms of violence, new forms of bureaucratic domination and of asceticism. Passionless, impersonal callousness, in which more persons than ever before in history are now killed or mutilated with the flick of a switch. (Gouldner, 1981, p 418)

He goes on to observe that 'there is no evolutionary trend towards kindness and happiness'. I do not think that Elias thought this either. What does need to be emphasised from these observations is that the 'civilising offensives' sponsored by contemporary welfare state actions aimed at integrating marginal populations into work, and the implementation of policies of incapacitation which fill up the prisons, must be understood in a context of *de-civilising processes*. This is precisely what Wacquant (2009) describes.

There are other areas that require development in Elias's work. A number of commentators have suggested that Elias paid insufficient attention to economic processes, even if he acknowledged their impact (see Newton, 2003) — in particular, that his perspective fails to appreciate fully that while the development of money, markets and credit can lead increasingly to dense chains of interdependency, they can also lead to *amoralism* and, in the period following Elias's death, exploitative relationships through the 'economic barbarity' of global neoliberal finance.

Monetarisation and markets have been described by Steven Messner and Richard Rosenfeld as leading to a state of institutional anomie in which the socio-cultural realm of civil society is unable to impose moral regulation on a disembedded market system (Messner and Rosenfeld, 2001). The exaggerated emphasis on the acquisition of money in a consumerist society encourages the pursuit of wealth by any means. It also tends to subordinate everything to the logic of money and markets. Institutional anomie is, therefore, the absence of social solidarity and the absence of predictability in social and economic exchanges because it is lubricated by selfish rather than other regarding values. More pointedly, Bruer (1991) draws attention to an important distinction overlooked by Elias between the regulatory and integrative impact of bourgeois competition law and the atomising influence of markets. He contrasts the socially integrative effects of the civilising process in bringing about orderly and peaceful socioeconomic exchanges in the developing bourgeois societies of early industrial capitalism and the disaggregating, asocial and individualising tendencies that underpin the capitalist market system today.

> The development of modern society … cannot be understood simply in terms of an expansion of social interdependencies, and competition cannot be seen simply as a medium which drives cultural formation to ever-more complex and higher levelled aggregates. More frequently, the opposite can also be observed. Social relationships, which

arose with bourgeois society, are decomposed, relations of solidarity dissipated or completely destroyed. Market societalization means an increase in interdependency *and* atomisation of the social, the increasing density and the negation of all ties – asocial sociability. (Bruer, 1991, p 407)

Disorder and conflict are embedded features of competitive capitalist market systems. The social disorganisation and occasional violence generated by economic processes are always present, especially in the marginal populations and communities who lose most in a competitive market society. An interpretation of the pacification associated with the theory of the civilising process that is more congruent with history might be that the visible manifestations of violence and interpersonal aggression are generally subdued, or placed 'behind the scenes', but they re-surface with the ebb and flow of the capitalist accumulation cycle precisely because the strength and density of the networks of interdependency which influence feelings of empathy, self-control and social inclusion fluctuate in line with economic activity. The conclusion being drawn here is that while Elias was partly correct to understand monetarisation as a force that transformed social relationships and economic exchanges, creating denser networks of interdependency as an integral feature of the *civilising process*, he should have presented a more balanced understanding of capitalist markets and market competition, especially in explaining the ever-presence of the *established/outsider* relationships that capitalism, and particularly its neoliberal version, creates. There is an absence of a discussion of the circumstances that might lead to a more intractable process of de-civilising at the margins of mainstream economy and society. Money, credit and trade develop in ways that are uneven, cyclical and which create hierarchy and conflict, and we need to understand how neoliberal market forces create the conditions for processes of de-civilising to take hold in a sustained and ongoing way. This is precisely the contribution that Wacquant has made to social and penal analysis by anchoring his conceptualisation of *advanced marginality* in the relentless and harmful atomising impact of neoliberal market forces on poor communities. In order to establish this point a brief detour into the association between the civilising process, violence and cycles of capital accumulation is helpful.

Civilisation, violence and the cycle of accumulation

The interconnection between the civilising process, economic development and the cyclical patterns of violence has been made by

Mares (2009). While drawing on the theory of the civilising process, he attempts to address the issue of recurring, or cyclical, patterns of violence through history which, he argues, Elias's theory does not explain, at least not in an explicit way. Key to understanding Mares' analysis is Giovanni Arrighi's thesis on the 'long centuries' (Arrighi, 2005, 2010). A key element of Arrighi's analysis has been to place contemporary problems relating to global financial crisis in a long-term historical context. He concentrates on the endemic problem of capitalism, that of managing its recurring problems of finding reinvestment for accumulated profits and money towards the end of a cycle of accumulation: over time there is a limit to the profitable expansion of trade and production, and capitalists at that stage seek alternative sources of profitability by retaining a larger proportion of their incoming cash flows in liquid form. Market niches are created for financial intermediaries who divert money away from productive and employment-creating activities. This can involve a form of financial serfdom in which financial expansion leads to 'accumulation by dispossession' through accelerating processes of de-industrialisation and asset stripping as the economy and society comes to be driven by financial rather than productive markets. The fundamental problem that results from this is that the change of phase from production to financial services has led to a sustained period of de-industrialisation and social dislocation in the English-speaking countries and the European Union (EU) from the 1980s onwards. And, of course, the expansion of risky ventures for liquid capital in search of profit led to the global financial crisis which began to unfold from 2008. In short there have been phases of expansion, consolidation and contraction in world cycles of accumulation. The political economy of the contraction phase is what is of particular interest with respect to advanced marginality, the de-pacification of social relations and de-civilising processes.

Dennis Mares (2009) helpfully tracks the historical phases of capitalist development and contraction described by Arrighi against homicides rates in order to augment Elias's theory of the civilising process. This analysis emphasises the cyclical reality of violence as a response to economic contraction. He uses trends in homicide because they are a relatively unambiguous and reliable measure of violence over time. So, drawing on the 'long century' framework, he argues that in periods of what Arrighi refers to as 'explosive expansion', the state is forced into a strategy of social coercion in an attempt to control a socio-political context where institutions are immature and legitimacy for many acts of governance are low. Mares refers to this phase as one of social disorganisation to capture that sense of social turmoil associated with early immigration into the large US cities such as Chicago in the early 20th century. In Elias's terms this is a stage with weak governance and legitimacy, high levels of division between *established* and *outsider* groups and the expectation that levels of interpersonal violence will be high. In the 'sustained expansion' period, increased state regulation and control, combined with increased *functional democratisation* and social mobility, should lead to a decline in interpersonal violence in a social context in which there is greater social incorporation into a society of outsider groups and social divisions become less pronounced. In the 'contraction phase', which typically is underpinned by an accumulation crisis leading to a flight of capital from trade, manufacture and production, to financial services and consumption, the resulting de-industrialisation causes social dislocation.

In these circumstances governmental institutions become undermined by a declining tax base and, therefore, unable to invest in the social amelioration programmes that Habermas (1976) argued are essential for maintaining legitimacy for a capitalist society where socially produced wealth is appropriated privately. Violence can be expected to increase in such periods together with informal economic activity and criminality. Mares' data largely supports this cyclical pattern: trends in homicide expand and contract in line with both Elias's thesis on the civilising process and Arrighi's social history of the cyclical phases of the capitalist accumulation. An important observation to underline at this point is that at each successive cyclical stage the capacity to reintegrate marginal occupational groups back into the economy and society diminishes (see Arrighi, 2005). Indeed a key feature of what Wacquant (2008) describes as *advanced marginality* is the 'functional disconnection from macroeconomic trends' of the 'precariat' – unemployment in 'urban sensitive areas' becomes increasingly impervious to economic growth (p 236). It is also at this point that the processes of *functional democratisation* are stalled (the process whereby people come to have increasingly more equal balances of power through the functional utility that they have for others and the expansion of this process to ever-extending networks of people and groups, both nationally and internationally).

Civilising offensives and problem populations

The central point to be stressed here is that the connection between violence, disorder and criminality *and* economic downturn and financial crisis can be understood by examining the work of Wacquant and Elias together. Wacquant's analysis of *advanced marginality* augments Elias's theory of the civilising process because it captures the emerging state response to neoliberal market crisis well. What Elias neglected, but which Wacquant adds, is an understanding of de-civilising processes that are intrinsic features of capitalist development and, in particular, its neoliberal impact on the *outsiders* living in the hyper-ghettos and *banlieues* today. Life in those marginal communities is shaped by a need to grapple with the social, occupational and political consequences of the crisis in capitalist accumulation that has manifested itself as the global financial crisis.

History informs us that the thrust of Elias's broad theory of the civilising process is credible because the sensitivities and mentalities that became embedded as a *second nature* in people in the modern era remain dominant for those fully incorporated into the *established* social, cultural and political institutions of the advanced societies. The abhorrence of interpersonal violence, the display of good manners and the expression of empathy for the needs and discomfort of others are evident today in a variety of circumstances and forms which cannot easily be erased by periods of economic uncertainty and unemployment. However, as Laurent Mucchielli (2010) suggests in relation to contemporary France, while there is evidence that societal pacification, and increasing legal regulation of even the most minor of behavioural infringements, testifies to a strong desire for a peaceful social order, the social interdependence and social solidarity on which that social security depends is undermined by economic cycles which lead to fluctuating levels of crime, racism and violence. The reaction to this instability is, invariably, populist political-led 'moral panics' against *the outsiders* who typically are those variously referred to as the 'underclass', NEETs (not in education, employment or training), neds (a derogatory term applied in Scotland to hooligans, louts or petty criminals) and Chavs who are stigmatised as the authors of that potential criminality. Today *social interdependence* has to be policed constantly by evolving strategies to manage the succession of 'moral panics' that accompany economic and social change and the marginalised problem populations created by an unforgiving neoliberal society. As suggested by Rohloff (2008), 'moral panics are processes of decivilisation: occurring where civilising processes break down and decivilising trends become dominant' (p 66).

Good manners and violence coexist, as they have always coexisted. However, what Wacquant's analysis of advanced marginality adds to our understanding of urban crisis and neoliberal public policy is that the problem populations that are constructed out of the chaos of economic crisis may be a more permanent feature of neoliberal societies because, increasingly, they are resistant to re-absorption back into the mainstream economy. Wacquant recognises this as a key problem of advanced marginality.

The comparative sociology of the structure, dynamics and experience of urban relegation in the US and the main countries of the EU during the past three decades reveals not a *convergence* on the pattern of the US ghetto, as the dominant media and political discourse would have it, but the *emergence* of a new regime of marginality on both sides of the Atlantic. This regime generates forms of poverty that are neither residual, nor cyclical or transnational, but indeed inscribed in the future of contemporary societies insofar as they are fed by the fragmentation of the wage–labour relationship, the functional disconnection of the dispossessed neighbourhoods from national and global economies, and the reconfiguration of the welfare state into an instrument for enforcing the obligation to work in the polarising city (Wacquant, 2007, pp 66-7).

De-pacification of the hyper-ghetto and the *banlieues*

Functional de-democratisation has been a particular effect of financial crisis and deindustrialisation. The work skills and intellectual capital tied to industrial enterprises in decline are quickly discarded, trapping the unemployed in their de-commodified status (Esping-Andersen, 1990). Those whose marginalised *outsider* status is combined with spatial isolation in these circumstances are typically stigmatised for the social dispositions that they cultivate as survival tools for life in the neglected hyper-ghettos and the peripheral communities of our major urban centres. Their idleness has typically become an issue of their personal motivation to find alternative work, or their willingness to accept unskilled minimum wage jobs, rather than the failures of economic policy, education or the market. It is the economic and social consequences of these processes that have become the focus of Wacquant's analysis of advanced marginality. His description of the consequences of neoliberalism connects well with Elias's perspective on pacification and violence because it draws attention to the return of social insecurity to the streets and neighbourhoods of large 'sophisticated' metropolitan centres. Advanced marginality can be conceptualised as a *figuration* that ties together agencies of the state and the occupants of the ghetto and the *banlieue* in a conflictual and hierarchical relationship constantly in friction: it takes a punitive form because of the absence of integrative economic and occupational connections between the marginalised populations and mainstream (legal) market processes.

The withdrawal of the social state from its welfare obligations leads to a reaction from the ghetto that is shaped by having to live increasingly in a 'society without a state'. The 'cultural tool kits' that are fashioned by those living in such marginal communities involve developing attitudes, skills and emotional predispositions that are antithetical to mainstream society but essential for their own social and economic survival (see Swidler, 1986; Duncan, 1999). Their mentalities are transformed by their routine engagement with hostility, interpersonal threat and, too often, only the coercive arm of the state. They develop the knowledge of what Anderson (1999) has referred to as the 'code of the street' and Miller (1958) described as the 'focal concerns of the working-class community' – skills that are too often lacking in empathy for the other.

The return of high levels of routine interpersonal violence to some urban areas today requires a sociological account that does not reduce explanation to the perverse incentives of a profligate welfare state or the mental frailties of an 'underclass'. Wacquant (2004) avoids this by drawing on Elias's theory of the civilising process explicitly in his description of the changing configuration of the black ghetto from the 1960s to the present. It is the only sustained piece written by him discussing Elias's thesis. In particular, Wacquant traces the transformation of the black ghetto from a socioeconomic space that contained a broad representation of social classes and institutions of civil society to a marginal enclave containing residual housing, ill-educated and unskilled residents who are united, not by common local institutions, customs and solidarity, but by their 'race' and common status as a dispossessed group who often compete violently and criminally against each other in an internecine war of survival. Central to this analysis is the use made of Elias's theory of the civilising process as a framework for exploring processes leading to advanced marginality. De-industrialisation leads to the flight of the middle classes from the ghetto in pursuit of social advancement and employment elsewhere. The shops and services dwindle as their customer base dwindles. The institutions of civil society shrivel through a lack of willing volunteers to maintain their functional buoyancy and, worst of all, unpredictability in social exchanges and the fear of interpersonal violence are re-established as an everyday problem. The only state agencies left after the withdrawal of the social state are the agencies of criminal justice geared to the zero tolerance management of urban promiscuity in a society that resolves fear of crime by supporting an ever-expanding penal system (see Simon, 2007, on government through crime). In this context the mentalities of the residents living in areas of urban decay accommodate to these new harsh realities.

At the heart of Wacquant's analysis is a critique of the retreating welfare state and the withdrawal of its protective safety-net against the harsh vagaries of neoliberalism, although the notion of welfare in the US context always requires qualification (see Pierson, 1990; Skocpol, 1992; Eitzen and Baca Zinn, 2000; Alesina and Glaeser, 2004). Table 5.1 summarises the main processes underpinning hyper-ghettoisation.

Table 5.1: The de-civilising process and the ghetto

Organisational desertification of the ghetto	Retreat of the welfare state and the degradation of the associative fabric in the ghetto Decline of municipal services Degradation of the schools
Social de-differentiation and economic informalisation	Functional and structural decrease in the local division of labour (churches and voluntary organisations substitute for state actions Rise of the informal economy
De-pacification of everyday life and erosion of public space	Increasing violence and murder Dying a violent death and going to prison become banal Children acquire modes of behaviour habituated to violence

There are two dominant features of this analysis that are related to the debate surrounding the contradictions in Elias's thesis. First, Wacquant shares with Gouldner (1981) that interpretation of the civilising process that points to the ambivalence surrounding state action: it is interpreted as a form of bureaucratic violence against the most economically and socially vulnerable who challenge the mores of a market society and require solutions for their plight requiring more rather than less state aid. Through the strategic withdrawal of collective social security and welfare obligations, the state engages in what amounts to a 'civilising offensive' to discipline those on the economic margins by bouncing them into precarious low-wage employment while building prisons and criminalising social policy for those intent on resisting that inducement. Table 5.2 summarises the main lines of argument.

While much of Wacquant's analysis is focused on the US, he acknowledges the difference between the survival of the disadvantaged living in Western Europe who, on the whole, remain supported by a safety-net of welfare services despite the global financial crisis, and the residents of the US hyper-ghettos struggling to survive in a post-welfare society, made even worse by the passing of the Personal Responsibility and Work Opportunity Act 1996. The differences between Europe and the US may only be a matter of degree (see Wacquant, 2008, pp 135-62). If there is a process of convergence, then it is underpinned by the standardising impact of subjugation to the relentless drive of neoliberalism.

Table 5.2: The penal state and the government of social insecurity

Withdrawal of the economic state	The global embedding of neoliberalism and dominance of market logics in all areas of life
Retraction/ retrenchment of the social state	A discernible shift from welfare to a workfare state, creating a 'trampoline' to bounce the 'precariat' into 'insecure employment'
Growth of the penal state	The carceral state emerges as a means of containing the 'precariat' – liberal at the top but punitive and interventionist at the bottom
Symbolic import of punishment	The 'symbiosis of the prison and the ghetto' is an embedded feature of a penal strategy focused on incapacitation at the expense of rehabilitative reintegration of offenders who challenge the mores of neoliberal market society

The US way of welfare support is very much grounded in racist and behaviourist assumptions that are stronger and institutionally fixed in deeper foundations in US history and society compared with Europe (see Alesina and Glaeser, 2004). While the US is in that sense different, and some might argue 'exceptional' in comparison with Europe, the differences are perhaps overstated. Stephen Mennell (2009) has suggested that it is perhaps not as 'exceptional' as is often presented. The feature that is common to both the US and Europe is the impact that markets and de-industrialisation have had on processes of *functional democratisation*. What becomes increasingly problematic in both the US and Europe today is the *functional de-democratisation* that is occurring in all Western societies in the wake of global financial crisis and de-industrialisation. Advanced marginality is a socioeconomic figuration that represents the most extreme form of *functional de-democratisation*, a process that is driven by neoliberal market forces that consign the flawed consumers of the advanced societies to the social and spatial periphery of a society predicated on materialism. The typical reaction to this process of relegation has been for increasing numbers of people to engage in informal economic activity. The main lubricant of that economy continues to be drugs which in turn requires occasional violence to 'rectify market irregularities'; people in those circumstances can become habituated to interpersonal aggressiveness and develop a preparedness for the unpredictable use of violence. De-civilising conditions develop quickly out of such a situation.

It is largely because the US exhibits de-civilising tendencies in a more manifestly clear way compared with the EU countries that it is treated as being 'exceptional'. In addressing issues of 'American exceptionalism' and the civilising process, Mennell captures this sense that the US is an extreme rather than exceptional case when he describes the distinctive features of US development not in the criminality of US society but in the inability of large numbers of Americans to control their murderous emotional impulses compared with Europeans, impulses that are fuelled by the extremities of wealth, deprivation and an acute worsening of racial fractionalisation despite the Obama Presidency.

> Processes of functional democratisation are certainly a feature of the modern world. But, I would argue, they are also accompanied by and entangled with movements in the opposite direction – towards *functional de-democratisation*. And they may bring with them *diminishing mutual identification*.... This can be seen both internally to the USA and externally. Internally – at odds with the traditional images of 'American exceptionalism' – socio-economic inequalities are vastly increasing, and rates of social mobility are not as great as is commonly believed. (Mennell, 2009, p 111, emphasis added)

It is at this point that the complementarity between Wacquant and Elias can be seen.

Psycho-genesis and the ethnography of the poor

If we are moving to conclude that Wacquant adds to Elias's theory of the civilising process by elaborating a more adequate framework for understanding de-civilising processes, one that is rooted in the sociological analysis of neoliberalism, then Elias adds to Wacquant's analysis of advanced marginality by pointing to the interconnection between socio-genesis and psycho-genesis: the agenda for studying advanced marginality must of necessity focus on those factors that lead to the transformation of mentalities in the US hyper-ghettos and peripheral housing estates and *banlieues* in Europe. Elias has shown that mentalities have a history and are shaped by the networks of sociability which include the structures of both work and civil society. When the links that connect those structures and social institutions to people and communities are destroyed, then we must expect there to be consequences for the sense of self-identity and emotional integrity of those cut adrift. We can formulate the issue more graphically, in terms of what Jock Young (1999) has metaphorically called 'social bulimia'. What he means by this is that neoliberalism has been responsible for the voracious devouring of people into the belly of consumerism and the pursuit of celebrity followed by their ejection as they are spewed out into the metaphorical gutter. The level of brutality of this process will determine how those who experience 'social bulimia' will act in the world because it will shape how they feel and react to their social exclusion. Significantly, the exclusion from mainstream social and economic activities in contemporary society is presented by Young (1999, 2007) as a consequence of wider forces which *actively* marginalise people: it is something that is done to people and not something that people do to themselves.

Understanding the psycho-genesis of advanced marginality as a *figuration* involving the interaction between local, national and international forces is important. Wacquant clearly wants to anchor his understanding of advanced marginality in this larger context, especially the global driving force of neoliberalism. His adopted methodology for documenting the consequences of 'social bulimia' is ethnographic observation grounded in an appreciation of the type of links and connections that Elias's sociology is built around and informed by the vision of social research gifted by Bourdieu.

> … ethnographic observation emerges as an indispensable tool, first to pierce the screen of discourses whirling around these territories of urban perdition which lock inquiry within the biased perimeter of the pre-constructed object…. But, lest one condemn oneself to monographic myopia, fieldwork cannot for a single moment do without institutional analysis, and vice versa…. It must be guided at every step by the methodical knowledge, itself constantly revised and enriched by the first person study of concrete situations, of the macro-structural determinants that, although ostensibly absent from the neighbourhood, still govern the practices and representations of its residents because they are inscribed in the material distribution of resources and social possibles as well as lodged inside bodies in the form of categories of perception, appreciation and action. (Wacquant, 2008, pp 9–10)

This view of ethnographic method is one that is appreciative of the human consequences of the relationship between 'macro-structural determinants' and their impact on the interior of 'human bodies', on the social, cultural and body capital of those who live in a state of *advanced marginality*. It must also encompass an appreciation of the impact on the emotional level, on the changes in empathy or the other-regarding sensibilities that Elias calls a *second nature*.

Wacquant's discussion of the territorial stigmatisation that accompanies advanced marginality points to the qualitative change in social relations and sense of solidarity in a wide range of communities in the US and Europe ranging from the South Side of Chicago to Moss Side in Manchester. The residents of 'old working-class towns and districts' display a decline in a sense of attachment to their area. In describing the sense of insecurity and the social and cultural dislocation that replaces the solidarity and mutuality that characterised the Fordist period of industrial society, Wacquant observes that the working-class areas of the past have now 'mutated into an empty space of competition and conflict, a danger-filled battleground for the daily contest for subsistence' (Wacquant, 2008, p 271).

What is perhaps lacking in this account of life in the marginal communities of urban US and Europe is a fuller description of the psycho-genesis of de-civilising processes that these developments presage. This has been addressed by Wouters (2007). For example, he has taken Elias's sociological reading of Freud and extended it to explain the socio-psychological reaction typical of living in a more individualistic culture which neoliberalism has partly created. Drawing on the Freudian conceptual framework used by Elias, he describes the processes of *informalisation* that characterise the loosening of the rigid 'harmonious inequality' that was a feature of Victorian and inter-war European society: a movement from a society populated by *superego-dominated personalities* to a society of *we-less superego-dominated personalities* through to a society today that is characterised by *ego-dominated self-regulation* which he describes in terms of the implanting of a *third nature*. Central to this version of the civilising process is an appreciation of the ways in which social change has an impact on character and sense of self. As Western culture has become more open and individualistic, people have become habituated to the new social conditions. Functional democratisation brings with it a 'controlled decontrolling of relationships of superiority and inferiority'. However, what becomes of those who experience a process of de-democratisation as their functional utility for mainstream society is lost? What are the consequences for those who must experience a process of '*uncontrolled* decontrolling' as the institutional anomie of the marketplace fractures the key integrative social institutions of economy and society and the state adopts an obsequious posture to markets by the sudden abrogation of its welfare obligations?

Sennett (1999, 2004; Sennett and Cobb, 1993) has begun to answer some of these questions by talking about the 'hidden injuries of class', the 'corrosion of character' and the consequences for 'respect' living in an age of inequality. He does so in order to draw our attention to the impact of a capitalist market society on how people *feel* about the impact of work and society on their lives and sense of worth. The anxiety and loss of dignity that results from the changing occupational structure and the changing nature of work today is described in a way that exposes the human and social costs of neoliberalism. The descriptions offered by Sennett concentrate on those who experience the deskilled, repetitive and low-paid work in the offices, shops and factories of the mainstream business economy. We are left to conjecture as to how even more dispiriting it might be for those consigned to a life of casualised and precarious menial jobs working for poverty wages without hope of social mobility. Jock Young (2007) has observed that the penury of the urban ghetto is not due to an unwillingness on the part of residents to work but to 'slave-like jobs'. It is precisely because the world of minimum wage work is so meaningless, sometimes full of discomfort and often demeaning that it frequently fails to achieve its integrative functions. It stimulates a sense of anger and of exploitation in a primitive way (see Hall et al, 1978). We need to know much more about the phenomenology of working life and the experience of menial labour (see Charlesworth, 2000). What is really important about this sociological focus on advanced marginality is the transformations that will take place at the level of psycho-genesis. The phenomenon that may be emerging in the hyper-ghettos is not the development of a *third nature* in which people adjust to the world of freedom and individualism in the wake of a long-term process of *informalisation*, but of a return to a *first nature* of primitive survival, devoid of any recognition of the superego in a me-dominated environment of social insecurity and rising interpersonal violence. Ferge (1999) has captured this sense of foreboding well.

> The consequences of the waning away of elements of civilisation in some parts of society are easy to think through (logically, if not morally). If conditions change so as to make scarce the knife and fork, inside toilet, hot water, and then water itself ... as well as privacy, then habits tied to them

have to change. All these changes, including the lowering of the level of shame and the weakening of many other self-restraints set in with tragic rapidity in the case of the homeless ... the non-poor become involved too. If the institutions of social security in general are weakening, the habits developed in relation to money, to time, to space, to self, and to others are all jeopardised. (Ferge, 1999, p 235)

Conclusion

There is a sense in which the argument advanced by Stephen Quilley and Steven Loyal (2005), specifically that Eliasian sociology provides a central theory for the human societies, might require further justification, but it is certainly a strong candidate to fulfil that role. The integration of state analysis with sociological and psychological levels of investigation is fairly unique and, when it is combined with an analysis of social figurations, the building blocks for a general theory are evident. The particular focus of Elias's perspective on pacification and violence certainly make it useful for augmenting Wacquant's analysis of advanced marginality. However, Elias's theory requires development with respect to de-civilising tendencies. The contradictions of the theory of the pacification and de-pacification of Western societies are grounded in an inadequate understanding of the effects of monetarisation and economic processes on social solidarity and relationships of interdependence. More particularly, the contemporary version of capitalist market society, driven by a global system connecting everyone and everything to a neoliberal economic network of interdependence, was not anticipated by Elias and has been inadequately integrated into his theory by his followers. Wacquant's relentless focus on the consequences of neoliberalism for the de-civilising of the marginal communities in the major cities and regions of the US and Europe has contributed to rectifying this weakness.

References
Alesina, A. and Glaeser, E. (2004) *Fighting poverty in the US and Europe: A world of difference*, Oxford: Oxford University Press.
Anderson, E. (1999) *The code of the street: Decency, violence and the moral life of the street*, New York: Norton.
Arrighi, G. (2005) 'Hegemony unravelling – II', *New Left Review*, vol 33, May-June, pp 1-27
Arrighi, G. (2010) *The long twentieth century: Money, power and the origins of our times*, London: Verso.

Bruer, S. (1991) 'The denouements of civilization: Elias and modernity', *International Social Science Journal*, no 128, May, pp 401-16.

Burkitt, I. (1996) 'Civilization and ambivalence', *British Journal of Sociology*, vol 47, no 1, pp 135-50.

Charlesworth, S.J. (2000) *A phenomenology of working class experience*, Cambridge: Cambridge University Press.

Duncan, C. (1999) *Worlds apart: Why poverty persists in rural America*, New Haven, CT: Yale University Press

Eitzen, S. and Baca Zinn, M. (2000) 'The missing safety net and families: a progressive critique of the new welfare legislation', *Journal of Sociology and Social Welfare*, vol 27, no 1, pp 53-72.

Elias, N. (1982) *State formation and civilisation*, Oxford: Blackwell.

Elias, N. and Scotson, J. (1965) *The established and the outsiders*, London: Frank Cass.

Esping-Andersen, G. (1990) *The three worlds of welfare capitalism*, Cambridge: Polity Press.

Ferge, S. (1999) 'And what if the welfare state fades away? The civilising process and the state', in S. Svalfors and P. Taylor-Gooby (eds) *The end of the welfare state?*, London: Routledge, pp 218-39.

Gouldner, A. (1981) 'Doubts about the uselessness of men and the meaning of the civilising process', *Theory and Society*, vol 10, pp 413-18.

Habermas, J. (1976) *Legitimation crisis*, London: Heinemann.

Hall, S., Critcher, C., Jefferson, T., Clarke, J. and Roberts, B. (1978) *Policing the crisis: Mugging, the state and law and order*, London: Macmillan.

Mares, D. (2009) 'Civilization, economic change and trends in interpersonal violence in Western societies', *Theoretical Criminology*, vol 13, no 4, pp 419-49.

Mennell, S. (2009) 'An exceptional civilizing process?', *Journal of Classical Sociology*, vol 9, no 1, pp 97-115.

Messner, S. and Rosenfeld, R. (2001) *Crime and the American dream*, Belmont, CA: Wadsworth.

Miller, W.B. (1958) 'Lower-class culture as a generating milieu of gang delinquency', *Journal of Social Issues*, vol 15, pp 5-19.

Mucchielli, L. (2010) 'Are we living in a more violent society? A socio-historical analysis of interpersonal violence in France, 1970s-present', *British Journal of Criminology*, vol 50, no 5, pp 808-29.

Newton, T. (2003) 'Credit and civilization', *British Journal of Sociology*, vol 54, no 3, pp 347-71.

Pierson, C. (1990) 'The "exceptional" United States: first new nation or last welfare state?', *Social Policy & Administration*, vol 24, no 3, pp 186-98.

Powell, R. (2007) 'Civilising offensives and ambivalence: the case of British Gypsies', *People, Place and Policy Online*, vol 1, no 3, pp 112-23.

Quilley, S. and Loyal, S. (2005) 'Eliasian sociology as a "central theory" for the human sciences', *Current Sociology*, vol 53, no 5, pp 807-28.

Rohloff, A. (2008) 'Moral panics as decivilising processes: towards an Eliasian approach', *New Zealand Sociology*, vol 23, no 1, pp 66-76.

Sennett, R. (1999) *The corrosion of character: Personal consequences of work in the new capitalism*, New York: Norton.

Sennett, R. (2004) *Respect: The formation of character in an age of inequality*, London: Penguin Books.

Sennett, R. and Cobb, J. (1993) *The hidden injuries of class*, New York: Norton.

Simon, J. (2007) *Governing through crime: How the war on crime transformed American democracy and created a culture of fear*, Oxford: Oxford University Press.

Skocpol, T. (1992) *Protecting soldiers and mothers*, Cambridge, MA: Harvard University Press.

Swidler, A. (1986) 'Culture in action: symbols and strategies', *American Sociological Review*, vol 51, pp 273-86.

van Kriekan, R. (1999) 'The barbarism of civilization: cultural genocide and the "stolen generation"', *British Journal of Sociology*, vol 50, no 2, pp 297-315.

Wacquant, L. (2004) 'Decivilizing and demonizing: the remaking of the Black American ghetto', in S. Loyal and S. Quilley (eds) *The sociology of Norbert Elias*, Cambridge: Cambridge University Press, pp 95-121.

Wacquant, L. (2007) 'Territorial stigmatisation in the age of advanced marginality', *Thesis Eleven*, no 91, November, pp 66-77.

Wacquant, L. (2008) *Urban outcasts: A comparative sociology of advanced marginality*, Cambridge: Polity Press.

Wacquant, L. (2009) *Punishing the poor: The neoliberal government of social insecurity*, Durham, NC: Duke University Press.

Wouters, C. (2007) *Informalization: Manners and emotions since 1890*, London: Sage.

Young, J. (1999) *The exclusive society*, London: Sage Publications.

Young, J. (2007) *The vertigo of modernity*, London: Sage Publications.

SIX

Beyond the penal state: advanced marginality, social policy and anti-welfarism

Lynn Hancock and Gerry Mooney

Introduction

Loïc Wacquant's extraordinarily extensive writing over recent years has sparked widespread commentary across a range of academic disciplines but notably, for our purposes, in criminology, social policy and urban studies. Many of those commentating on *Urban outcasts* (2008), *Punishing the poor* (2009a) and *Prisons of poverty* (2009b) in the UK and Europe express support for Wacquant's overall analysis and the contributions his insights make to the way we assess and conceptualise neoliberal state-craft, penality, the restructuring of welfare and its implications. In this vein, writers have sought to extend, modify and qualify Wacquant's analysis in the light of empirical observations in a variety of settings, further comparative analysis and theoretical fine-tuning within an overall appreciative framework. We adopt the same kind of stance in this chapter. The themes we explore focus on Wacquant's (2008) work on 'advanced marginality', what this means in the contemporary UK and the role of territorial stigmatisation in the production of marginality. This occupies an important position within his overall approach which arguably has not received the same level of attention as some of his other concepts.

Wacquant has placed important emphasis on the interrelationships between social welfare and criminal justice. We explore a number of aspects which are somewhat overlooked by Wacquant – in particular, we highlight that representations of 'the urban poor' as a 'problem' category in the population (both historically and contemporarily) are significant aspects not only of advanced marginality but also of social policy interventions (understood in their broadest sense). Further, advanced marginality and the construction of particular disadvantaged populations as problematic are also enabled and reinforced by what is increasingly being referred to as 'poverty porn' and 'penal pornography'. Wacquant has given some attention to the latter (2009a, p xii). He observes that:

> ... [t]he law-and-order merry-go-round is to criminality what pornography is to amorous relations: a mirror deforming reality to the point of the grotesque that artificially extracts delinquent behaviours from the fabric of social relations in which they take root and make sense, deliberately ignores their causes and their meanings, and reduces their treatment to a series of conspicuous position-takings, often acrobatic, sometimes properly unreal, pertaining to the cult of ideal performance rather than to the pragmatic attention to the real. (Wacquant, 2009a, pp xii–xiii)

Our argument in this chapter is that 'poverty porn' can be read in a similar way. Moreover, the pervasiveness of both types of pornographies, we suggest, is critical for understanding punitive social and criminal justice policies. The overall thrust of the chapter, then, provides support for Wacquant's approach but also seeks to take it forward with respect to the critically important role played by social policy more generally.

Advanced marginality and stigmatisation: 'poverty porn'

Advanced marginality

Loïc Wacquant's thesis on advanced marginality distinguishes six features that characterise this emergent condition:[1] (i) 'flexible', unstable patterns of wage labour and the production of insecurity and social disintegration; (ii) the 'functional disconnection from macroeconomic trends' (2008, p 236) such that the most marginal groups and neighbourhoods remain untouched during periods of economic growth and the life chances of residents remain persistently depressed; (iii) 'territorial fixation and stigmatisation' (2008, p 237) – advanced marginality is concentrated in particular locations in cities and those who reside outside such locales as well as within them regard such places as 'urban hellholes' (2008, p 238) that are dangerous, degraded and degrading; (iv) territorial or spatial alienation and what Wacquant refers to as the 'dissolution of "place"' (2002, 2008, p 241) as community-based affiliations and bonds are shattered, and residents withdraw from a public space that is increasingly characterised by conflicts and divisions; (v) 'loss of hinterland' (2008, p 243), by which the author means the depletion of the means of social support for workers who in earlier periods (under Fordism, 1945–75) during a cyclical downturn would have been able to find support from relatives, neighbours and local institutions. Such support may have taken the form of informal working, but the link between the formal and informal economy and the path to regular employment would have been facilitated by such connections that have now been ruptured. Furthermore, collective means of representing and resisting are rendered mute by (vi) 'social fragmentation and symbolic splintering' (2008, p 244) as trades unions find difficulty organising beyond the workplace and the myriad of pressure groups find little traction or common ground. Wacquant's emphasis on the language and labels frequently used to describe populations in this setting is of importance ('new poor', 'excluded', 'underclass', 'yobs', etc); it 'speaks volumes on the state of *symbolic derangement*' (2008, p 245; original emphasis). As we show below, however, the labelling and construction of 'the urban poor' in media and popular discourses both order and mobilise support for punitive anti-welfarism and at the same time diminish the potential for collective responses.

Wacquant (2002, 2008) is clear that the six key features of 'advanced marginality' form an ideal type analysis and a framework for 'hypothesis making' and empirical refinement. The existence or absence of features, conditions or attributes that contrast with Wacquant's descriptors do not therefore challenge his thesis. Flint (2009) observes, for example, how religious organisations have developed rather than withdrawn or diminished in 'segregated neighbourhoods' in the UK. Rather than being regarded positively, however, Islamic institutions and mosques in UK neighbourhoods in some British cities are frequently portrayed as threatening and dangerous and are construed as signifying a process of 'Islamisation' (Flint, 2009). Observations such as these invite theoretical modification in the light of empirical evidence drawn from different cities and their varying social compositions and histories.

The dissimilarities between urban conditions and the treatment of marginalised groups under Fordism and the plight of the least advantaged in the contemporary period of neoliberal state formation are over-played, however. As Piven (2010) argued, Wacquant tends to ignore the strong continuities in welfare provision in the US historically; welfare support has always been highly conditional and woefully underfunded. In the UK, the history of social policy teaches us to avoid too romantic a view of the Keynesian welfare state and Fordism (Hughes and Lewis, 1988; Williams, 1989; see also Mayer, 2010).

The division of the working class into 'deserving' and 'undeserving' categories, which pre-dates the post-war welfare settlement, has remained a persistent theme. Furthermore, the experiences of poor women, black and minority ethnic groups and people with disabilities in the struggle for access to welfare and equal treatment in welfare provisioning caution against idealism when reflecting on the 1945–75 period (see, for example, Gordon, 1986; Smith, 1989; Briar, 1997). Indeed, during the 1980s the New Right employed the arguments made by feminist groups and left critics of an unresponsive welfare system (selectively) to make their case for reforms during the Thatcher governments in the 1980s (King, 1987).

The main strengths of Wacquant's 'advanced marginality' thesis centre on the challenges it poses to the dominant political, media, popular and, indeed, some academic discourses around the 'underclass'. The thesis contests and rejects many of the 'folk concepts' and 'folk theories' that appear to inform policy formulation in the UK, and instead focuses steadfastly on the role of the state in the production of advanced marginality. In so doing, Wacquant's concern to centre the relationships and entanglements between welfare and penal policy for the regulation of marginalised groups is insightful, although the broad-brush approach tends to obscure the way systems of welfare and punishment have been enmeshed over a long period for 'deviant' women, for example (Gelsthorpe, 2010).

Wacquant's analysis is strongly grounded in the US context where welfare and penal policies remain largely unique in important ways (Mayer, 2010). Moreover, his arguments centre primarily on the penal state (and 'workfare' to a lesser extent), and as a consequence other policy areas have tended to be neglected:

> Housing, education, immigration or urban development are all policy areas, whose goals, strategies, and instruments have been significantly reconfigured so that they, too, contribute to regulating and controlling urban marginality. (Mayer, 2010, p 99)

Wacquant's focus may derive from the different meanings that are attached to the concept of 'welfare' in different settings (Gelsthorpe, 2010; Daly, 2011). In the UK welfare (or social welfare) tends to encompass income maintenance, education, health, housing (allowances and provision), social services and so on; in the US 'welfare' 'is conceived narrowly as relating to the means-tested, residual "assistance" dimensions of state provision' (Gelsthorpe, 2010, p 380).

We return later to the ways in which policy developments in some of the areas noted by Mayer (2010), above, have operated to control, regulate and remake welfare-dependent 'problem populations' as low-paid flexible labour in the UK context.

'Poverty porn'

The role of the media in shaping ever more punitive welfare and criminal justice policies receives remarkably little attention in Wacquant's work, yet it has been recognised as one of the major factors explaining variations in punitiveness between the UK and other nation-states (Norway, for example; see Green, 2008). As Nelken (2010, p 336) notes, 'the role of the media is another story – but it's not Wacquant's story'. However, the pervasive media attacks on people in poverty – including some of the most disadvantaged groups in the UK today – from the 24/7 news media, in newspapers and on television – reinforces and reconstructs dominant popular and political attitudes to poverty and welfare more generally. Poverty porn, in its various formats, focuses on individual failures and deficiencies. Programmes such as *Jeremy Kyle*, *Tricia*, *The Fairy Jobmother* and the like exemplify this genre. As Aitkenhead (2010) described the latter:

> *The Fairy Jobmother* ... is essentially *Supernanny* for the unemployed. In each episode, the 43-year-old Yorkshirewoman [Hayley Taylor] moves in with a family of longterm benefit claimants, observes the habits of the household, then produces a plan of action. From ordering a young man to fix his front tooth ("Sorry, but you look like a thug") to teaching interview technique ("No! Not 'Hiya'! You've got to say 'Hello'"), Taylor tackles every obstacle on the journey out of joblessness, undeterred by the mandatory tears and rage of the participants' 'narrative arc'.

In programmes such as these, 'dysfunctional' working-class families are contrasted with the 'normality' of middle-class lives; 'backward-looking' attitudes among the poor are rendered shameful; middle-class values associated with self-improvement and aspiration are revered. These programmes, designed to titillate and entertain, invoke anger and indignation and a way to 'know' working-class lives in a manner wholly de-contextualised from a critical understanding of the broader historical and structural processes that shape them. Wacquant (2008) powerfully explains and explores the impact of territorial stigmatisation on the residents of 'defamed' and 'tainted' urban spaces. Further, he notes that:

> The effects of territorial stigmatisation are also felt at the level of public policies. Once a place is publicly labelled as a 'lawless zone' or an 'outlaw estate', outside the common norm, it is easy for the authorities to justify special measures, deviating from both law and custom, which can have for effect – if not for intention – to destabilise and further marginalise their occupants, and submit them to the dictates of the deregulated labour market, render them invisible, or drive them out of a coveted space. (2008, p 240)

The kind of special measures he refers to include welfare reform (workfare) in the US in the form of the Personal Responsibility and Work Opportunity Act 1996 and the removal of large housing projects to disperse the poor from the 'ghetto' (Wacquant, 2008, p 240). Many of these insightful observations resonate in our own research. We would, however, wish to highlight the ways in which the print and broadcast media (and arguably the web is a potent tool here too) act *in concert* with policy makers to reproduce stigmatisation and justification, not only of special measures for 'defamed localities' but also of more widespread welfare reforms. The 'problem' of welfare is portrayed as being intrinsic to, and symbolised by, but not restricted to, the boundaries of 'problematic communities'.

A clear example of how 'neighbourhoods of relegation' (Wacquant, 2008, p 239) are presented is provided by the four-part BBC Scotland reality television programme *The Scheme*, the first two parts of which were broadcast in Scotland in May 2010. In this instance the community of a deprived social housing estate ('scheme' in Scotland), Onthank in the town of Kilmarnock in Ayrshire, was presented for public consumption as entertainment. The series provoked a great deal of debate and controversy across Scotland and beyond, reflected in considerable press coverage and presence on social networking sites and online discussion forums. The programme purported to offer a 'warts'n'all' 'reality-based' account of life in this particular housing scheme. Moreover, it positioned the viewer in judgement over the behaviour and lifestyles of those exhibited. In showcasing the problematic or dysfunctional aspects of family relationships, unemployment, alcohol or drug taking, it provided no insight into the underlying causes (such as the devastating economic change in this part of East Ayrshire) or contexts (of widening social inequalities) of social problems.

One of the most powerful criticisms of *The Scheme* – and 'poverty porn' more generally – is that it caricatures poverty and people experiencing poverty in a manner that demarcates subject from context; its episodes offered a vision, and a very partial and flawed understanding of poverty, which did not consider the underlying social and economic factors that work to generate and reproduce poverty over time and in particular locales. The focus in the documentary was on one housing scheme, and on only a handful of individuals and families who resided there. *The Scheme* relied on a largely behaviour-centred perspective focused on cultural and behavioural norms, lifestyles and attitudes that work to keep people in poverty. Furthermore, as the cameras rested on the possessions of those experiencing severe poverty and through the camera's gaze on the plasma TVs and other goods, use of alcohol and tobacco, we learn that many of those in poverty are 'flawed consumers' (Bauman, 2004) and that, as these are 'non-essentials', therefore the benefits claimants receive must be 'too much'.

For viewers, *The Scheme* fits into a schema of understanding; the view that council estates are synonymous with 'problems' has a long history in the UK (Johnstone and Mooney, 2007). Indeed, the negative 'messages' about publicly subsidised housing were being disseminated via various national housing policies, politicians and policy makers long before contemporary mass communication (Hancock, 2008). So, '[b]y the time New Labour came to power in 1997 there was a ready-made stock of largely negative terms, imagery and signifiers [for council housing] that were to find renewed vitality and generally uncritical usage in the early years of the 21st century' (Johnstone and Mooney, 2007, p 128). Moreover, programmes such as *The Scheme* reflect and constitute a sense-making framework in which to connect with contemporary narratives and stories about welfare 'in crisis' in the contemporary UK. This is perhaps most explicitly captured in the 'Broken Society' idea.

The labels 'Broken Society' and 'Broken Britain' have passed into wider popular and media discourses about the social and moral health of the UK in the news media. As with other anti-welfare narratives over recent decades, part of the potency and pervasiveness of the 'Broken Society' idea is the pliability of the term; it is capable of being deployed without evidence for a tremendously diverse assortment of social problems. For Conservatives such as Iain Duncan Smith and the Centre for Social Justice (CSJ), the 'Broken Society' finds its origins in 'broken families'. Teenage pregnancies, one-parent households living in a 'dependency culture', these are the staple diet of such perspectives. Consequently, stable marriages and a two-parent family life are regarded as central to 'mending' 'Broken Britain', thereby reducing levels of poverty. But the primary route out of poverty is through work. The absence of a 'habit' of work coupled with a willingness to be 'flexible' and 'mobile' are conceptualised as the major barriers to employment; there is no recognition that unemployment has structural causes or of long-term economic disinvestment in disadvantaged neighbourhoods and regions.

A key moment in this new mythology around 'Broken Britain' – or Broken Scotland more particularly – was the 2008 Glasgow East by-election (Mooney, 2009). The hotly contested Westminster seat, previously a Labour stronghold, invoked a great deal of media attention as a consequence of the power struggles between New Labour and Gordon Brown and the Scottish National Party and Scottish First Minister Alex Salmond. For our present purposes what is important is that Glasgow East was portrayed overwhelmingly in negative terms; dramatic newspaper headlines centred on high mortality rates and so-called 'worklessness' in the local population. Again, as was the case with *The Scheme* television programme, there was little acknowledgement of the East End of Glasgow's struggle with long-term economic decline or disinvestment over a long period after Clydeside's heavy industry and manufacturing industries had largely disappeared. Instead, one commentator spoke of the 'desolation' of Easterhouse, a large post-1945 'peripheral' housing estate, and of 'broken families', that this is a 'Broken Society'. Glasgow East was first and foremost presented and represented as a place of misery, apathy and despair. *The Times* journalist Melanie Reid (2008) referred to the council estates of the East End as 'Glasgow's Guantanamo'.

Media and political commentary act to influence and shape each other, and visits to the Glasgow East constituency by David Cameron and Iain Duncan Smith in 2008 played a key role in shaping much of the social commentary of the media during the election. Duncan Smith had visited the area in February 2008 to launch a CSJ report detailing what he identified as the key problems having a impact on the area, *Breakthrough Glasgow*. Using a language that came to be taken up in many of the newspaper reports of the election, Glasgow East was held up to exemplify the 'Broken Society'.

Of course, 'poverty porn', when combined with 'anti-crime' or 'penal pornography' (Wacquant, 2009a), constitutes the most potent imagery and does so in the most dramatic form when a high profile crime-related story unfolds in the national news media. This happened after the sentencing of Karen Matthews in December 2008 when the then Conservative leader David Cameron stated that:

> The verdict last week on Karen Matthews and her vile accomplice is also a verdict on our broken society. The details are damning. A fragmented family held together by drink, drugs and deception. An estate where decency fights a losing battle against degradation and despair. A community whose pillars are crime, unemployment and addiction.... How can Gordon Brown argue that people who talk about a broken society are wrong? These children suffered at the very sharpest end of our broken society but all over the country are other young victims, too. Children whose toys are dad's discarded drink bottles; whose role models are criminals, liars and layabouts; whose innocence is lost before their first milk tooth. What chance for these children? Raised without manners, morals or a decent education, they're caught up in the same destructive chain as their parents. It's a chain that links unemployment, family breakdown, debt, drugs and crime. (Cameron, 2008)

Poor families and communities and the 'problems' they create both for those directly affected but also the wealth and security of the 'law-abiding majority' are reported and repeated in the print, broadcast and web media, especially the UK tabloid press. The deeply rooted and rigid distinctions between the 'deserving' and 'undeserving poor' are forged, reworked but always sustained in social policies and popular culture, as they have been over a long period, but are seen most clearly in what is now described as 'poverty porn'. In the wake of the worldwide financial crisis in 2008 and, in particular, as governments have tried to make the case for welfare spending cuts in response to this crisis, media coverage has both reflected and moulded official discourses.

Iain Duncan Smith on Benefits Britain

BRITAIN'S shirkers' paradise shame with hordes of work shy benefit claimants was blamed last night for much of our economic mess. (*The Sun*, 1 December 2010)

Exaggerated stories and extreme examples used by newspapers are employed uncritically in official pronouncements to justify the claims being made in the Coalition's £81 billion deficit reduction programme (to be achieved by 2014–15). Similarly, the state exploits public anxiety, shaping the case for populist and punitive 'solutions' (Hall et al, 1978).

Impact of 'poverty porn'

Stryker and Wald's perceptive (2009) research on how 'compassion' was redefined to secure the imposition of strict time-limited welfare assistance and stringent work requirements as *progressive* measures in the US government's Personal Responsibility and Work Opportunity Reconciliation Act 1996 is informative in the context of the UK Conservative-led Coalition government's attempts to redefine 'fairness' in their justification for welfare spending cuts during 2010. These authors note how the pre-1996 welfare system in the US was constructed as lacking compassion, damaging those who received assistance and rooting them in, rather than alleviating, their poverty. Taken in this way, 'the logic behind [perversity] rhetoric is impeccable – if assistance is actually hurting the poor by creating dependence, then denying [assistance] is not cruel but compassionate' (Somers and Block, 2005, quoted in Stryker and Wald, 2009, p 522). Stryker and Wald's discourse analysis centres on debates in Congress and related documents. It does not aim to assess how the news media framed the debates or public and popular opinion in response to them. They do, however, emphasise how taken-for-granted stereotypes and assumptions about 'deserving' and 'undeserving' welfare recipients – and how these are both gendered and racialised – are pivotal backdrops to the struggle for the redefinition of 'compassion'.

The debates in and around the Emergency Budget delivered by the Chancellor (George Osborne) on 22 June 2010 provide one example (among many) of how media coverage both follows and shapes official discourses. The speech announced wide-ranging changes to Housing Benefit and the Local Housing Allowance (which supports low-income tenants in the private sector). The stated aims of the reforms were:

> … to provide a fairer and more sustainable Housing Benefit scheme by taking steps to ensure that people on benefit are not living in accommodation that would be out of the reach of most people in work, creating a fairer system for low-income working families and for the taxpayer. It will avoid the present situation where Housing Benefit recipients are able to live in very expensive properties in areas that most working people supporting themselves would have no prospect of being able to afford. (DWP, 2010a)

Chancellor George Osborne said: 'Today there are some families receiving £104,000 a year in Housing Benefit'. However, when challenged later, a spokesperson for the Department for Work and Pensions (DWP) conceded that 'We don't have any figures on how many people are claiming that rate' ... but 'a search of the *Daily Mail* and *The Sun* newspaper websites would throw up stories of people being paid the same if not more' (Booth, 2010). A *Telegraph* investigation involving 24 London boroughs revealed just three households claiming this amount (Raynor, 2010).

As the justification in the quotation above indicates, the Conservative-led Coalition government is engaged in efforts to redefine 'fairness' in terms that can be imagined by 'most people in work' and 'the taxpayer' (although many who claim housing and related benefits *are* in low-paid work) and away from any notion of 'redistribution' (see also DWP, 2011). In the context of increasing economic and social insecurity (Young, 2007), exaggerated claims, together with the portrayal of flagrant 'pathological' behaviour and 'flawed consumption' (Bauman, 2004) of the types described, and founded on a long history of 'scroungermania' (Cook, 2006, p 53), mobilise support for harsher and more punitive forms of welfarism.

Moral tutelage

In addition to its broader legitimising role, poverty porn, especially as it is represented in *Jeremy Kyle, Tricia, The Fairy Jobmother* and other 'self-transformational television' programmes (Skeggs, 2009, p 628), stress self-improvement and self-help (Skeggs, 2005). They employ 'expert' narratives and the emphasis is squarely on the normality of middle-class lives, and the dysfunctionality of poor working-class ones. The drive for an 'aspirational culture' is both implicit and explicit. Tutelage reaches beyond programme participants of course: audiences are invited to adjudicate on the 'deserving' and 'undeserving' and to feel victimised by those deemed 'undeserving'. The BBC television series *Saints and Scroungers* (in 2009) provides a good example. Its web pages inform us: 'Dominic Littlewood follows fraud officers as they bust the benefits thieves stealing millions of pounds every year, while charities and councils track down people who actually deserve government help'. The programme reminds us that 'we', the law-abiding taxpayers, are being 'robbed' by the 'scroungers'; we acquire the impression that it is easy to obtain welfare benefits (as evidenced by the supposed prevalence of 'scroungers'). Indeed, poverty porn as moral tutelage goes further; the degraded lives of working-class people work also as a warning by invoking the fear that personal 'failure' will lead to the 'flawed' and 'deviant' lifestyle of 'the poor'. Manifestations of class-based antipathy, reinforced by periodic 'moral panics' (Cohen, 1972), forge the view that 'something has to be done about such groups'.

'Social fragmentation and symbolic splintering'

'Poverty porn' works to further the process of 'social fragmentation and symbolic splintering' (Wacquant, 2008, p 244) by reinforcing classed, gendered and racialised social divisions. Media coverage provides a major avenue through which groups acquire 'knowledge' of each other's views and standpoints. This is particularly the case for 'policy elites' and politicians whose sense of detachment from 'public opinion' makes them particularly interested in the 'window' offered to them by the media (Indermaur and Hough, 2002, p 204, quoted in Hancock, 2004, p 60). Residents who have chosen to live in 'fenced-off enclaves' or 'gated communities' (Blandy, 2008) acquire their main understanding of other social groups through the media too. However, we should also acknowledge that residents occupying different tenures and employment statuses within so-called 'mixed communities' tend not to form social relationships (Tunstall and Lupton, 2010), and, in a context where positive representations of working-class people are notable by their absence, poverty porn offers up distorted, decontextualised and sensationalised accounts of the behaviour, attitudes and dispositions of marginalised groups.

It is important to stress that the way working-class people are represented in poverty porn and in media coverage more generally shapes not only the way the precariat, that is, those on the most insecure and vulnerable edges of the proletariat, are regarded but how more affluent groups – the 'included' – come to see themselves (see Young, 1999, 2007). Haylett (2001, p 365) puts it thus: 'middle-class dependency on working-class "backwardness" for its own claim to modern multicultural citizenship is an unspoken interest within the discourse of illegitimacy around the white working-class poor'. Furthermore,

> In these circumstances a representative middle class is positioned at the vanguard of 'the modern' which becomes a moral category referring to liberal, cosmopolitan, work and consumption based lifestyles and values, and 'the unmodern' on which this category depends is the white working-class

'other', emblematically a throwback to other times and places. (Haylett, 2001, p 365)

These unspoken class interests were reflected in New Labour's urban regeneration and social policies where socially excluded families and communities were defined as 'the problems to be fixed' (Morrison, 2003) and through which the 'unruly' could be remade as 'civilised' neoliberal subjects (Gray and Mooney, 2011). In this way we would emphasise that the state's moral tutelage takes multifarious forms, through the state's influence on the mass media and other 'cultural systems', but also through a variety of policy programmes (Hall et al, 1978).

Beyond the penal state?

As Mayer (2010) noted, Wacquant places emphasis on the penal state to the neglect of other policies – housing renewal, urban regeneration and education, for example – which operate to control, regulate and remake welfare-dependent 'problem populations' as low-paid, flexible neoliberal subjects. Furthermore, the inclusion of these broader policy areas exposes both the complexity of state transformation and its variation in different geo-political settings (Mayer, 2010), each of which tend to be downplayed in *Urban outcasts* and *Punishing the poor*, for example. Their consideration raises three further key points for us in the current UK context: (i) the infusion of market rationalities and the opportunities opened up for private capital in the delivery of welfare and service provision in each of these areas; (ii) the role of politics; and (iii) the resistance to the privatisation of social welfare on behalf of both providers and 'consumers' of services.

The inclusion of policy areas beyond the 'penal state', of course, raises wider questions about social reproduction, regulation and social control which were prevalent under Fordism and the Keynesian welfare state in the UK. Efforts to control and regulate behaviour have, however, been significantly extended over recent years (Crawford, 2006). As Crawford notes, 'few aspects of social life have been left out of this zealous gaze' (2006, p 456). The most economically marginal have borne the brunt of the new policy tools developed to secure compliant behaviour (Anti-Social Behaviour Orders, Acceptable Behaviour Contracts, Parenting Orders), including the strengthening of the conditions that must be met to secure welfare benefits. Nevertheless, as Crawford argues, regulatory mechanisms have been extended to all manner of institutions (schools, hospitals, universities, for example), and social settings – including state agencies – although this is not to say they have been realised in the ways regulators envisaged or that they are coherent and uncontested (Crawford, 2006).

The expansion of market rationalities, privatisation and the introduction of quasi-markets to discipline and contest state welfare provision clearly reflects attempts to re-shape the role of the state in the period from Thatcher's 1979 government as well as to redraw the relation between providers and 'consumers' in social welfare. Perhaps the most explicit example is found in the 'Right to Buy' legislation introduced for council tenants in 1980. Similarly, government attempts to widen opportunities for private sector penetration and capital accumulation, through public–private partnerships (PPPs), private finance initiatives (PFI) and the like in housing renewal, urban regeneration, education and health, for example, fit firmly in this logic. The corporate 'land grabs' that became a feature of efforts to stimulate the renaissance of Britain's post-industrial cities through the gentrification of 'neighbourhoods of relegation' under New Labour provide a good example, not least because of the way 'territorial stigma' was employed to justify 'special measures' (Gray and Mooney, 2011). Further, the targeting of policing efforts towards the most marginal groups was justified in order to bring about or sustain the 'urban renaissance' (Raco, 2003; Hancock, 2007; Coleman, 2009).

It would be a mistake, however, in our view to see the policy frameworks in which these developments emerged as being about the manifestation and furtherance of neoliberal ambitions alone or, even more, simply about disinvestment (although this has occurred in notable policy areas such as local authority-provided housing). Although New Labour's (1997–2010) stance towards neoliberalism was relatively uncritical and supportive, and punitive measures were developed to coerce welfare dependants into low-paid work, considerable investment was made in so-called 'problem places'. Programmes such as the National Minimum Wage (introduced in 1999), Sure Start (1998) and in England, the New Deal for Communities (launched in 1998), and the National Strategy for Neighbourhood Renewal (2001), for example, were aimed at supporting workers and communities in the most disadvantaged areas and, at the same time, worked to recreate flexible, low-waged labour. Neoliberalism cannot, however, be seen as the *only* logic (see also Gelsthorpe, 2010; Piven, 2010, with regard to penal policy). It is important, then, to recognise other aims and functions including state legitimisation, 'public opinion', internal Labour Party politics and priorities, and the relations between central government, local councils and the devolved governments and assemblies, for example.

The Housing Market Renewal Initiative (HMRI), New Labour's flagship urban programme, clearly represents some of the main contradictions at the heart of New Labour's urban policy. The overarching aim was to arrest market decline in areas that had experienced 'market failure' in the declining post-industrial cities.[2] In Liverpool, as elsewhere, the initiative formed part of the city's 'urban renaissance' ambitions (City of Liverpool, nd, para 2.5; see also Allen, 2007). Attracting higher income groups and revenue by boosting the number and proportion of higher-rated Council Tax-banded properties was envisaged as the way to address the problems of marginalised communities. Large-scale clearance (demolition) of properties aimed to address over-supply and to facilitate new developments in partnership with private and third sector property developers. Like other British cities, Liverpool aimed to compete with other cities, regionally and globally, to attract investors and consumers. Widening the city's 'cultural offer' through consumption-based and 'culture-led' projects, such as Liverpool's European Capital of Culture status during 2008, was regarded as the approach through which middle-class repopulation and inward investment would be secured. The initiative attracted £1.2 billion from central government between 2002 and 2008 and another £1 billion was committed for 2008–11 (Long, 2010). The Conservative-led Coalition withdrew funding for HMRI, however, in the government's Comprehensive Spending Review in October 2010.

Urban programmes such as these, and others pursued under the previous Thatcher and Major Conservative governments, raise questions about the displacement and dispersal of supposed 'problem populations' *and* their concentration. However, they also invoke questions about the role of *politics* that, in our view, is insufficiently addressed in the core texts we have been primarily concerned with in this chapter (see also Piven, 2010). As we have seen, the Conservative-led UK Coalition government is engaged in concerted efforts to redefine 'fairness' in order to force a step-change towards forcing welfare-dependent 'problem populations' to take up low-paid, flexible labour. The proposal to cut Housing Benefit by 10 per cent for people claiming Jobseeker's Allowance[3] for 12 months or more, irrespective of their efforts to find work, labour market disadvantage or experience of discrimination, indicates the punitive approach advocated by the government. The proposal was withdrawn in February 2011 in the face of opposition; it nonetheless indicates the government's direction of travel.

Proposals current at the time of writing in May 2011 to reduce the Local Housing Allowance from the median (50th percentile) of rents in Broad Rental Market Areas[4] to the 30th percentile from October 2011 and increase subsidies in line with the Consumer Prices Index, rather than the Retail Price Index (which includes housing costs) will diminish the pool of available properties for rent and reconfigure how and where the poor are housed in urban space. The 'shared room rate' – which was a lower level of benefit for those aged up to 25 – was widely regarded as requiring significant subsidy from the lower earnings (or benefits) of young people even before the reduction in subsidy to the 30th percentile of rents (House of Commons Work and Pensions Select Committee, 2010). Henceforth it will apply to those aged up to 35. Many commentators believe that low-paid workers in London will be forced to move away from the city. Meanwhile in the capital and elsewhere, more exclusively affluent areas and 'ghettoisation' for the most disadvantaged will be encouraged. The DWP informed the House of Commons Work and Pensions Select Committee (2010) that it 'is to discuss the impact of people moving address and needing to find new childcare, schools and health services', and that 'some customers will need to move away from extended family support networks; this however reflects the choices that most people in work also have to make' (2010, p 44). The erroneous view that Housing Benefit and Local Housing Allowance are 'out-of-work' benefits is reflected here; these representations also show the version of 'fairness' that is being promoted. The evil of 'welfare dependency' was centred again in the government's blanket overhaul of welfare – Universal Credit (DWP, 2010b) – that embeds a strict regime of conditionality for out-of-work benefits, including unprecedented penalties for not fulfilling prescribed conditions (up to three years' loss of benefits). The structural causes of poverty, unemployment, uneven development, discrimination and low wages have been erased from current policy discourses.

Space precludes an exploration of the cuts to welfare spending and local government expenditure that are bearing a large share of the government's £81 billion deficit reduction programme (2014–15) and their implications in this chapter (see Yeates et al, 2011). We do, however, wish to place some emphasis on the importance of the political resistance that is currently being mobilised in response to not only the UK government's austerity strategy but those of Western governments who are implementing similar reductions to public spending following the bailout of the banks in the wake of the world-wide financial crisis. Wacquant is clear that his is 'a *selective excavation*' (2009a, p xix; original emphasis) which does not explore ambiguities and contradictions or 'efforts to resist' (p xix) the penal state. In his view:

> This (over) simplification is an unavoidable *moment* in the analysis of the surge of the penal state in the neoliberal age and a cost well worth paying if it gets students and activists of criminal justice to pay attention to germane developments in poverty policies and, conversely, if it alerts scholars and militants of welfare – as traditionally defined – to the urgent need to bring the operations of the overgrown penal arm of the Leviathan into their purview. (2009a, pp xix-xx; original emphasis)

From our perspective, revealing the tensions, ambiguities, contradictions and efforts to resist are also important for our scholarship and politics. Efforts to oppose government proposals and policies, from the sale of council housing and the privatisation of utilities in the 1980s to students' resistance against the marketisation of higher education, health providers and 'consumers' opposition to reforms to the National Health Service in England during 2010-11, among many others in the contemporary period, have revealed the neoliberal ambitions of governments to wider publics. The surge in protest movements during 2010–11 has revealed in sharp focus that policy areas and the broader ideological canvass are sites of struggle, which can be opposed, rather than an unstoppable juggernaut against which resistance would be futile. Likewise, the kinds of protests we are witnessing at the time of writing[5] caution against the view that collective means of representing and resisting have been effectively muted, and against the forces that 'fragment' and 'splinter' (Wacquant, 2008, p 244), these movements are all the more remarkable.

Conclusion

This chapter has explored how Wacquant's approach can be enhanced and strengthened by extending his arguments to consider some of the ways in which the misrepresentation and othering of the poorest and most disadvantaged sections of the urban working classes are part and parcel of social welfare in general, and that the making and remaking of 'problem populations' is not only characteristic of advanced marginality. As highlighted here, there is a complex interconnection between the construction of the impoverished urban poor and the development and implementation of harsh, punitive anti-welfare policies. Further, and contrary to Wacquant's tendency to play down the conditionality and punitiveness that has long characterised welfare provision in different national contexts, we have argued that social welfare has always been characterised by the mobilisation of particular 'problem population' narratives, even if the language and conceptualisation of these may have changed over time.

In highlighting a range of social policy areas in the contemporary UK, such as housing and urban regeneration, for example, that lie beyond the penal state as described by Wacquant, we are able to grasp many of the ways in which efforts to manage and control populations have been extended in recent times. In our view the focus on these policy areas works to further reinforce the overall thematic and conceptual approach offered by Wacquant.

In extending our discussion here to include an analysis of poverty porn and penal pornography we have argued that an understanding of these is also crucial for our appreciation of the construction of punitive criminal justice and social policies. We have shown that both forms of pornography contribute to anti-welfarism – and anti-poor narratives and policy making. In so doing we have also highlighted that such narratives are driven by particular class interests, and represent a particular classed view of problematic populations.

The driving force behind the penal state and the increasingly harsh and punitive social policy making highlighted in this chapter is founded on class antagonisms – and class hatreds – heightened in periods of economic crisis. The extension of penality and punitivism, therefore, are best understood as part of longer and ongoing class struggles.

Notes

[1] Wacquant's use of the term 'advanced' is intended to denote that the features of marginality he discusses are not temporary, neither will they be addressed by free market expansion; rather they are 'ahead of us' (2008, p 232).

[2] The 'Pathfinders' were centred in nine areas in the North and Midlands initially, extending to 12 in 2005 (Long, 2010).

[3] At the time of writing (2011) £53; £45 per week for single young people aged 16-24; £67.50 for those aged over 24; £105.95 for a couple aged 18 or over.

[4] Administrative units for calculating rents and subsidies.

[5] For example, the march of half a million people against the cuts and for an 'alternative' in London on 26 March 2011; the thousands engaged in demonstrations for collective bargaining in Wisconsin in February 2011; the speed at which UKuncut has become a global anti-cuts movement undertaking

actions daily to oppose cuts and clamp down on corporate tax avoidance; local protests to stop cuts and closures to libraries and youth centres, and national days of action (three to date) in support of benefit claimants and against their defamation (see, for example, Benefitclaimantsfightback, 2011 in relation to the latter).

References

Aitkenhead, D. (2010) 'Hayley Taylor: I've felt what the unemployed feel: losing confidence, staring at four walls', *The Guardian*, 12 July (www.guardian.co.uk/tv-and-radio/2010/jul/12/hayley-taylor-fairy-jobmother-unemployment).

Allen, C. (2007) *Housing market renewal and social class*, London: Routledge.

Bauman, Z. (2004) *Work, consumerism and the new poor*, Buckingham: Open University Press.

Benefitclaimantsfightback (2011) 'Atos picketed, *Daily Mail* mobbed and invaded, Westminster Council told', National Protest Against Benefit Cuts (http://benefitclaimantsfightback.wordpress. com/2011/04/15/atos-picketed-daily-mail-mobbed-and-invaded-westminster-council-told/).

Blandy, S. (2008) 'Secession or cohesion? Exploring the impact of gated communities', in J. Flint and D. Robinson (eds) *Community cohesion in crisis: New dimensions of diversity and difference*, Bristol: The Policy Press, pp 239-58.

Booth, R. (2010) 'Budget 2010: Housing benefit figures come under scrutiny', *The Guardian*, 23 June (www.guardian. co.uk/uk/2010/jun/23/budget-housing-benefit-figures-scrutiny?INTCMP=ILCNETTXT3487).

Briar, C. (1997) *Working for women? Gendered work and welfare policies in twentieth century Britain*, London: UCL Press.

Cameron, D. (2008) 'David Cameron: There are 5 million people on benefits in Britain. How do we stop them turning into Karen Matthews?', *Daily Mail* (Mail Online), 8 December (www.dailymail. co.uk/news/article-1092588/DAVID-CAMERONThere-5-million-people-benefits-Britain-How-stop-turning-this.html).

City of Liverpool (nd) 'New heartlands: creating neighbourhoods of the future, Housing Market Renewal Initiative (HMRI), Liverpool Delivery Plan' (www.liverpool.gov.uk/Images/HousingMarketRenewalDeliveryPlan.pdf).

Cohen, S. (1972) *Folk devils and moral panics: The creation of mods and rockers*, Oxford: Martin Robertson.

Coleman, R. (2009) 'Policing the working class in the city of renewal: the state and social surveillance', in R. Coleman, J. Sim, S. Tombs and D. Whyte (eds) *State, power, crime*, London: Sage Publications.

Cook, D. (2006) *Criminal and social justice*, London: Sage Publications.

Crawford, A. (2006) 'Networked governance and the post-regulatory state?', *Theoretical Criminology*, vol 10, no 4, pp 449-79.

Daly, M. (2011) *Welfare*, Cambridge: Polity Press.

DWP (Department for Work and Pensions) (2010a) *Impact of changes to local housing allowance from 2011* (www.dwp.gov.uk/local-authority-staff/housing-benefit/claims-processing/local-housing-allowance/impact-of-changes.shtml).

DWP (2010b) *Universal Credit: Welfare that works*, Cm 7957, London: The Stationery Office (www.dwp.gov.uk/docs/universal-credit-fulldocument.pdf).

DWP (2011) 'Fairness finally restored to the Housing Benefit system as new rules come into force', Press Release, 1 April (www.dwp.gov.uk/newsroom/press-releases/2011/apr-2011/dwp036-11.shtml).

Flint, J. (2009) 'Cultures, ghettos and camps: sites of exception and antagonism in the city', *Housing Studies*, vol 24, no 4, pp 417-31.

Gelsthorpe, L. (2010) 'Women, crime and control', *Criminology and Criminal Justice*, vol 10, no 4, pp 375-86.

Gordon, P. (1986) 'Racism and social security', *Critical Social Policy*, vol 6, no 17, pp 23-40.

Gray, N. and Mooney, G. (2011) 'Glasgow's new urban frontier: "civilising" the population of "Glasgow East"', *City*, vol 15, no 1, pp 4-24.

Green, D.A. (2008) *When children kill children: Penal populism and political culture*, Oxford: Oxford University Press.

Hall, S., Critcher, C., Jefferson, T., Clarke, J. and Roberts, B. (1978) *Policing the crisis: Mugging, the state and law and order*, Basingstoke: Macmillan.

Hancock, L. (2004) 'Criminal justice, public opinion, fear and popular politics', in J. Muncie and D. Wilson (eds) *Student handbook of criminal justice and criminology*, London: Cavendish.

Hancock, L. (2007) 'Is urban regeneration criminogenic?', in R. Atkinson and G. Helms (eds) *Securing an urban renaissance: crime, community and British urban policy*, Bristol: The Policy Press.

Hancock, L. (2008) 'The criminalisation of places', *Criminal Justice Matters*, vol 74, no 1, pp 22-3.

Haylett, C. (2001) 'Illegitimate subjects? Abject whites, neoliberal modernisation and middleclass multi-culturalism', *Environment and Planning D: Society and Space*, vol 19, pp 351-70.

House of Commons Work and Pensions Select Committee (2010) *Changes in Housing Benefit announced in the June 2010 Budget*, London: The Stationery Office.

Hughes, G. and Lewis, G. (eds) (1988) *Unsettling welfare*, London: Routledge.

Johnstone, C. and Mooney, G. (2007) '"Problem people", "problem places"? New Labour and council estates', in R. Atkinson and G. Helms (eds) *Securing an urban renaissance: Crime, community, and British urban policy*, Bristol: The Policy Press, pp 125-39.

King, D.S. (1987) 'The state and the social structures of welfare in advanced industrial democracies', *Theory and Society*, vol 16, no 6, pp 841-8.

Long, R. (2010) 'Housing Market Renewal Pathfinders', Research Briefing, House of Commons Library SN/SP/5220, 14 May, pp 1-8 (www.parliament.uk/briefingpapers/commons/lib/research/briefings/snsp-05520.pdf).

Mayer, M. (2010) 'Punishing the poor – a debate', *Theoretical Criminology*, vol 14, no 1, pp 93-103.

Mooney, G. (2009) 'The "broken society" election: class hatred and the politics of poverty and place in Glasgow East', *Social Policy and Society*, vol 8, no 4, pp 437-50.

Morrison, Z. (2003) 'Cultural justice and addressing "social exclusion": a case study of a Single Regeneration Budget project in Blackbird Leys, Oxford', in R. Imrie and M. Raco (eds) *Urban renaissance? New Labour, community and urban policy*, Bristol: The Policy Press, pp 139-62.

Nelken, D. (2010) 'Denouncing the penal state', *Criminology and Criminal Justice*, vol 10, no 4, pp 331-40.

Piven, F.F. (2010) 'A response to Wacquant', *Theoretical Criminology*, vol 14, no 1, pp 111-16.

Raco, M. (2003) 'Remaking place and securitising space: urban regeneration and the strategies, tactics and practices of policing in the UK', *Urban Studies*, vol 40, no 9, pp 1869-87.

Raynor, G. (2010) 'Housing Benefit reform: a toxic battleground', *Telegraph* (www.telegraph.co.uk/news/politics/8097684/Housing-benefit-reform-A-toxic-battleground.html).

Reid, M. (2008) 'A political timebomb in Glasgow's Guantanamo', *The Times*, 3 July.

Skeggs, B. (2005) 'The making of class and gender through visualising moral subject formation', *Sociology*, vol 39, no 5, pp 965-82.

Skeggs, B. (2009) 'The moral economy of person production: the class relations of self performance on "reality" television', *The Sociological Review*, vol 57, no 4, pp 626-44.

Smith, S.J. (1989) *The politics of "race" and residence: Citizenship, segregation and White supremacy in Britain*, Cambridge: Polity Press.

Somers, M. and Block, F. (2005) 'From poverty to perversity: ideas, markets, and institutions over 200 years of welfare debate', *American Sociological Review*, vol 70, no 1, pp 260–87.

Stryker, R. and Wald, P. (2009) 'Redefining compassion to reform welfare: how supporters of 1990s US federal welfare reform aimed for the moral high ground', *Social Politics: International Studies in Gender, State and Society*, vol 16, no 4, pp 516-57.

Tunstall, R. and Lupton, R. (2010) *Mixed communities: Evidence review*, London: Department for Communities and Local Government (www. communities.gov.uk/documents/housing/pdf/1775206.pdf).

Wacquant, L. (2002) 'The rise of advanced marginality: notes on its nature and implications', in P. Marcuse and R. van Kempen (eds) *Of states and cities*, Oxford: Oxford University Press, pp 221-39.

Wacquant, L. (2008) *Urban outcasts: A comparative sociology of advanced marginality*, Cambridge: Polity Press.

Wacquant, L. (2009a) *Punishing the poor: The neoliberal government of social insecurity*, Durham, NC: Duke University Press.

Wacquant, L. (2009b) *Prisons of poverty*, Minneapolis, MN: University of Minnesota Press.

Williams, F. (1989) *Social policy: A critical introduction*, Cambridge: Polity Press.

Yeates, N., Haux, T., Jawad, R. and Kilkey, M. (2011) *In defence of welfare*, Social Policy Association (www.social-policy.org.uk/downloads/idow.pdf).

Young, J. (1999) *The exclusive society*, London: Sage Publications.

Young, J. (2007) *The vertigo of late modernity*, London: Sage Publications.

SEVEN

Loïc Wacquant, gender and cultures of resistance

Lynda Measor

Introduction

Loïc Wacquant focuses on sections of the urban proletariat who are 'the most marginalised' in the post-industrial world. He denounces, with Old Testament fury, contemporary neoliberal policies that assign men and women, respectively, to the carceral and assistantial wings of the state. Wacquant considers some very crucial and important issues, and while this chapter offers some criticism, it aims mainly to buttress the insights developed by the approach he takes. Wacquant offers relatively little detail about the pains of the daily lives of the 'precariat'.

The central concern in this chapter is that he gives scant consideration to evidence of resistance, contradictions or 'counter-publics' (Fraser, 1990), arising from the ranks of the dispossessed. As Mayer observes, 'struggles do not seem to exist' (2010, p 98). Accordingly, my first aim in this chapter is to develop our understandings of the conditions these 'urban outcasts' encounter, and of the responses they make, by analysis of ethnographic data, generated in research with UK teenage mothers. This approach asserts the importance of considering the view 'from below', and the development of insights into the perspectives of those 'caught in the cracks and ditches of the new economic landscape' (Wacquant, 2009, p xiv). It is drawn from critical sociology and social history work that emphasises the study of 'distinctive activities of freedom' (Linebaugh, 2003, p 3) and the development of 'vernacular publics' (Sarkar, 1997, p 37) which indicate the continued vitality of what Bahktin has referred to as the 'second life of the people' (Bakhtin, 1984).

Wacquant also pays little attention to gender in this recent work (Gelsthorpe, 2010; Mayer, 2010). Accordingly, the second aim of the chapter is to consider data drawn from a study of 'young welfare mothers' to enhance our understandings of the significance that dimensions of gender inequality have in assembling and reinforcing the conditions of this 'precarious fraction of the proletariat' (Wacquant, 2009, p 310).

Wacquant offers support for an approach which works 'to develop more complex and more differentiated pictures of the "wretched of the city"' (2008, p 2). He argues that 'enrolling ethnographic observation' is necessary both to capture their social predicament' and for 'the moment of theoretical construction' (Wacquant, 2008, p 10). Accordingly, the chapter argues that it is not solely their predicaments we need to know more about, but their individual and collective responses and resistance to them. This chapter aims to identify ways 'urban outcasts' seek to resist assignations with carceral and assistantial agencies, and the assignments of both *location* and *identity* plotted out for them in neoliberal systems.

Empirical work: the UK study

This chapter is based on data generated in the UK with 'young welfare mothers' (Bell et al, 2004), those affected *directly* by assistantial rather than the carceral branches of the neoliberal state. It is important to acknowledge that there are difficulties using data generated with women – and data from the UK – in a commentary on Wacquant. The defence rests on Wacquant's argument that: 'Welfare recipients and inmates have germane social profiles and extensive mutual ties that make them the two gendered sides of the same population' (2009, p 16).

It is the case that much of the research into 'advanced marginality' and 'urban outcasts' has focused on men and on carceral agencies (Mayer, 2010). A focus on women highlights the lack of explicit attention to issues of gender in Wacquant's approach.

> While we benefit from Wacquant's theoretical analysis enormously, closer attention to empirical studies of women, welfare and penality on the ground might add to or extend his analysis of the ways in which economic, race, class and gender relations are anchored across state structures. (Gelsthorpe, 2010, p 381)

Empirical data allow us to 'hear from women themselves' about their circumstances. It offers illustrations of their responses, allows insights into their resistance and opportunities for understandings of the agency that princesses, if not queens, of the 'welfare arts' practise. The focus also has implications for theoretical frameworks Wacquant both employs and avoids. Feminist work asserts that theory developed without gender in its warp and its weft makes for poor theory (Gelsthorpe, 2010; Mayer,

2010). Highlighting women allows us to elaborate understandings of the role gender plays in processes and systems that ensure that 'the poor are always with us'.

There are also difficulties in using data generated in the UK. One critique of Wacquant's work is that conclusions drawn from the US do not directly translate to Europe or BRIC nations (Brazil, Russia, India and China) (Lacey, 2010, p 778). But while there are important differences between the welfare systems of the UK and those of the US, it is possible to develop some insights from data drawn from women ('teenage parents' and 'welfare mothers') who are similarly stigmatised in both settings.

'Resistance', 'agency', 'contradictions' and 'counter-publics'

The central argument is that Wacquant devotes little attention to evidence of resistance or agency from those who occupy the *banlieues*, *favelas* and ghettos of the contemporary world or to the significance of contradictions there. He considers opposition in comments about urban disorders erupting from the ranks of young, poor men in Europe (2008, p 22). He questions what meanings we should draw from such outbreaks of collective violence 'from below', refuting an analysis that they are evidence only of social pathology. 'Collective action' of 'poor city dwellers', can, he argues, continually engender new meanings, which 'open up a possible space for collective demands and social critique' (Wacquant, 2008, p 12). Neither the possibilities nor the potential are systematically followed up in Wacquant's work, and while they are valued as 'disruptive and recalcitrant', these men are not portrayed as potent actors capable of effective action (Candeias, 2007, cited by Mayer, 2010, p 99).

A number of well-developed academic approaches can be drawn on to 'physic' Wacquant's portrayal of the 'de-proletarianised'. Sociological theories of deviance, resistance and agency based on careful and long-term ethnographic work alert us to the activities of the powerless and the dispossessed (Becker, 1963; Jefferson et al, 1975; Bourgeois, 1998; Young, 1999). Approaches from social history are particularly useful. There is a long, distinguished pedigree of work on resistance and social movements which elucidates 'history from below' represented by E.P. Thompson (1968), Hobsbawm (1971), Eley (1994), Linebaugh (2003) and their ilk. Innovative perspectives have developed insights into 'subaltern' worlds and increased understandings of 'weapons of the weak' (Scott, 1987) and the significance of small-scale resistance.

Political theory associated with Habermas's work on the 'public sphere' (1989) and Nancy Fraser's insights into 'counter-publics' is also relevant (1990).

These approaches encourage a search for evidence of agency from the poor of the 'global parish' while of course remaining alert to its limitations.

> It allows us to see how people living in conditions and amidst presuppositions inherited from the past, and so not of their choice – still strive to make their own history. (Sarkar, 1997, p 54)

Such approaches are corrective, they move from a view of class, caste and other oppressive systems as fixed and measurable entities. The problem with such approaches is that they:

> ... tended to rip the wretched of the earth from the possibility of agency or creative initiative. (Sarkar, 1997, p 53)

Habermas's work on the 'public sphere' (1989) and Fraser's discussion of the 'counter-public' (Fraser, 1990) provide important insights here. Habermas considers how the 'civil public' is transformed into the 'political public' and particular groups come to dominate both political discourse and taken-for-granted assumptions. While this public sphere is defined as 'universal', Fraser argues it excludes marginalised groups who develop 'counter-publics':

> ... parallel discursive arenas where members of subordinated groups invent and circulate counter discourses to formulate oppositional interpretations of their identities, interests and needs. (1990, p 58)

A focus on this range of sociological, historical and political theory highlights important 'silences' in Wacquant and asks us to attend to the activities and evidence of the agency of the dispossessed in the neoliberal state.

Exploitation and cultures of resistance

'History from below' developed sophisticated insights, producing carefully nuanced accounts of people and situations they studied. Their theoretical arguments are important in this context. E.P. Thompson rejected the persistent tendency of many Marxists to make class into a fixed thing – to 'reify it into merely a set of people who had a determinate connection with a particular kind of production relations' (Sarkar, 1997, p 53). The problem was that it was usually followed by an abstract reading of what class consciousness, and therefore styles and forms of resistance ought to be at a given stage of history. E.P. Thompson asked instead that we track how economic realities and forms of exploitation, located in 'a particular equilibrium of social relations', were translated into the actions of everyday life and informed the specifics of the 'weapons of the weak' and configured their resistance to exploitation and repression.

Such an approach is not alien to Wacquant's intentions and justification as this focus on subaltern realities lies in Wacquant's recent work. He states he has turned his back on discourse analyses that abstract themselves except in the most general terms from the realities of production and social relationships. He specifically recommends we 'wed the virtues of a materialist analysis inspired by Karl Marx and Friedrich Engels' (2009, p xv). He asks that analysis pay attention to:

> ... the changing relations that obtain in each epoch (and particularly during phases of socioeconomic upheaval) between the penal system and the system of production. (Wacquant, 2009, p xvi)

Despite these assertions, however, there is relative silence in Wacquant's work about the detailed workings of contradictions and paradox present in contemporary circumstances. There is an absence of any focus on dialectic forces which assert that any system that develops will have *both* emancipatory possibilities and novel 'closures' within it. This has the effect of presenting the precariat as one, undifferentiated mass, their individual characteristics and differences ironed flat. When sent to prison or assigned to welfare regimes, they obey and trudge off to their places, exhibiting little evidence of resistance.

There is therefore little sense of any movement or the possibility of movement within the context of late modernity – it is a bleak and featureless landscape. Urban outcasts are without agency as people, but the other consequence is that they are members of a world that is 'forever still, unmoving, trapped at the end of history' (Linebaugh, 2003, p 9). Wacquant's lack of interest in documenting contradictory pressures in the state or in tracking resistance from those most exposed to its brutalities has the consequence of excising the fulcrum for movement or change.

These difficulties arise from Wacquant's allegiance to certain of Foucault's theoretical assumptions. Linebaugh argues Foucault's tendency is to make 'the rulers of government and society seem all powerful' (2003, p 3). The state's operations are presented as all-pervasive – they effectively suffocate resistance and dissension within their domain. They are portrayed as homogeneous, without internal tensions. Critics of Foucault have noted the determinism and the static qualities associated with these elements of his analysis and the consequent lack of attention given to a politics of resistance and agency (Ramazanoglu, 1993).

Contradictions and the dialectic

By contrast, subaltern studies are clear that to move forward in our understandings of the contemporary world we cannot simply indulge in nostalgia for the 'lost verities of orthodox Marxism' (Sarkar, 1997, p 52). New insights are required. Sarkar's definition of the *dialectic* sees it not as representing 'totalising laws of development but rather an openness to the possibilities of tensions and contradictions in the heart of all processes' (Sarkar, 1997, p 79). The search for such tensions and contradictions must therefore lie at the heart of our research. While Wacquant's work is crucial in drawing attention to the neoliberal and globalising processes that have created and fixed 'urban outcasts', some difficulties lie in the picture he presents of the all-powerful state. While a focus on the state is not core to this chapter, reference to Harvey's work is useful here (Harvey, 2007). He argues, according to Campbell, that Wacquant presents the neoliberal policy web as seamless, without identifying contradictions (Campbell, 2010). Mayer concludes, 'there is still work to do in figuring out a coherent and sufficiently dialectical sketch of a theory of the neo-liberal state' (2010, p 101). There is also a need to sketch, in some detail, how the people exposed to the deprivations and degradations of prisons, ghettos and welfare agencies respond and resist, and it is to that issue that we now turn.

Documenting resistance is important – it allows us purchase on 'lived relations and meanings' of the precariat (Wacquant, 2008, p 9). Empirical evidence of agency allows understanding of how 'processes of insubordination and defiance grow' (Sarkar, 1997, p 58), and fosters our awareness of the 'vernaculars of crime', the configurations of 'making and taking' specific to a particular time and space (Linebaugh, 2003, p xxvii). It celebrates the potential for the human creativity that flourishes in the cracks and spaces of the 'soft city' (Raban, 1974) where the 'second life of the people' is staged (Bakhtin, 1984). It is important, of course, that we do not return simply to older – and heavily criticised – versions of Marxist analysis that focused on any manifestation of resistance and 'sanctified' it as evidence that the 'final' eschatological struggle was well under way against the grotesque inequalities of the world we inhabit – and create. By contrast, it is important to work with an acute awareness of the limits of resistance and the fragility of agency.

We now turn to consider the implications such theoretical approaches have for empirical work with the precariat. Subaltern studies focused specifically on the *informal cultural* forms that resistance might take. E.P. Thompson (1968) panned for empirical evidence of 'multiple appropriations' of hegemonic culture by the proletariat. Modes of leisure, autonomous rituals and ways of defining independent satisfactions and views of life within the constraints of class, gender and context were key issues. All imply that elements from dominant practices and discourses will be incorporated and recognise that only partial autonomy is possible. Profound mutual conflict is likely between different groups as Eley documented in his work on 'counter-publics' and a 'proletarian public' (1994, p 75).

Empirical work and Wacquant

Wacquant presents a picture of the 'assistantial' classes as a deprived people flattened by brutal circumstances that fix them in place. They are a colourless, uniform group, Lowry-like stick figures bent by cold Chicago winds or agitated by the Brazilian heat. From a theoretical standpoint the argument has been that this is both a limited picture and a limited perspective. We now turn to consider data drawn from qualitative research with 'young welfare mothers' in the UK, aiming to add detail to Wacquant's account, and to illustrate resistances and 'agency' shown and 'counter-publics' asserted by young women and young men who occupy deprived and marginal places in society. Seeking to link theory to micro-data is fraught, but an effort Wacquant also espouses.

> The more abstract theorizations – such as the analytical sketch of 'advanced marginality' always gain from being solidly harnessed to a carnal grasp of the historical experience for which they purport to account. (Wacquant, 2008, p 10)

Urban outcasts with prams

Research exists which indicates that 'becoming' a 'young, single mother' can be considered an act of resistance in our society.[1] Spender (1980) argued that young women without educational qualifications saw early motherhood as an escape route from the world of poorly paid and exploitative labour. Wacquant suggested neoliberal policies strip residents of marginalised communities of the means to *produce* their own material wealth and well-being (2008, p 48). Having children indicates agency and evidences the ability to re-(produce) the self when all other means are under threat (Hearn, 1987; Faludi, 2000). Agency can be involved in having babies – solid material factors motivate some young women (Measor, 2006). In deprived urban settings many recognise the ineffectiveness of statutory agencies to secure their safety (Lea and Young, 1984; Coleman et al, 2002). Young women make sexual relationships with sons of 'names' – local families possessing 'reputation', resources and respect. Having their children, often without formal commitments from the young men, secures some degree of protection from these informal sources.

Despite resistant intentions, data from the teenage pregnancy study suggest choosing to become a 'young welfare mother' nevertheless provokes important disapproval. While the exercise of sexuality by young women is no longer straightforwardly stigmatised in our society, arguably conception and early motherhood subsidised by the welfare state remains a source of dishonour. The research allows glimpses of the 'moral denunciation' (Wacquant, 2009, p 293) to which young mothers are exposed. Government, civil society and media tread dishonour into members of the 'fallen' and 'assistantial' classes (Hanna, 2001; Kirkman et al, 2001; Seamark and Lings, 2004; McDermott and Graham, 2005). Eruptions of *local* stigmatising classifications are also significant. Young men originating from the same deprived community as these 'welfare mothers' exercised *their* agency and named the 'female offences' of 'young welfare mothers':

> Greg: '"Little dirt" – she got pregnant by a black man.'

> Jimmie: 'Those girls are dirty little scum-bags in this estate.'

> Gary: 'Like another breed of humans.'

'Race' and place play a role, but sexual behaviour counts most in making these young welfare mothers one of the 'species of moral trash' in the local as well as the wider social worlds (Wacquant, 2009, p 225). The young men identify them as doubly tainted, because they are 'depraved' within the confines of their own 'deprived' communities. Their pregnancy revealed their sexuality – and it is a rampant and unacceptable kind of sexuality for a woman.

> Tom: 'You get these 12-year-olds gagging for it. Men are up for it every night but women only want it like every other day or once a week or whatever.'

> Wayne: 'Men have to do it like that, if they don't it could cause the man to explode.'

> Tyrone: 'But not women. But this lot are gagging for it.'

In the cultural context of the peripheral, deprived community in which these data were generated, young men claimed that the visible exercise of sexuality classified 'welfare mothers' as outside of the category of 'feminine'. The specific data state the case in an extreme form, and raise issues about how widespread such views are. They nevertheless show how many living in 'tainted' neighbourhoods, exposed to the worst effects of the economic hollowing of their communities, 'join their voices to the dominant chorus of denunciation of deviant and delinquent categories' (Borges, 2009, p 720) produced by neoliberal policies. We see claims made by young men for power to classify and stigmatise in these data, their agency is exerted by asserting power to denounce young women. Wacquant delineates welfare mothers and street criminals as 'twin detached and deformed categories in contemporary society' (2008, p 362). He elides the two categories, but these ethnographic data indicate the need to focus on hierarchies made of those classifications by those who live in and under them. Welfare mothers and street criminals are not simply twin categories – the young men bid to establish hierarchy. 'Being' a street criminal does not, the young men assert, carry identical cultural dishonour as 'being' a 'young welfare mother – gender and sexuality are fundamentally implicated.

We need analysis of how gender dimensions operate in relation to class and 'race' that Wacquant privileges. Theories of patriarchy, and studies of male 'urban outcasts', indicate how such men employ and deploy their women to secure masculine identity for themselves and to withstand undermining brutal economic and political structures (Campbell, 1993; Bourgois, 1998; Faludi, 2000). The young men quoted in these data occupy the bottom of the socioeconomic heap, a place with few rewards. They fight to place women (and 'subordinated' males) beneath themselves to reflect back different status messages and secure symbolic strengths (Willis, 1979) and economic resources (Bourgois, 1998). Gender theory alerts us to how women are critically involved in the ways *men* make class and 'race' inequalities more tolerable for themselves. The successful domination of men articulates with women and cannot be ignored in understanding dimensions of inequality. Gendered analyses are not prioritised in Wacquant, but are needed when scrutinising what also sustains the marginalisation, assistantialisation and penalisation of the 'precariat'.

Resistance and 'deflecting the taint'

Data from the UK study indicate 'young welfare mothers' were well aware of the 'discreditable identity' associated with being a 'teenage mother' on welfare (Plummer, 1975, p 27). They allow us to examine resistance they mobilised to the discourses, classificatory positions and stigmatised location to which they were directed. Their narratives indicated elements from mainstream culture were appropriated, and separating self from stigma was fundamentally connected with the creation of classifications and divisions within the category of 'welfare mother'.

Presentation of the self and particular behaviour sought to ward off negative labels for the individual:

> Gemma: 'I don't particularly act as if I am a single young mum. A lot of people don't even think of me as that – if I am not with Imogen....'

> Annette: 'Well, you don't, do you? When I look at myself I wouldn't think of myself as a single mother.'

Some took personal, emotional refuge in previous identities – a previous sense of self allowed some protection from the labels:

> Susie: 'I was the last person in the world that anyone would think of as getting pregnant. I was not the type to get pregnant. I was predicted to get all A stars in my GCSEs. I wanted to do GCSEs and then A levels and college and have a career. A lot of girls in my year were more of the type to get pregnant than me.'

Many narratives simultaneously relied on producing distinctions between the self – who is a 'good' mother – and the 'other' kinds of 'bad' 'welfare mothers'. Material factors were of obvious significance. Some young mothers spelled out their respectability, confirmed by their continuing partnership with the child's father and his 'proper' employment status:

> Mel:'Yeah, well my boyfriend works at the train station, but he's worked there for five years so it's regular and everything, which is good. I don't think there's anyone down there in that group with their babies that can say that.'

Material factors were key to demonstrating advantage, but also to condemning 'others':

> Gina:'Yusuf has a good job. We've got a really nice flat. It's so different with some of them in that group … they are on their own and in bed and breakfast. And there's people that have babies to get houses.'

Gina's comment about young mothers having babies to obtain local authority social housing is interesting. A 'teenage' mother deployed right-wing discourses to distinguish herself from what she sees as much less respectable counterparts who collect 'welfare'.

In an attempt to deflect stigma some 'young welfare mothers' plotted strategies for slipping out of welfare provision, aware of the additional 'social taint' associated with residual housing.

> Jillie:'You were sort of seen as a stereotyped single young mum, put away in a little council flat, you know, but I have chosen specifically not to go into council or even housing association housing 'cos I don't want that, you know to be seen like that.'

> Mandy: 'I didn't want Moordown or Westhaven. All the mums on their own live in either Moordown or Westhaven. And I sort of said to them, I said, you know I don't want to really go to those areas, I don't mind anywhere else. And then we ended up in Wishton which was pretty good.'

Material realities were important but Iris Marion Young has drawn our attention to the different kinds of respect that are coupled to them

(1992), which these young women wished to avoid. Some 'welfare mothers' asserted their ambitions; emphasising their aim to make a 'better life' for themselves and their children was what distinguished them.

> Clare: 'I blew it basically. I was a really strong-headed teenager that thought I knew the world and now I'm paying for it the hard way. But I'm doing it, I'm going to college now in September ... doing it now so I'm not going to be one of them dossy mums, I'm going to finally do it, but I've done it the long way round.'

The data indicate few collective efforts, the preferred tactic was to defend the 'self', avoid actions that spoke of 'doing single young mum' and assert personal, creditable identities aimed at distinguishing the self from the 'stigma label' (Plummer, 1975).

Wacquant identified the deep reluctance to 'acknowledge the collective nature of their predicament' in dispossessed, marginal groups (2008, p 184). These data offer evidence of the 'inclination to develop strategies of material and symbolic distancing' (p 184) that he suggested indicates the 'desolidarizing effects of territorial stigmatisation' (p 5). They foster our awareness of how strategies of resistance mobilised by the 'assistantial' classes were reliant on mutual antagonism discussed earlier in this chapter in relation to 'subaltern' studies (Eley, 1994).

'Consoling plots' – being a good mother

Within the data, however, there is also evidence of discourses offering more creative strategies and opportunities for agency. For instance, for 'young welfare mothers', a central element in their claims for positive identity concerned the quality of their mothering. The discourse of 'good mother' centred on competence demonstrated by practices with their children that affirmed they were the 'right kind' of mother. Crucial to this gambit is the ability to point to healthy, happy babies.

> Judy: 'No. I mean everyone can see that, you know, she's ... she's thriving basically and I think I'm doing a very good job.'

> Jan: 'I look young though and in the shop the other day ... the woman at the counter and she looked at me, I was like "Yeah, my son". She goes, "You're a bit young" ... she

goes, "Oh you look a bit young to be a mum", I said, "Well I'm not!" It's just ... I am a bit young but I'm a great mum.'

Gina: 'Again I think I come across, this is just from what people tell me ... and especially my health visitor she said the other day "I think you've done really, really well".'

Discourses of 'good mother' are powerful in most cultures and these young women called on them as a resource for resistance (Yardley, 2008). A number of studies have argued the appeal to the deep and profound importance of motherhood seeks to throw off the cultural dishonour of the particular position and secure a less contaminated self (Yardley, 2008, p 283; see also Duncan, 2007). The young women quoted here assert significant personal worth – they claim to be doing an important job very well, and it confers creative goodness on *them*.

Young 'welfare mothers' spoke frequently about how to perform and attain the positive identity of 'good mother' throughout this study. At its heart were notions of responsibility for the child. Emma stressed the daily, careful work involved – 'doing' mothering was defined as a demanding craft.

Emma: 'I don't know, it is so scary thinking like, God, you've got to teach her how to go to the toilet, you've got to teach her to have manners.'

Emma grasped for 'good mother' identity, emphasising nurture, child development and 'proper' integration of the child into society. The two examples she chose, while commonplace, were particularly revealing, for shame will result *for*, but crucially *from*, a child who cannot perform bodily control and relate to people in ways that demonstrates 'proper' behaviour, recognise the significance of respect and hence verify 'proper' mothering. What is noteworthy is the involvement of 'young welfare mothers' in producing 'categories for symbolic affirmation and self-identity' (Borges, 2009, p 719). In this regard, their resistance work is not entirely based on establishing negative categories which condemn 'others' and elevate the self.

The importance of classifications *between* categories of 'young mothers' was nevertheless clear for them. The resistance of those claiming the 'good mother' status frequently focused on the assertion that they were not one of the 'bad' kind (McDermott and Graham, 2005). In their narratives it was possible to discern what signalled the differences. We have already identified some material factors relating to income and housing – it is also clear that dress and appearance were important – but mothering practices and sexual behaviour were especially crucial.

> Mel: 'The way they dress, big, yeah, big gold ear-rings and Croydon "facelift" hair – tight scraped back – so it pulls your face up – no surgery needed – all that sort of stuff and they're always shouting "Oy! You little bugger! Come back here" and everything – shouting at their babies. I would never, ever shout in the middle of the street to my baby to do something. I couldn't do that. I think I hate that. But you see so much of it!'

The strongest features of this mothering code identified by welfare mothers were the weight of responsibility, the demand for instinctive nurturing and the need for self-sacrifice (Baker, 2009, p 282). Many claimed this status, but denied it to 'others' because they failed to 'perform' the critical duties. While we can discern evidence of strategies of coping and escape in these data, they remain entirely individual and cannot promote any collective demands.

For the young welfare mothers I interviewed, the critical factor in defining those who fail to achieve 'good mother' identity was that they had maintained the life and activities that characterised their pre-parent status.

> Jillie: 'My friend she got bored with her son, she was out every night doing loads of drugs and things like that all night. She was leaving her son with her mother and going out every night getting drunk and stealing cars.'

> Julie: 'She is the worst mother I have ever met. I think 'cos she is never with her baby, it is always with her mum and she is never home, doing drink, doing drugs, whatever she is just a useless mum.'

Welfare mothers who claimed 'good mother status' employed some of the same indicators of dishonour in their accounts as the young men quoted earlier. 'Being' respectable was central, and continent sexual behaviour key in demonstrating respectability.

> Angie: 'This girl Claire, she's 21, one of these ... well, she has all these 15-year-olds.... She sleeps with all of them

really....Well, one of them got her pregnant she don't know which. She takes no notice of her kid, she just shouts at her all the time.'

It was important to position one's self as distant from such mothers:

Kelly: 'I started going downhill when I went to stay with Claire. I had to get out.'

Any young woman who displayed emotional difficulties in coping with 'doing' mothering was also categorised as 'inadequate' and defined as a useful foil for demonstration of the strengths of the self.

Tanya: 'There's some people, there's a girl at my other young mums group and if I was her social worker I'd be there every day. She really looks down every time she comes in and she's told me she tried drowning her baby once. But I think for me, people see me and they really don't think I've got a problem.'

The accounts enhance our grasp of the 'self understandings of those who are arbitrarily lumped together in this analytic fiction' of 'welfare mother' (Wacquant, 2008, p 48). They offer evidence of the sorts of resistance welfare mothers mobilised to their 'othering', indicating their interrogation of 'the toxic metaphor of the 'welfare queen' (Peck, 2010, p 105). The narratives remind us of the significance of categorisations which condemned 'others' while elevating self. It is important to note, however, that there is evidence of the creation of more positive assertions, in the discussion of the 'good mother'. A 'superior classification' (Yardley, 2008) is authenticated by thriving babies, happy, sociable toddlers and restrained, respectable, sexual and material lifestyles. In discussions about what makes a 'good mother', additional positive affirmative identities were put forward by the 'young welfare mothers', and this is explored in the next section of this chapter.

Less tangible discourses about the 'specialness' of motherhood are discernible in these data. Some 'young welfare mothers' made complex claims about 'motherhood' which offered a more collective, but crucially a symbolic social challenge to the dishonoured category to which they were 'delivered'. They made claims for a 'self-identity' which was positive in its own right, and not just in silhouette against the 'other' mothers. It was based on what they had 'produced' physically and also by the work they had invested in their baby as they 'mothered'.

Young 'welfare mothers' employed narratives and languages that both formulated and enhanced the claims they made in their stories, in a number of surprising ways. They made a bid for protection for their children but also for their 'self' in unexpected references to profound aspects of human experience. Baker discusses discourses of the 'essentially sacred and sacrificing endeavour' of motherhood (2009, p 285). The self-sacrificing aspects of mothering have already been explored here and elsewhere (Baker, 2009). It is the twin notions of the 'sacred' endeavour of motherhood and the claims that 'motherhood' can be 'redemptive' (Baker, 2009, p 285) that we now consider. The terms used – *sacred endeavours* and *redemptive acts* – are lofty, and hardly ubiquitous in the language of contemporary sociology of deprivation and deviance; they need careful handling. The concepts involved are unlikely to be expressed directly by young, poor women; it is important, nevertheless to acknowledge that such references are present in the narratives that 'young welfare mothers' employed.

That a young woman makes 'a mistake' which is embodied in the birth of a child is a well-established idea, a commonplace, 'small phrase' in our repertoire that nonetheless has poisonous social implications. 'Young welfare mothers' used the word 'mistake' in ways that repay attention. They spoke of 'mistakes' with a display of emotion that is difficult to convey in a written account of their words, but demonstrated to the researcher its profound significance to them. The quotes selected are a small selection of those generated in the research. The language repeated with ubiquitous frequency throughout the interviews was unvarying and remained intact across respondents. The 'hegemony' of the wording draws the researcher's attention, although at first glance it is prosaic and empty.

> Julie: 'You can't look at him now and say he was a mistake, can you?'

> Kim: 'Having them here. That does change it. Yeah, it does.'

The 'young welfare mothers' again challenge prevailing stigmas. At the simplest level they seek to restore the purity of the life granted to the child, to allow that child to slip from the stigmatising swaddling. One young woman made the views of many clear:

> Tracey: 'He's a lovely, lovely boy.'

She aimed to draw the sting of the dishonour of the child's birth. The 'young welfare mothers' confronted the language of 'a mistake', to deflect the taint it smears on the baby, but also on the mother. In this way the young welfare mothers reappropriated the negative language used about them as mothers to represent themselves in a more positive light.

> Julie:'But the thing is … I'm living in it.… I'm quite happy to live with it, that's the best mistake I ever made in my life!'

> Tracey:'Yeah, yeah, yeah!'

At the most straightforward level 'young welfare mothers' drew on discourses of our 'taken-for-granted' admiration and connection with children to de-stigmatise the child born to teenage parents who may well be dependent on welfare.

They go on to demand we reconsider them, the mothers, too. They appeal to our collective recognition of the colossal significance of birth – the familiar yet profound event. The *words* they chose were simple, utterly banal, but the *claims* made were not. The young women spoke of the startling and weighty feelings they experienced once 'you have them here'. They were feelings for which they made an important claim – they 'change everything' and wipe clean the stigma. The 'young welfare mothers' challenged discourses, labelling the conception and birth of their children as 'wrong' and claimed a kind of redemption for themselves in the nature and experience of creating a life. They referred to the 'redemptive' nature of birth – but they also seemed to draw on a notion of the 'sacred' (Baker, 2009, p 287). They asserted the cardinal significance of 'making' life, and insisted on the special and revered significance of the 'baby'. Their subsequent work, of careful, caring, responsible and responsive mothering, abolishes the stigma from themselves and affirms a positive self. In their accounts 'young welfare mothers' in an inexplicit way called on the 'sacred aura' of motherhood to sanctify and make right their motherhood' and their 'selves' (Romito, 1997; Baker, 2009, p 280). They implicitly appealed to discourses about fertility and life they asserted were universal and timeless. Their bid was to values that transcended their own time and certainly their own economic circumstances.

The words the young mothers used were simple; they failed by academic or literary standards to express the profound qualities that the experiences of creating life and giving birth produced for 'them' and ultimately for 'us' too. But, by using simple words, the young women remain connected to the deep feelings that conception and new life provoke in 'us' as human beings (Erikson, 1994). They found access to discourses and references that prevail above and beyond their scorned neighbourhoods and blemished bodies and identities.

Resistance and agency: when the disorderly speak

In the introduction to this chapter, the suggestion was made that Wacquant pays relatively little direct attention to evidence of resistance among the dispossessed and marginal peoples he discusses: the precariat are, it seems, a crushed and cringing fragment. By contrast, through empirical work, this chapter has attempted to provide evidence of members of the 'assistantial classes' acting with some agency. Similarly, Hartsock drew attention to the significance of moments when agency is demonstrated, when the diverse and disorderly 'others' begin to speak, to chip away at the social and political power of the 'Theorizer' (1987, p 195). Such moments are discernible in the data presented here as 'welfare mothers' both queried and disrupted classifications to which they were directed and the power those classifications had to locate them to identities and assignations in the neoliberal state.

Benhabib's account of subjectivity is significant in this context. She 'stresses that individuals have agency not because they choose their circumstances but because they make sense of them' (1991, p 350). Young welfare mothers were acutely alert to the stigma of their position, and worked to ameliorate it materially, emotionally and symbolically. They challenged the 'given' meanings of what they were told about themselves, and what they deserved. This involved purloining and employing, 'taking and making' (Linebaugh, 2003, p xxvii) elements of established discourses and transforming them for their own purposes. Such strategies of resistance highlight how those without power can deny the particular authoritarian insights into 'reality' specified by those who have power. Such actions challenge those who construct and fortify the 'public sphere' (Habermas, 1989) and build 'counter-publics' (Fraser, 1990).

The young women elaborated their own views of life, and discovered the independent satisfactions in life that Thompson (1968) asserts are representative of subaltern resistance. The limits of the weapons that they were able to invent must be acknowledged. The 'small resistances' engaged in by 'young welfare mothers' will not change the world or neoliberal governing practices. They fail to threaten prison walls; they do not open the welfare coffers of the richest states in the world. As Campbell points out, their actions will not fundamentally contest the rise of the penal state (2010). The resistance was partially dependent on drawing sharp distinctions between themselves and 'others', their agency purchased from the balance sheets of 'others'. They achieved 'partial insights' into the material and symbolic oppressions they encountered which in part allowed for the inequalities to be reproduced (Willis, 1979).

Conclusion

Wacquant focuses on the implications of globalised industrial production and neoliberal politics for the 'precariat'. He highlights 'the scaffold of closed factories and empty freeways' that sculpted their position (Bonvin, 2009, p 306). He illuminates the plight of those most perilously affected with 'imaginative passion'. He shifts the lens of blame from the individual to the structural, and the new focus is welcome.

This chapter raises no fundamental or overall disagreement with Wacquant's focus; the chief concern in this chapter rested on fleshing out the meanings that contemporary structures and conditions have for their victims. While Wacquant's work analyses new structures in which 'precariat' lives are lived, it does not always pursue the responses and reactions that result. There is little recognition or analysis of how and where 'practices of insubordination and defiance grow' (Sarkar, 1997, p 58). In this chapter I have considered how we can look for the ways that new 'counter-publics' are debated into existence, and for evidence of where the weak forge new weapons.

Wacquant's work does not consider gender in any detail, emphasises 'masculinist' perspectives and does not trace the intricate ways that gender-based differences play out in the contemporary world he analyses. We need both data and theoretical perspectives to develop further intersectional understandings of the carceral and the assistantial state. In this chapter we have explored ethnographic details of the ways young women exposed to advanced marginality experienced and responded to the positions in which they were placed.

Empirical material permits us to sketch faces onto the stick figures of the oppressed, and render them more human by attention to their troubles and pains. Academic work which emphasises detailed empirical study and incorporates subaltern, feminist and post-colonial insights into analysis of the strategies used by the precariat offers insights into 'silences' inhabiting Wacquant's recent work.

Note

[1] The research referred to here consisted of a project on teenage pregnancy in rural and seaside areas, see Bell et al, 2004 and Measor, 2006. All quotations cited later are drawn from this research project.

References

Baker, J. (2009) 'Young mothers in late modernity: sacrifice, respectability and the transformative neo-liberal subject', *Journal of Youth Studies*, no 3, June, pp 275-88.

Bakhtin, M. (1984) *Rabelais and his world* (translated by H. Iswolsky), Bloomington, IN: University Press.

Becker, H.S. (1963) *Outsiders*, New York: The Free Press.

Bell, J., Clisby, S., Craig, G., Measor, L., Stanley, N. and Petrie, S. (2004) *Living on the edge: Sexual behaviour and young parenthood in seaside and rural locations*, Hull: University of Hull for the Department of Health.

Benhabib, S. (1999) 'Sexual differences and collective identities: the new global constellation', *Signs*, vol 24, pp 335-61.

Bonvin, J.-M. (2009) 'Review of *Urban outcasts: A comparative sociology of advanced marginality*', *Critical Social Policy*, vol 29, no 2, pp 303-5.

Borges, G.A. (2009) 'Review of *Urban outcasts: A comparative sociology of advanced marginality*', *International Sociology*, vol 24, no 5, September, pp 718-72.

Bourgois, P. (1998) 'Just another night in a shooting gallery', *Theory, Culture & Society*, May, vol 15, no 2, pp 37-66.

Campbell, B. (1993) *Goliath: Britain's dangerous places*, London: Methuen.

Campbell, J.L. (2010) 'Neo-liberalism's penal and debtor states: a rejoinder to Loïc Wacquant', *Theoretical Criminology*, vol 14, no 59, pp 59-73.

Candeias, M. (2007) 'Das unumoglices prekariat oder das Scheitan an den Widerspruchon pluraler Spaltungen', *Das Argument*, vol 271, no 49 (3), pp 410-67.

Coleman, R., Sim, J. and Whyte, D. (2002) 'Power, politics and partnerships: the state of crime prevention on Merseyside', in G. Hughes and A. Edwards (eds) *Crime control and community: The new politics of public safety*, Cullompton: Willan Publishing, pp 86-108.

Duncan, S. (2007) 'What's the problem with teenage parents? And what's the problem with policy?', *Critical Social Policy*, vol 27, no 3, pp 307-34.

Eley, G. (1994) 'Nations, publics and political cultures: placing Habermas in the nineteenth century', in N.B. Dirks and G. Eley (eds) *Culture/power/history: A reader in contemporary social theory*, Princeton, NJ: Princeton University Press.

Erikson, E. (1994) *Identity and the life cycle*, New York: W.W. Norton & Company.

Faludi, S. (2000) *Stiffed: The betrayal of modern man*, New York: Vintage.

Fraser, N. (1990) 'Rethinking the public sphere: a contribution to the critique of actually existing democracy', *Social Text*, vol 25/26, pp 56-8.

Gelsthorpe, L. (2010) 'Crime and crime control', *Criminology and Criminal Justice Studies*, vol 10, no 4, pp 375-86.

Habermas, J. (1989) *The structural transformation of the public sphere*, Cambridge, MA: The MIT Press.

Hanna, B. (2001) 'Negotiating motherhood: the struggle of teenage mothers', *Journal of Advanced Nursing*, vol 34, no 4, pp 456-64.

Hartsock, N. (1987) 'Rethinking modernism: minority versus majority theories', *Cultural Critique*, vol 7, pp 187-206.

Harvey, D.C. (2007) *A brief history of neo-liberalism*, Oxford: Oxford University Press.

Hearn, G. (1987) *The gender of oppression: Men, masculinity and the critique of Marxism*, London: Henderson.

Hobsbawm, E. (1971) *Primitive rebels*, Manchester: Manchester University Press.

Jefferson, T., Clarke, J. and Hall, S. (1975) *Resistance through rituals*, London: Routledge.

Kirkman, M., Hillier, L. and Pyett, P. (2001) 'I know I'm doing a good job: canonical and autobiographical narratives of teenage mothers', *Culture Health and Sexuality*, vol 3, no 3, pp 279-94.

Lacey, N. (2010) 'Differentiating amongst penal states', *British Journal of Sociology*, vol 61, issue no 4, December, pp 778-94.

Lea, J. and Young, J. (1984) *What is to be done about law and order*, Harmondsworth: Penguin.

Linebaugh, P. (2003) *The London hanged: Crime and civil society in the 18th century*, London: Verso.

McDermott, E. and Graham, H. (2005) 'Resilient young mothering: social inequalities, late modernity and the "problem" of "teenage" motherhood', *Journal of Youth Studies*, vol 8, pp 59-79.

Mayer, M. (2010) 'Punishing the poor – A debate. Some questions on Wacquant's theorizing the neoliberal state', *Theoretical Criminology*, vol 14, no 1, pp 93-103.

Measor, L. (2006) 'Young women, community safety and informal cultures', in P. Squires (ed) *Community safety: Critical perspectives*, Bristol: The Policy Press, pp 181-93.

Peck, J. (2010) 'Zombie neoliberalism and the ambidextrous state', *Theoretical Criminology*, vol 14, no 1, pp 104-10.

Plummer, C. (1975) *Stigma: An interactionist account*, London: RKP.

Raban, J. (1974) *Soft city*, New York: The Harvill Press.

Ramazanoglu, C. (ed) (1993) *Up against Foucault: Exploration of some tensions between Foucault and feminism*, London: Routledge.

Romito, P. (1997) 'Damned if you do and damned if you don't: psychological and social constraints on motherhood in contemporary Europe', in A. Oakley and J. Mitchell (eds) *Who's afraid of feminism? Seeing through the backlash*, London: Penguin.

Sarkar, S. (1997) *Writing social history*, Oxford: Oxford University Press.

Scott, J.C. (1987) *Weapons of the weak: Everyday forms of peasant resistance*, New Haven, CT: Yale University Press.

Seamark, C. and Lings, P. (2004) 'Positive experiences of teenage motherhood: a qualitative study', *British Journal of General Practice*, vol 54, no 508, pp 813-18.

Spender, D. (1980) *Learning to lose: Sexism in education*, London: Women's Press.

Thompson, E.P. (1968) *Them of the English working class*, Harmondsworth: Penguin.

Wacquant, L. (2008) *Urban outcasts: A comparative sociology of advanced marginality*, Cambridge: Polity Press.

Wacquant, L. (2009) *Punishing the poor: The neoliberal government of social insecurity*, Durham, NC: Duke University Press.

Willis, P. (1979) *Learning to labour: How working class kids get working class jobs*, London: Routledge.

Yardley, E. (2008) 'Teenage mother's experiences of stigma', *Journal of Youth Studies*, vol 11, no 6, December.

Young, I.M. (1990) *Justice and the politics of difference*, Princeton, NJ: Princeton University Press.

EIGHT

Women, welfare and the carceral state

Denise Martin and Paula Wilcox

Introduction

Loïc Wacquant, in his recent series of publications, has outlined an impressive thesis to explain penal expansionism in the US (Wacquant, 2009a) and the adoption of these policies elsewhere in Europe (Wacquant, 2009b). His account of a seemingly more punitive state is linked to the neoliberal programme of welfare retreatism and inextricably linked to penal regulation. In *Punishing the poor*, Wacquant is persuasive in his argument, providing extensive evidence to support his contentions. In particular, he draws our attention to the precariousness of poor women and the extent to which they are disciplined and controlled by the state through an emphasis on 'workfare' rather than welfare. As he suggests,

> The activation of disciplinary programmes applied to the unemployed, the indigent, single mothers, and others "on assistance" so as to push them onto the peripheral sectors of the employment market, on one side and the deployment of an extended police and penal net with a reinforced mesh, in the dispossessed districts of the metropolis, on the other side are the two components of a single apparatus for the management of poverty that aims at effecting the authoritarian rectification of the behaviours of populations recalcitrant to the emerging economic and symbolic order. (2009a, p 14)

Wacquant then distinguishes these two components along gendered lines, suggesting that women are the recipients of the regulatory 'workfare' programmes (pointing out that 90 per cent of welfare recipients are mothers) and men the receivers of 'prisonfare'. He argues that what we are seeing is a 'remasculinising' of the state where 'the quartet formed by the police, the court, the prison and the probation or parole officer assumes the task of taming their boyfriends, or husbands and their sons' (2009a, p 15). However, as Gelsthorpe (2010) rightly argues in her analysis of Wacquant's recent work, his thesis would have benefited from a further exploration of how 'both social and penal policy over the past two decades in particular have escalated the punitive outcomes for women' (p 377). In addition, Gelsthorpe examines the ways in which the remasculinisation of the state has had an impact on women who have been treated both within welfare and penal systems with distinct features of moral tutelage apparent in a number of policies. Wacquant's work has also been criticised for failing to adequately deal with the ambiguities and unevenness of these developments elsewhere (Nelken, 2010). Drawing on literature, policy developments and an evaluation of a recent programme for women offenders in the UK, this chapter aims to demonstrate that while Wacquant's work provides a useful explanatory tool, it fails to fully demonstrate the experience of female offenders in the UK context and some of the contradictory patterns that have emerged.

Privileged targets of the penal state

Wacquant (2009a, 2009b) demonstrates clearly, through the use of data, the links between the reduction in welfare spending and corresponding increases in prison budgets and spending on more punitive mechanisms to attempt to control the moral deficiencies and criminality associated with the lower echelons of society. He argues that rising concerns relating to wider socioeconomic instabilities, like the precarious labour market and the uncertain futures of the middle class, add to concern about those on the edges of society. These marginalised groups then become what Wacquant refers to as 'privileged targets'. The privileged targets of the above shifts in welfare retraction and neoliberal politics are namely those that belong to a 'population considered "contemptible" and expendable in the post-civil rights and post-welfare era' (p 195). The two groups that Wacquant refers to in particular are the growing population of African American young men that occupy prison places in the US and sex offenders who have become 'dangerous' categories in need of punitive and restrictive sanctions to keep them in check. While these two groups are given special attention, Wacquant's analysis does account for other marginalised groups including women. His attention to women's experience of poverty and marginalisation through 'workfare' and their position in unstable economics identifies them also as 'privileged targets'. Wacquant argues that the 'moral individualism', evident in the approach of the US to welfare reform, is notable in the introduction of the Personal Responsibility and Work Opportunity Reconciliation Act 1996, which served to reduce welfare dependency and encourage a shift towards waged labour. As Wacquant (2009a) argues, this shift in policy demonstrated a 'tenacious ideology of gender and the family that makes poor unwed mothers (and fatherless children) into abnormal, truncated, suspect beings who threaten the moral order and who the state must place under harsh tutelage' (p 81).

   This approach to welfare reform was not just evident in the US but was also witnessed in other countries, and this withdrawal of welfare has also had further far-reaching consequences on women in the UK.

Women as privileged targets in the UK

The responsibility of all to work was central to New Labour policy, as seen in the consultation paper *No one written off: Reforming welfare to reward responsibility*: 'for those capable of working there will be no right to a life on benefits' (DWP, 2008, p 12). Within this discourse lone mothers were privileged targets because of their lack of paid work and, over time, they were increasingly being compelled into work. This, despite the fact that women largely retain their traditional caring role and the position of many women in the labour market remains insecure, the majority located in part-time, low-paid jobs, homeworking and teleworking. Lone mothers continue to be regarded as privileged targets providing key fodder for the penal state (Wacquant, 2009a). The recent economic recession and cuts in public spending are having far more intense impacts on women than men, as women are more likely to work in the public sector, and marginalised women bear the responsibility for managing poverty in families (Lister, 2009). Research assessing the impact of the Coalition government's cuts, tax increases and benefits changes makes it clear that single-parent families, especially those headed by women, will be one of the worst affected groups, facing services cuts equivalent to over 10 per cent of their household income. In cash terms this means that single-parent families may lose up to £1,900 worth of services per year, with the major losses being felt in education, housing and social care (TUC, 2010). Insecurity and poorly paid employment are key factors in women's offending, and currently over half of those classified as poor are in employment (Toynbee and Walker, 2008) and hence more vulnerable to offending; in one survey, '54% of women said that having no money was the reason for their crime; another 38% said it was because they needed to support their children and 33% said it was because they had no job' (survey of imprisoned women and mothers, 1994, cited in Home Office, 2003, p 6).

Compared to the general population, women offenders frequently lack education and skills and there is an awareness of the stigma which can prohibit them from achieving employment on leaving prison:'I'm unemployable because I have a criminal record' (cited by Deedes, 2008). In a study of young women in young offender institutions, nine out of ten had left education by age 17 (90 per cent) and only a quarter (27 per cent) were employed prior to imprisonment (Douglas and Plugge, 2006, pp 6, 7). Women's plans for resettlement are also less likely to be linked to training and employment than men's (Niven and Stewart, 2005). This supports Wacquant's idea that imprisonment has become a way of managing those (but in this case women) who are socially and economically marginalised (Gelsthorpe, 2010, p 378). As Carlen and Tombs (2006, p 339) suggest, some women are, and always have been, more likely to be imprisoned for the complexity of the anti-social, gendered and exclusionary nature of their living conditions.

Women offenders, welfare and the penal state

Women who are incarcerated suffer increased risks of mental illness, self-harm and even suicide in women's prisons. As the governor of the women's prison HMP Styal recently commented: "I'd never experienced anything like it, and I know my colleagues in male prisons hadn't. In a male prison almost twice the size, you'd probably have, on a daily basis, about half a dozen prisoners on ACCT[1] procedures – at risk of self-harm. At Styal there are about 50 a day, on special observation for self-harm" (quoted in Chatterton, 2010).

Welfare problems are not, of course, unique to women prisoners, but as much of the literature surrounding women offenders has shown, women have 'gender-specific' problems that are distinguishable from their male counterparts (Carlen, 2002; Fawcett Society, 2004; McIvor, 2004). Indeed, many of the women in prison in the UK have acute vulnerability *before* they are convicted and incarcerated; women offenders are much more likely than men to be victims of domestic and sexual violence and their experience of violence both in childhood and as adults is a key risk factor for their offending (Rumgay, 2004; Hollin and Palmer, 2006); 50 per cent have experienced domestic violence and abuse (compared with 6 per cent of men) and 33 per cent have experienced sexual violence (*Hansard*, 25 November 2009). Two issues are important here: (i) it is common for victims to experience multiple incidents of sexual or domestic abuse,[2] usually over long periods of time, before seeking support or reporting such abuse. This intensifies the difficulties of those trying to recover from such abuse and it has to be said that, despite improved levels of support, these continue to be inconsistent and patchy across the country; and (ii) it highlights the blurring of boundaries between offender and victim, which the public are often unaware of, and politicians feel it is in their interests to ignore. Ignorance of this overlap has many concrete impacts on how women are treated when they leave prison for the outside world.

Up to 80 per cent of women in prison have diagnosable mental health problems; the comparable figure in the community is less than 20 per cent. O'Brien et al (2001) found that 66 per cent of women in prison have symptoms of neurotic disorders compared with 16 per cent in the general population and 70 per cent have two or more diagnosed mental health problems; female prisoners account for 5 per cent of the total prison population and yet account for 50 per cent of all self-harm incidents (HMIP, 2010); the proportions are higher for younger female offenders. In relation to suicide, over one third attempted suicide prior to imprisonment and, between 2002 and 2009, 55 women prisoners actually killed themselves (Prison Reform Trust, 2010). In relation to drug misuse and harm, 70 per cent need clinical detoxification on entry to prison (Ministry of Justice women's team, cited in Cabinet Office, 2009). Another significant problem for women in prison that is not included in the official prison statistics but which also has a negative impact on women offenders' welfare is the prevalence of women's sexual exploitation within prison that has been documented (Chesney-Lind and Irwin, 2008).

Women are usually the primary carers for elderly relatives and children. Women's continuing role as carers of children means that they are far more likely to have children dependent on them; in a recent inspection of women's prisons, 'fifty-five per cent of survey respondents said that they had children under 18' (HM Inspectorate of Prisons, 2010). At least one third of these mothers are lone parents before imprisonment and only 25 per cent of children of women prisoners live with their biological or current fathers; and only 5 per cent of children of imprisoned mothers are able to stay in their own homes during their mother's absence (Epstein, 2008). Childcare, therefore, figures strongly in women offenders' lives and influences their experiences in prison more than it does men. Also there is the concomitant damage done to children's lives since each year it is estimated that more than 17,700 children are separated from their mothers by imprisonment (Prison Reform Trust, 2009). Prison disrupts family relationships due to women's prisons often being geographically distant from family members and the consequent difficulties of visiting; one third of women prisoners also encounter problems with sending and receiving mail that adds to the loneliness and isolation of imprisonment.

Coming out of prison women often find they are even more marginalised: "It's like being punished again" (quoted in Deedes, 2008). Pre-release they report feelings of ambivalence, gate-fever and institutionalisation with huge worries about letting their families down again. Fear of coming out of prison and how they are going to adapt to the outside world exist alongside an awareness of the stigma they will face: "I feel fear, loathing, disgust and shame. I walk down the street with a big red streak painted down my front" (quoted in Deedes, 2008). Post-release women report an unexpectedly intense emotional reaction and that the stigma was far worse than they had expected; financial hardship, lack of information and guidance and lack of support are common. Family support is viewed positively, but relationships with family are complicated due to the fact that, for example, family members may be on drugs or alcoholic, and adapting back into family life is not straightforward, with many feeling isolated: "Outside is harder than inside" (quoted in Deedes, 2008).

Housing and accommodation are constant concerns as many women lose their homes while in prison. As we have seen the majority of women receiving custodial sentences get short sentences, mainly six months or less, which is long enough to lose their accommodation but often too short a time to arrange another home, and so women prisoners are less likely than men to have accommodation arranged for them on discharge from prison. As a result, at worst 60 per cent of women prisoners do not have homes to go to on release (HM Prison Service, 2008) and many lose all their possessions as well.

This account of women offenders' experience is reflected in both *Punishing the poor* and *Prison of poverty*, and as already stated, Wacquant's analysis draws our attention to these connections between welfare, exclusion and penality. However, his analysis fails to demonstrate that women's experiences of prison and welfare are often multidimensional and contradictory. The next part of this chapter examines how Wacquant's framework provides us with only a partial story.

Contours and ambiguities: a more complex picture of women, welfare and the carceral state in the UK

Wacquant demonstrates an appreciation of his own limitations. In the prologue to *Punishing the poor*, he suggests:

To paint patterns that are not fully congealed, whose elements crystallise at varying paces, and whose effects have yet to ramify fully across the social structure and play out over the long run (in the case of workfare), requires that one exaggerate the meshing of trends tying punishment and marginality, at the risk of giving the impression that penalization is an irresistible totalising principle that crushes everything in its path, (Wacquant, 2009a, p xix)

Wacquant proposes that this exaggeration is necessary to expose scholars of criminal justice and welfare radicals to the 'overgrown penal arm of the Leviathan' (2009a, p 20). However, this overemphasis on the extent of the punitive upsurge and social insecurity fails to recognise the contradictions and contours which are evident when we more closely examine the experience of female offenders in the UK. Gelsthorpe (2010) argues that Wacquant's arguments do not go far enough in providing us with an account of women's experiences in the UK and that further analysis of other interrelated notions of moral tutelage that have an impact on women are required. What is evident in Gelsthorpe's (2010) analysis is how Wacquant's identification of moral tutelage and the remasculinising of the state play out in other areas of women's lives. A good example here is particular notions of parenting and motherhood (Gelsthorpe, 2010). As Gewirtz (2001) argues, implicit in New Labour's approach was re-socialisation and re-education, which has as its ultimate aim the eradication of class differences by reconstructing and transforming working-class parents into middle-class ones. Rodger (2008) notes a disconnect between policies aimed at supporting children and families. One the one hand, the government is encouraging responsibilisation through work which is seen as investing in children's future security and ending dependency cultures. On the other hand, families are being criticised for not managing to adequately support or 'parent' their children. Parr and Nixon's (2008) work explored the use of family intervention projects aimed at reducing the eviction of 'anti-social' families, and found that the majority of these projects were aimed at female-only households and that there was a tendency to blame female tenants for the 'inappropriate' behaviour of their male partners or teenage sons. A similar finding is also seen in the use of Parenting Orders, which have been predominantly given to lone mothers (see Holt, 2008).

Gelsthorpe (2004), exploring Garland's work and the so-called retreat from penal welfarism, suggests this doesn't fully account for female offenders' experiences. The perception of women's offending as different from men's is a theme that has persisted within the criminal justice system. Women's status as mothers, their welfare and social standing are taken into account in relation to their treatment in the criminal justice system. The perception of them as 'troubled' rather than 'troublesome' has continued to be a key theme in decisions about how to sentence them. Gelsthorpe (2004, p 9) argues that:

> ... rather than this displacing the penal-welfare approaches in sentencing and in prison regimes and so on the two strategies co-exist. There is no contradiction here, but a complex interweaving of discourse.

This point is supported by Sim (2009), who also suggests that the shift towards a punitive era is perhaps overstated and there is a need to appreciate continuity in penal policy. He argues that a historical perspective tells us about the ever-present pains of imprisonment and that punitive policies have played a part in previous prison regimes. In addition, Sim also appreciates the continuation of penal welfarism alongside these seemingly more punitive regimes. As Zedner (2002) states, the retraction of penal welfarism has been exaggerated. She points to the continued use and expansion of probation and community penalties, as well as rehabilitation being a continued objective of the prison service and the search for evidence of 'what works' in reducing offending behaviour. Finally Sim (2009) points to pockets of resistance in relation to prisoners rights groups who can challenge the status quo. He does, however, stress, that liberal reform groups in particular have had limited success in transforming dominant penal discourses. In relation to female offenders this has led to a coupling of penal and welfare treatment (Gelsthorpe, 2004, 2010). There is evidence to suggest that in the sentencing of women, a custodial sentence is seen as the best route for women, as in prison there is a chance to resolve some of the problems or issues that they face in their lives. This is supported by Barry and McIvor (2010), whose research with practitioners and policy makers in Scotland found that there was a perception that female offenders were 'up-tariffed' as sheriffs believed women were more able to access services that would assist them in prison. As was stated by one professional,

> 'I do think that [sheriffs will] use Corton Vale [Scotland's only dedicated female prison] to get them a health service ... sheriffs see women as quite vulnerable and maybe requiring help and they do accept that it is very difficult for

women to access services within the community.' (quoted in Barry and McIvor, 2010, p 32)

Even women themselves see custody as an advantage at times. As Vickers and Wilcox (2011) suggest, for those women who have often been subject to abuse, prison can provide a safe haven for a short period of time.

This point is further illustrated by Jackie Tombs in her scrutiny of penal policy in Scotland at the end of the 1990s. Tombs argues that the publication of *Women offenders: A safer way* (Social Work Service and Prisons Inspectorate for Scotland, 1998, cited in Tombs, 2004, p 68), following a spate of suicides at Corton Vale, emphasises the need to consider a more gender-specific policy towards female offenders; it further questions the effectiveness of penal responses and suggests a shift towards decarceration. In general the document identifies issues including poverty and emphasises a twin-track approach where prison is reserved only for the most serious offenders (Tombs, 2004, pp 69-70). Despite this commitment, what Tombs demonstrates is an inability to pursue such a policy of decarceration. One final point that Tombs does make in her analysis of penal reductionism in Scotland is that room did remain for this strategy to be adopted. However, she was also clear to suggest that this type of policy could not be left to the courts alone and that rather than just thinking about the futility of incarcerating women for minor offences, the 'language of morality' is rarely applied in this process.

Pat Carlen (2002) identifies the process of 'carceral clawback' that she suggests undermines all attempts to introduce more lenient penal policies towards female offenders. She argues that the continued investment in prison as a place that can offer something else other than punishment helps to sustain its existence as the primary form of punishment. Carlen suggests that there are a number of reasons for, first, that democratic governments need in some way to justify its existence despite the often recognised 'pains of imprisonment', second, that prison regimes are still a major stakeholder in the utilisation of 'psy' therapies, and finally, that reform groups' acceptance of their failure to reduce the prison population has meant a shift of focus towards not reducing but assisting in the formation of prison regimes. Hannah-Moffat (2002), in her research on Canadian penal policy, suggests that while attempts to introduce a gender-focused penal strategy did improve the conditions for some women in prison, she argued that the 'sinister elements of incarceration persists' (p 203).

A similar picture has emerged in penal policy in England and Wales, as outlined by Hedderman (2010) who suggests that New Labour were slow to respond to the needs of women offenders despite recognising their social exclusion. This is witnessed in the time that it took New Labour to recognise existing research and reports. Hedderman (2010, p 48) identifies the *Reducing reoffending by ex-prisoners* report published by the Social Exclusion Unit, which clearly identified those in prison as the most socially disadvantaged. It was not until 2004 that the Women's Offending and Reduction Programme (WORP) was developed. WORP acknowledged continuing inequalities between men and women applying to the treatment of women offenders and focused on 'addressing their particular needs and characteristics' (2004, p 3). However, as Hedderman states, the underlying messages were that these needs would be met within existing funding and structural arrangements. It was not for another couple of years that government policy truly started to shift.

While penal reform for women has faced a number of contradictions and a path of mixed fortunes, over the last few years there has been a move towards dealing with female offenders in a different way. *The Corston Report* (2007), which highlighted female prisoners' high levels of complex personal needs, intertwined with intense family relationship problems in contexts of poverty, was very influential. Corston proposed fundamental reforms recommending improved sentencing, more community interventions and the development of a network of support/supervision centres. Alongside this it recommended the introduction of smaller residential units for women whose offending was so serious and/or violent that an alternative to custody would be inappropriate.

A changing context

The government responded to *The Corston Report* (2007) by announcing the setting up of a Reducing Reoffending Inter-Ministerial Group to provide governance and linked to a new cross-departmental unit responsible for women and criminal justice. The Together Women Programme (TWP) was funded for three years as the government's Demonstration Project to offer a centre to provide holistic and individual support packages to reduce women's offending and to divert women 'at risk of' offending. In February 2010, the Corston Independent Funders' Coalition (a group of 21 charitable trusts, foundations and individual philanthropists) was established to sustain a shift from imprisonment to community sentencing for vulnerable women offenders, and the Ministry of Justice announced the creation of the Women's Diversionary Fund. This was a £2 million fund to divert women from custody and focus on: (i) supporting organisations to develop new one-stop shop services for women offenders; (ii) developing existing one-stop shop services further; and (iii) building the capacity of the women's offending sector. The Women's Centres Forum is the new umbrella body for the 38 women's community and diversion projects now operating across England and Wales. The work of the voluntary sector is to be supported by partnerships that include probation, prison and police, and also health agencies and many others with common aims of reducing crime and reoffending, as well as social exclusion.

The local context: the South East and Brighton and Hove

Offender Management Services are organised on a regional basis in England and Wales and the South East is one of the largest regions. Statistics from the Director of Offender Management in 2010 revealed that over the previous 10 years the female prison population had been rising twice as fast as the male (200 per cent), from an average of about one-and-a-half thousand (1,560) in 1993 to around four-and-a-half thousand (4,463) in 2006. Despite this rise in numbers, women in prison still represent a very small proportion of the total prison population, at about 5 per cent of a total of 85,447 in England and Wales as at April 2011. Nevertheless the value to society of moving such women out of prison is significant – a New Economic Foundation study found that 'For every pound invested in support-focused alternatives to prison, £14 worth of social value is generated to women and their children, victims and society generally over ten years' (Lawlor et al, 2008, p 2).

There was recognition in Brighton and Hove that women experience high and multiple levels of inequality (see Brighton and Hove, 2007) and particularly those with additional vulnerabilities such as lone parents, Black and minority ethnic groups, lesbian, bi-sexual and trans-gender groups, women with low work skills, or mental health difficulties and older women. The Assistant Chief Officer for Sussex Probation highlighted a specific need for counselling services and a cognitive-based group work programme for women offenders in relation to the regional criminogenic need linked to 'thinking and behaviour'. A multiagency partnership approach was seen as particularly useful in terms of engagement with women and the Inspire project was awarded a government grant in November 2009 to begin this work (see www. justice.gov.uk/news/newsrelease051109c.htm).

A gender-sensitive approach at community level

The Inspire project was designed to provide positive alternatives for women. It was developed by the Women's Services Strategic Network (WSSN), a partnership of Brighton and Hove women's voluntary sector organisations set up by Brighton Women's Centre (BWC) in 2007. WSSN offers a strategic approach to the development of women's services across Brighton and Hove, aiming to provide a holistic, empowered, cohesive women's sector working together to provide continuity of care and representation for women across the city. WSSN comprises five organisations: BWC, Threshold (BHT), Rise, Brighton Oasis Project and Survivors' Network. The core value at the centre of Inspire is broadly 'to create a safe space in which women can be supported and assisted in creating alternative and positive futures, diverted from crime and custodial sentences', and the programme has five objectives: (i) to provide additional and enhanced services in the community for three groups: women at risk of receiving a custodial sentence, women offenders and women at risk of offending; (ii) to build on and improve existing third sector, community-based women's services; (iii) to ensure coordination of services for women at an early stage in order to tackle the factors that lead to social exclusion and hence the heightened risk of offending; (iv) to work in partnership with local criminal justice agencies to divert women from custody and increase compliance rates by providing integrated packages of support that meet the needs of vulnerable women; and (v) to work with mainstream services outside of the criminal justice sector to facilitate women's access to specialist services and their integration into mainstream services at the end of their support package.

Inspire in practice

> 'Sometimes when I come out of a session, I feel happy, just more in control ... sometimes I skip all the way to the bus stop.'

The Inspire project became operational in April 2010 as a partnership project, a new way of working. Inspire brings together five women's agencies in Brighton and Hove that are involved in tackling the complex range of support needs that women offenders and those at risk of offending need to be able to access with each partner specialising in supporting women with a range of needs, such as domestic violence, sexual abuse, substance and alcohol use, self-esteem, life skills, mental health and psychological well-being. Members of the Inspire partnership have long been associated with providing support to women who are disadvantaged socially and economically. The project has a Service Level Agreement with Sussex and Surrey Probation to deliver women-centred specified activities and unpaid work at Inspire. Of particular importance has been the integration of services for female offenders with general provision for women and the provision of 'women-only' spaces; women contrasted this with attending at probation offices: "Going to probation was a constant reminder of what I had done; I kept meeting other people who were the same [still offending]".

Women-only services, especially those that draw on feminist research and practice, will draw on a different construction of gender than that used by, for example, the judiciary that historically has taken a harsher stance against those women rejecting feminine norms (Chesney–Lind and Shelden, 1997). This is very important to female participants who feel more secure and who say: "Women come here just as women, without a label" (quoted in Paget, 2011)[3].

Women are referred to Inspire in a range of ways: by the court as part of a Specified Activity Requirement (SAR), and this represents the majority of referrals, or, if they are seen to be 'at risk' of offending through an assessment, using the 'At Risk Toolkit'. Inspire case workers also attend the local police custody suite to encourage diversion at this early stage and provide advice and advocacy to reduce the risk of custody. The case workers also link in with the Mental Health Court Pilot at Brighton Magistrates' Court and provide access to specialist support packages and specified activities. And finally, some women refer themselves on a voluntary basis. The case workers also provide in-reach support at HMP Bronzefield and support packages for women in resettlement and provide alternatives to custody for those on remand/bail. Following referral women are assessed by a case worker and an enabling package of interventions and activities, tailored to the particular woman's needs, is agreed, thus meeting the SAR requirements. These activities can be at partner agencies or at other specialised services, and through this support package women can start to address some complex issues.

The women who are referred attend various aspects of Inspire at a range of different partner agencies. Many reported the time of referral as a point when their lives had been extremely chaotic, troubled and out of control. Decentralisation in the creation and administration of penal policy has been called a 'responsibilisation strategy' by Pat O'Malley (1992), shifting responsibility away from the state and on to others such as organisations, the community and individuals. Women-centred services are more likely to challenge the personal responsibilisation discourse and contextualise women's situations. However, women themselves, not surprisingly, have taken on board the dominant discourse of being personally responsible, as we can see from these comments: "I felt incredible shame at needing help"; "I was a lost cause"; "I knew I was dangerous".

Inspire workers are aware of women's familial responsibilities and the impact of women's offending on their children and the wider family; awareness of whether a woman is integrated into her community or isolated; and their histories of physical and sexual violence and alcohol/drug dependencies. As one woman said: "[This relationship] helped me put into perspective a lifetime of addictions". In terms of the subjects of welfare and penal policies – the discourse is often one of personal responsibility – where choice is key, people have to own up not only to their offences but to the bad choices they made that led them to offend, 'from choices of whom to associate with to how to make money to what kind of relationships to be in" (Haney, 2004, p 345).

Modern technologies of governance, drawing on a rational actor model, focus on the individual, emphasising self-control, self-management and self-regulation (Feeley and Simon, 1992; Garland, 2001) – projects of the self. Therapeutic corrections may be premised on their emotional and social instability. 'When applied to women in the welfare and penal systems, strategies of individualization are often cloaked in promises of female "empowerment" – as ways to teach women self-reliance, self-respect and self-esteem. Such promises may serve to convince the women administering these projects that their approach is transformative; many even represent themselves as advocating a feminist vision of women's equality' (Haney, 2004, p 347).

Dependency discourse also tends to focus on the individual – who and what they have chosen to be dependent on – welfare benefits, alcohol/drugs and/or the wrong type of man; frequently social structural vulnerabilities having an impact on women are transformed into personal pathologies. We would want to argue that working in a gender-sensitive way works in opposition to this approach. But although we agree that it is crucial for workers and women to see that social structural issues such as homelessness and poverty are central, nevertheless, because of the experiences women have had there really is also an issue with self-confidence and a need to feel personal control.

The relationships formed in the Inspire programme are significant: "I can't put it into words, [without her] I would have been in prison". Over time this relationship served as a checking-in place for women and fostered a growing sense of trust. What is clear is that this relationship, with at its core non-judgement, positive regard, empathy and reliability, provides Inspire with a crucial role in assisting women to make different choices, feel confident enough to change, to experience both positive role modelling and positive human relationships. This was borne out in many responses, and this is a sample of those comments: "I know I can trust her"; "[This relationship] helped me put into perspective a lifetime of addictions"; "I can talk about anything".

The approach is one more of interrelationship with woman offenders not seen as solely responsible – a more non-judgemental relationship is built between woman and worker/s: "There is so much warmth, a lot of love"; "I know I can trust her"; "I can talk about anything". For example, women offenders' previous experiences of domestic and sexual violence, rather than indicating victimisation, 'become risk factors indicating their potential for self-destruction, passivity, and thus irresponsibility' (Haney, 2004, p 345). In Inspire feminist discourse makes clear the contexts of social structures and power relationships in which women are located and rather than emphasising individual choice in previous experiences emphasises structural issues and contexts.

Positive relationships are not, however, confined to those made with project workers; the value in meeting other women in similar circumstances cannot be underestimated. In particular, support for women experiencing domestic violence, whose children have been removed, and in particular, the value of bringing women for whom offending was 'out of character' – an 'I wasn't myself' experience – together may be of enormous value. The time required in working in the ways described in the Inspire project is likely to be slow and painstaking, taking longer than working in a crisis-focused way, as the quote below makes clear:

> The principal challenge to the criminal justice and offender management systems is therefore not dramatic, but much more demanding. It means working with persistence and determination to make and build upon improvements each of which may be small but, when taken together, make a

real impact on the problem. (Esmee Fairbairn Foundation, 2004, p 1)

The issue here is whether projects such as Inspire will be allowed the space and time to develop in such a way or whether the continued alignment of punitiveness and welfare will continue. As Hedderman (2010) proposes, despite some suggestions of success as a result of *The Corston Report*, it seems to be having little effect on the number of women receiving short custodial sentences. Also previous attempts to alter approaches towards female offenders have tended to integrate prison and community penalties into one with little progress in altering the punitive outcomes experienced by them (Carlen and Tombs, 2006) or altering the situation in which they find themselves.

Conclusion

The Inspire project indicated a shift of focus and more holistic approach to female offenders; what this illustrates is that there is room for alternative responses to prison to exist and there is also room for programmes that can effectively work with female offenders and change their lives. This is somewhat ignored in Wacquant's analysis, and demonstrates that when considering the experience of offenders, there is a need to do this on a local and gendered basis. Saying this, questions remain about the underlying features of strategies to reduce the impact of the penal system and welfare systems of women. The need for female offenders to take responsibility for their actions still features in alternative programmes, indicating that individual responsibility and the need to alter one's behaviour are requirements of such schemes. While some may argue that this can lead to adaptations in women's self-esteem, it may do little to resolve the multiple problems that female offenders face. It is not simply a process of rethinking the offending behaviour, but finding ways to resolve some of the multiple issues and precarious positions women face. While there is the promise of a 'Rehabilitation Revolution' by the Coalition government, cuts elsewhere in welfare and social support systems are likely to undermine attempts at penal reform. As Wacquant so eloquently suggests, these system are inextricably linked. In addition, the ambition to substantially reduce the number of women in prisons in the UK is yet to be realised.

Notes

[1] The Prison Service uses a care planning system called ACCT (Assessment, Care in Custody and Teamwork) for prisoners at risk of self-harm or suicide. ACCT has been in place in all establishments since April 2007.

[2] The legal definition of domestic violence now extends beyond intimate partners to include acts perpetrated by extended family members, as well as acts such as forced marriage, and other so-called 'honour' crimes.

[3] All the quotations from participants in the Inspire project are taken from Georgina Paget (2011), which is the first evaluation report for Inspire.

References

Barry, M. and McIvor, G. (2010) 'Professional decision making and women offenders: containing the chaos', *Probation Journal*, vol 57, no 1, pp 27-41.

Brighton and Hove (2007) *Developing appropriate strategies for reducing inequality in Brighton and Hove, Phase 1: Identifying the challenge: Inequality in Brighton and Hove Phase 1 final report*, December (www.brightonhove.gov.uk/downloads/bhcc/equalities/OCSI_ReducingInequalityReview_phase_1_full_report.pdf).

Cabinet Office (2009) *Short study on women offenders*, London: Social Exclusion Taskforce.

Carlen, P. (2002) 'New discourses of justification and reform for women's imprisonment in England', in P. Carlen (ed) *Women and punishment: The struggle for justice*, Cullompton: Willan Publishing, pp 220–36.

Carlen, P. and Tombs, J. (2006) 'Reconfigurations of penality: the ongoing case of women's imprisonment and reintegration industries', *Theoretical Criminology*, vol 10, no 3, pp 337-60.

Chatterton, C. (2010) 'Vulnerable women in the justice system, women's centres and the Corston Agenda', Speech, Prison Reform Trust, London, 22 June.

Chesney-Lind, M. and Irwin, K. (2008) *Beyond bad girls: Gender, violence and hype*, London: Routledge.

Chesney-Lind, M. and Shelden, R.G. (1997) *Girls, delinquency, and juvenile justice*, Pacific Grove, CA: Brooks and Cole.

Corston, B. (2007) *The Corston Report, A report by Baroness Jean Corston of a review of women with particular vulnerabilities in the criminal justice system*, London: Home Office.

Deedes, R. (2008) 'Women leaving prison', Unpublished paper given at Sussex Probation Workshop, 17 June, Stanmer House, Brighton.

Department for Work and Pensions (DWP) (2008) *No-one written off: Reforming welfare to reward responsibility,* Green Paper, Norwich:TSO.

Douglas, N. and Plugge, E. (2006) *A health needs assessment for young women in young offender institutions,* Oxford: University of Oxford (www.yjb.gov.uk).

Epstein, R. (2008) 'Paying the price: children of parents in prison', *Justice of the Peace,* 28 June, pp 415–18.

Esmee Fairbairn Foundation(2004) *Crime, courts and confidence: Report of an Independent Inquiry into Alternatives to Prison,* London:Esmee Fairbairn Foundation (www.esmeefairbairn.org.uk/docs/Coulsfieldreport.pdf).

Fawcett Society (2004) *A report of the Fawcett Society's Commission on women and the criminal justice system,* London: Fawcett Society.

Feeley, M. and Simon, J. (1992) 'The new penology: notes on the emerging strategy of corrections and its implications', *Criminology,* vol 30, pp 449–79.

Garland, D. (2001) *The culture of control: Crime and social order in contemporary society,* Oxford: Oxford University Press.

Gelsthorpe, L. (2004) 'Back to basics in crime control: weaving in women', *Critical Review of International, Social and Political Philosophy,* vol 7, no 2, pp 76–103.

Gelsthorpe, L. (2010) 'Women, crime and control', *Criminology and Criminal Justice,* vol 10, no 4, pp 375–86.

Gewirtz, S. (2001) 'Cloning the Blairs, New Labour's programme for the resocialisation of parents', *Journal of Educational Policy,* vol 16, no 4, pp 365–78.

Haney, L. (2004) 'Introduction: gender, welfare and states of punishment', *Social Politics,* vol 11, no 3, pp 333–62.

Hannah-Moffat, K. (2002) 'Creating choices: reflecting on choices', in P. Carlen (ed) *Women and punishment: The struggle for justice,* Cullompton: Willan Publishing, pp 199–219.

Hedderman, C. (2010) 'Government policy on women offenders: Labour's legacy and the coalition's challenge', *Punishment and Society,* vol 12, no 4, pp 485–500.

HMIP (Her Majesty's Inspectorate of Prisons) (2010) *Women in prison: A short thematic review,* July (www.justice.gov.uk/inspectorates/hmiprisons/docs/Womens_Thematic_2010_rps_.pdf).

Hollin, C.R. and Palmer, E.J. (2006) 'Criminogenic need and women offenders: a critique of the literature', *Legal and Criminological Psychology,* vol 11, pp 179–95.

Holt, A. (2008) 'Room for resistance, Parenting Orders, disciplinary power and the production of the bad parent', in P. Squires (ed) *ASBO nation: The criminalisation of nuisance*, Bristol: The Policy Press, pp 203-22.

Home Office (2003) *Statistics on women and the criminal justice system*, London: Home Office.

Lawlor, E., Nicholls, J. and Sanfilippo, L. (2008) *Unlocking value: How we all benefit from investing in alternatives to prison for women offenders*, London: New Economics Foundation (www.neweconomics.org/publications/unlocking-value).

Lister, R. (2009) 'Women in the recession: Gender relations and the economic crisis', Compass/Fawcett meeting, 6 May (www.fawcettsociety.org.uk/documents/compassfawcett.pdf).

McIvor, G. (ed) (2004) *Women who offend*, London: Jessica Kingsley Publishers.

Nelken, D. (2010) 'Denouncing the penal state', *Criminology and Criminal Justice*, vol 10, no 4, pp 331-40.

Niven, S. and Stewart, D. (2005) *Resettlement outcomes on release from prison*, Findings 248, London: Home Office.

O'Brien, M., Mortimer, L., Singleton, N. and Meltzer, H. (2001) *Psychiatric morbidity among women prisoners in England and Wales*, London: The Stationery Office.

O'Malley, P. (1992) 'Risk, power and crime prevention', *Economy and Society*, vol 21, pp 252-75.

Paget, G. (2011) 'Inspire: positive alternatives for women, An evaluative report', Unpublished evaluation.

Parr, S. and Nixon, J. (2008) 'Rationalising family intervention programmes', in P. Squires (ed) *ASBO nation: The criminalisation of nuisance*, Bristol: The Policy Press, pp 161-78.

Prison Reform Trust (2009) *Bromley Briefings Prison Fact File*, London: Prison Reform Trust.

Prison Reform Trust (2010) *Bromley Briefings Prison Fact File*, London: Prison Reform Trust.

Rodger, J. (2008) *Criminalising social policy, anti-social behaviour and welfare in a de-civilised society*, Cullompton: Willan Publishing.

Rumgay, J. (2004) 'Scripts for safer survival: pathways out of female crime', *The Howard Journal*, vol 43, no 4, pp 405-19.

Sim, J. (2009) *Punishment and prisons: Power and the carceral state*, London: Sage Publications.

Tombs, J. (2004) 'From a safer to a better way: transformations in penal policy for women', in G. McIvor (ed) *Women who offend*, London: Jessica Kingsley Publishers, pp 82-98.

Toynbee, P. and Walker, D. (2008) *Unjust rewards: Exposing greed and inequality in Britain today*, London: Granta.

TUC (Trades Union Congress) (2010) *Where the money goes: How we benefit from public services*, London: TUC.

Vickers, S. and Wilcox, P. (2011) 'Abuse, women offenders and the criminal justice system', *Criminal Justice Matters*, vol 85, no 1, pp 24-5.

Wacquant, L. (2009a) *Punishing the poor: The neoliberal government of social insecurity*, Durham, NC: Duke University Press.

Wacquant, L. (2009b) *Prisons of poverty*, Minneapolis, MN: University of Minnesota Press.

Zedner, L. (2002) 'Dangers of dystopia in penal theory', *Oxford Journal of Legal Studies*, vol 22, no 2, pp 341-66.

Section 3
Urbanisation, criminality and penality

NINE

Illicit economies and the carceral social zone

Vincenzo Ruggiero

There are several interconnected issues raised by Loïc Wacquant's work which reflect not only general sociological and criminological concerns, but also pertain to specific areas of debate, including the function of imprisonment, the notion of illicit markets, the interpretation of violence, the concept of collective action and the new ways of superseding neoliberal philosophies.

In an analysis of the continuity between the prison and the ghetto, Wacquant (2001) argues that both host a surplus population, the human waste discarded by the productive system and ignored by the welfare state. The growth of these two receptacles of marginality, he remarks, is not a response to growing crime, but to growing poverty; not a reaction to criminal insecurity, but to social insecurity: in brief, the war against poverty has turned into war against the poor. An expansion of this analysis is found in the more recent *Punishing the poor* (Wacquant, 2009), where Wacquant discusses how the current workfare philosophies are intertwined with the retrenchment of inclusive assistance and policies, and the expansion of custodial punishment. The control of the economically disadvantaged is thus described as a result of fear and resentment on the part of the better-off, a reassertion of institutional strength, an outmoded exhibition of the moralising role of the state. Warehouses for the dispossessed, prisons testify to a politics of 'class cleansing' implemented against undesirable populations and neighbourhoods whose very existence may be disturbing, hence the urge to make them coercively disappear. What makes the prison system different today, according to Wacquant, is that 'it does not carry out a positive economic mission of recruitment and disciplining an active workforce. The prison serves mainly to warehouse the precarious and deproletarianized fractions of the black working class in the dualizing city' (Wacquant, 2009, p 208). Is, then, the growth of custodial penalties a mere reflection of the decline of the welfare state and the criminalisation of marginality?

We have two distinct issues here, the former relating to the punishment of social insecurity rather than criminal insecurity, the latter pertaining to the manifest or latent function of punishment itself. What follows may add to Wacquant's analysis while suggesting a slight change in the focus of theoretical inquiry.

Criminalisation of indolence

One would assume that with the phrase 'social insecurity', Wacquant intends to convey a notion of social disorder that is constructed in particular ways around certain groups, and widely used to serve certain particular interests. The appeal to 'social disorder' may contribute to mobilising despair as a political weapon rather than demands for justice. Appropriated by powerful groups, and turned into fear, it reflects, reshapes and reinforces the status quo (Shirlow and Pain, 2003). In common understandings 'social disorder' is associated with behaviour involving potentially threatening strangers (Sampson, 2009), like in Wacquant's elaboration 'social insecurity' is linked with marginalisation and poverty. In other words, punishment is disjointed from the potential criminal nature of the threat experienced and is aimed at specific categories of feared individuals. In this respect, Wacquant's analysis might benefit from some supplementary observations about 'human waste' and the perception of certain groups as troublesome. The emphasis, however, can be placed on useless people who fail to act as consumers. My proposed change of focus, in other words, sets off with the hypothesis that what is feared and punished is less the criminal capacity of these groups than their indolence, and specifically their absence from markets and their relative deprivation (Ruggiero, 2010a). Let us see some precedents to this analysis.

In the words of Walter Benjamin (1999), market economies display a pure cult of the useful. It is inevitable, therefore, that uselessness is associated with disorder. Markets enact a constant, dreamless, celebration involving consumers as relentless adorers: they take on the traits of a religion. Grown as parasites of Christianity, market economies keep the essence of parasitic systems at their core, while incorporating new types of religion. By absorbing the 'juice' of religion, they replace religious authority, managed by clerical apparatuses, with economic authority, managed by anonymous powers that are just as sacred. These systems are victorious less because they are superior than for their 'cult of possession'. According to Benjamin, the opening hours of shops remind one of liturgical calendars, in a cult that is more concrete and imperative than its religious counterpart (Gaeta, 2008).

Sure, such systems are never completely accomplished, but they will be in the coming kingdom of universal well-being. Here, the mixture of secular and transcendental order is decisive: the kingdom of God will only come with the total dominion of the economic sphere. As a preliminary suggestion, I would like to note that this obtuse faith in progress still affects the perceptions of order and disorder in contemporary societies. Productive activities and consumption remain today the only signs of social health and acceptable order. Even the concept of anti-social behaviour, and Wacquant's 'social insecurity', in the last analysis, might be associated with indolence and failure to play a role in the marketplace.

Social insecurity and disorder, therefore, signal unproductive lifestyles and absenteeism from markets. Wacquant's idea that punitive measures make poverty disappear echoes Lefebvre's (2003) critique of cities which prevent the constitution of a group, of a subject: it is not a coincidence, Lefebvre remarks, that whenever threatened, the first thing power restricts is the ability to linger or assemble in the street. If not devoted to consumption and the celebration of the powerful, conquerors and death, then streets have to be stripped of their political potential, and turned into 'blind fields', areas that we resist, turn away from, and struggle against. Areas of disorder. This was the character of Haussmann's urbanism, that 'gutted Paris according to plan and deported the proletariat to the periphery of the city' (Lefebvre, 2003, p 109).

Social order became governed by 'straight lines, alignment and geometric perspective', more suitable for the intervention of the army called on to confront the crowd. Social order, in sum, expresses itself through the void: 'empty space, broad avenues, plazas of gigantic proportion open to spectacular processions' (Lefebvre, 2003, p 109). Fear steps in when spaces are populated. What is important to note, here, is that the perception of disorder leads to processes aimed at making the street apolitical, that is, to the creation and perpetuation of social enclaves banned from shaping the urban. The urban community is the result of collective action by social agents, subjects acting in successive thrusts, 'discontinuously releasing and fashioning layers of space' (p 109). Social groups, while acting with and/or against one another, forge the qualities and properties of urban space. Excluded groups are not allowed to create space. 'The merchant bourgeoisie, the intellectuals, and politicians modelled the city. The industrialists demolished it. The working class never had any space other than that of its expropriation, its deportation: segregation' (Lefebvre, 2003, p 128).

Excluded groups are expected to populate the other place, the place of the other, the place of anomie. This is Lefebvre's concept of heterotopy, which should be assimilated to a notion of chaos, formlessness, a menacing site that can explode, whether or not such a possibility is realistic. Wacquant may want to recognise that this process precedes and attends to the disappearance of poverty he hypothesises.

The fear of relative deprivation

We are facing a paradox: excluded from the market and its religion, materially denied the opportunities to develop a form of loyalty for 'controlled consumption', banned from collective formulations of political uses of the street, marginalised groups are expected to express a social sensibility that has been taken away from them. That such groups are automatically assimilated to ideas of chaos and disorder is not surprising, because these ideas provide an explanation of a social issue that would otherwise remain 'unknown'. There is a need to make sense of 'urban disorder' and 'diversity'. Nietzsche (1968) suggests that in turning something that is unknown into something that is known we feel a sense of lightness and power. The unknown is dangerous, disquieting, worrying, and our instinct tends to suppress it: any explanation is better than no explanation. In the past, hostile beings, 'nasty spirits' and hysterical women were mistaken for devils and witches, and yet this infamous mistake brought the pleasure of a spiritual discovery, of truth. Enemies, in other words, were 'spiritualised', so that they could confer legitimacy on inquisitors. The translation of the unknown into the known produces righteousness; stigmatisation provides a rational escape from chaos, while disorder is strongly associated to the presumed indolence characterising groups on the margins.

It is also worth noting some aspects of the relationship between perceptions of disorder and inequality. The idea of urban disorder emerges with the very birth of the urban, and accompanies the whole history of sociological thought. However, the demand for order increases in periods in which the demand for political participation declines, as if by removing the signs of marginalisation the social problems connected to it could be eliminated. In such periods, concerns about disorder find unwitting support in criminological theories, particularly theories hinging on notions of disadvantage. I am thinking of concepts such as 'relative deprivation', according to which many disadvantaged people, when surrounded by the wealth they cannot reach, feel that they have a right to portions of it. Hence their alleged or potential engagement in illicit activity, the official means for achieving wealth being denied to them. It would be worth investigating whether such concepts have by now gained currency even among the police and the judiciary who, predicting that the condition of disadvantage inevitably leads to crime, respectively arrest and convict the marginalised, because sooner or later they will be forced to do so anyway. If this is the case, growing perceptions of disorder or insecurity are the result of parallel perceptions that social injustice is reaching dangerous levels: what is feared is not disorder or crime, but the potential consequences of astonishing increases in inequality.

The function of custodial punishment

Punishing poverty may be a sadistic way of inflicting pain on those already suffering from a painful social condition. This is not, of course, what Wacquant argues, although the function he attributes to the prison system in general remains unclear. He does stress that the punitive turn cannot be simply explained with the shift from a traditional industrial mode of production to a flexible post-Fordist system of work. In his view, there is a specific efficacy in the symbolic power of punishment that purely materialistic analyses may fail to account for. His view that punishment does not perform an economic mission in terms of forging and disciplining sectors of the labour market has already been mentioned. But to sum up his analysis, the penal state is said to perform a number of complementary tasks: warehousing the surplus population, keeping the marginalised in the condition of labouring poor and reassuring the fearful middle classes (De Giorgi, 2010). It may be useful, in this respect, to locate Wacquant's analysis within a framework of 'cultures of punishment' with which sociologists and criminologists are familiar. Les us start with some classics.

By becoming citizens human beings acquire dignity. But there are exceptions: dignity is lost by citizens who commit crime, which makes them mere tools of state choices (Kant, 1996). Crime makes an individual a bondsman, a *servus in sensu stricto*, the property of the state. The penal state, as examined by Wacquant, seems to incorporate this Kantian notion: rulers have the right to punish wrongdoers or, to avoid any equivocation, to 'inflict pain upon them'. Kant does not hide his views behind periphrases, nor does he share the awe with which penal reformers look at the concept of rehabilitation. Punishment means inflicting pain and can never be used as a means to 'promote some other good for the criminal himself or for civil society'. Rehabilitation, instead, implies that a human being is treated 'merely as a means to the purposes of another' (Kant, 1996, p 104). Punishment is the logical consequence of a conduct that the rulers define as crime: it is a categorical imperative. While for Kant we should avoid being infected by pain and leave the sovereign exercise the right to punish, in Hegel it is offenders who have a right to be punished. For Hegel, crime and punishment constitute a single category; wrong in itself carries the presuppositions and the necessity for a moral emendation disguised beyond a legal repressive measure. In sum, Hegel sees wrong and the institutional responses to it as a single whole, as interwoven components of a discrete notion. Against reformers who advocate punishment only if its beneficial effects can be proven, he retorts, first, that punishment need not be useful, and second, that it need not be deterrent, because this would imply that offenders are not free individuals. Deterrence threatens people, be they offenders or otherwise, as if they were dogs, which we menace by raising a stick. Punishment based solely on such a ground is itself a form of wrong, because it does not contain any respectful vision of the people addressed, their rationality and their personality (Hegel, 1952).

It is difficult to determine whether the symbolic function of custody Wacquant attributes to the expanding penal state contains some of these idealistic elements, in other words, whether his analysis is suggesting that contemporary punitiveness marks the return to sacred visions of authority. If this is the case, Wacquant would find also in Durkheim a source of inspiration. Durkheim turns Hegel upside down: it is not the intrinsic nature of an act that produces the ensuing punishment, it is the fact that the act violates a rule. Conducts which cause identical material consequences may be 'blamed or not blamed according to whether or not there is a rule forbidding them' (Durkheim, 1974, p 43). Durkheim accompanies this argument, which contains an *ante litteram* element of labelling theory, with the observation that there is no strong relationship between the harm caused by an act and the intensity of the institutional response to it. For example, in the penal law of most societies, murder is regarded as the greatest of crimes. However, he argues, an economic crisis or stock market crash can disorganise the social body more severely than an isolated homicide. 'No doubt murder is always an evil, but there is no proof that it is the greatest of evils. What is one man less to society? What does one lost cell matter to the organism?' (Durkheim, 1960, p 72). In the elaboration of Wacquant individuals do not have to violate a rule to be punished, unless by rule we mean a conformist lifestyle totally devoted to producing and consuming. Also in Durkheim, however, punishment is not meant to respond to evil, but only to vent our instinct of vengeance on those we regard as morally outrageous: 'Punishment, thus, remains for us what it was for our fathers. It is still an act of vengeance. What we avenge is the outrage to morality' (Durkheim, 1960, pp 86-9). Put differently, we inflict various degrees of suffering and hardship on offenders, not because we may benefit in a material sense from it, but to mark the moral strength of a message we intend to convey (Garland, 1990). Punishment, then, is not for offenders, but is a means for boosting the common moral order, the *conscience collective*. It reassures and regenerates the righteousness of the law-abiding community, while also meting out in legally sanitised fashion our need for revenge (Ruggiero, 2003, 2010b).

All of this may help locate Wacquant's analysis of the symbolic function of punishment, particularly his view that the penal state performs the task of reassuring groups and classes that the moral fabric of society is effectively protected. As for his assertion that punishment does not perform a significant economic mission, some clarification is necessary if we are to fully understand his interpretation. Broadly distinguishing critical approaches to the analysis of punishment, two extreme positions can be observed: the former emphasises the institutional function of imprisonment, while the latter stresses its material function. The first is embedded in the notion of retribution and, in its extreme manifestations, addresses imprisonment as a means for the destruction of bodies. The second looks at prison as a regulatory tool and mainly focuses on the productive use of bodies. Of course, analyses adopting a mixed approach are numerous, but for the sake of clarity here the two positions will be kept theoretically and empirically separate. Founding, celebrated theorists of the respective approaches are Rusche and Kirchheimer (1968) on the one hand, and Michel Foucault (1977) on the other. However, if we are to draw a complete theoretical map, an additional element should be added. Contemporary prison systems, for example, can be identified as a synthesis of the institutional and the material function. Although the former seems to be prevailing, the latter is far from having become redundant. The institutional function is undergoing a technical evolution and manifests itself in the metaphorical annihilation of those prisoners who are deemed impervious to treatment. The material function, in turn, is also undergoing wide modification. We can still employ the term 'material' because it conjures up a notion of productivity, but suggests that it should not be assimilated to the notion of the workhouse nor with that of 'prison as factory' of early capitalism (Melossi and Pavarini, 1977). Prisoners' work and exploitation mainly takes place beyond the prison walls, notably in those social areas where marginalised activities and precarious jobs intermingle with overtly illegal activities. We could term these areas *carceral social zones* to which a variety of forms of control and punishment are addressed, including, when softer forms prove unsuccessful, the threat of physical and mental destruction. In such areas, the general and individual deterrent roles of punishment are not only directed to repeat or unmanageable offenders but also to the excluded populations in general (Ruggiero, 2010b).

Carceral social zones, that elsewhere I have described as *bazaars* (Ruggiero, 2000), host a mixture of official and illegal activities, and witness a constant flow of commodities and service delivery whose nature may be legal or otherwise. In such areas, 'crime as work' means that poorly paid regular work, unregistered jobs, under-employment and criminal activity proper are not part of a definitive occupational choice. In them, people 'commute' from one activity to the other, and in doing so expose themselves to the institutional as well as the material aspect of punishment. To remark that those inhabiting these areas are met with increasingly punitive measures is to provide a partial picture of the relationship between punishment and the material condition of those punished. In other words, the concept of repression is insufficient (Wacquant, 2008a), as it leaves out the 'educational' content of state intervention. If we attempted to apply Rusche and Kirchheimer's model of interpretation to the carceral social zones, enormous problems would arise, in that such zones do not display the conventional traits of labour markets, nor do they show neat distinctions between employment and unemployment. Even if we decided to adopt a 'long cycle' or 'long wave' of, respectively, economic development and incarceration (Melossi, 2003), problems would remain, because in the carceral social zone, unemployment, semi-employment, under-employment and illegal work co-exist, at times in the same person. On the other hand, it has to be stressed that the educational or material function of punishment, in these areas, does not cease to be exercised. The marginalised, the under-employed, the occasional workers, the petty criminals and all the others whose lifestyle and economic activity straddle legality and illegality, are 'trained' to remain and survive in their areas of exclusion, like their counterparts in the past centuries were trained to the discipline of industrialism. Prison discipline aims at lowering their social expectations, an aspect that leads us back to the concept of rehabilitation so spurned by German idealist philosophers. Prisoners are deemed rehabilitated when they accept that they are to remain in that specific sector of the labour force and inhabit the carceral zone assigned to them. This 'criminal' labour force and the adjacent marginalised labour force constitute the repository of the prison population, the human reserve on which custody, with its diverse degrees of harshness and rehabilitative rhetoric, projects its shadow.

The economy of the outcasts

Returning to the continuity between the prison and the ghetto, another contribution by Wacquant deserves to be reviewed. His *Urban outcasts* is a passionate study of ghettos and *banlieues*, of their moral and material economy, and of the relationships between the growth of such enclaves and recent, general, politico-economic developments. Perceived as lawless zones, at times as 'no-go wild districts', such urban areas appear to be characterised, at first sight, by a uniform degree and quality of destitution, violence and despair. Wacquant's (2008b) comparative study of 'advanced marginality' remarks that these territories of deprivation, owing to the halo of danger and dread that enshrouds them, are typically depicted in monochrome tones. His is an attempt to show how urban marginality, instead, takes different forms related to space and state intervention and according to the class characteristics found in specific contexts and epochs. He focuses on the US Black Belt and the French Red Belt (the peripheral working-class areas that were the traditional stronghold of the left). In both places social life may appear equally chaotic and brutish, but only in the former does socio-spatial relegation assume the traits of a hyper-ghetto; nor is it appropriate to regard such a distinct configuration of marginality as the inevitable destiny of European exclusionary areas. The US hyper-ghetto, we are told, is an amalgam of racial discrimination, class inequality and state inaction, where the retrenchment of the welfare state and the shrinking of occupational opportunities are compensated by intensive police activity and the constant threat of the penal apparatus.

The declining urban peripheries of European cities and the African American ghettos could be therefore described as two distinct socio-spatial formations, produced by different institutional logics of segregation. Higher levels of isolation and hardship are found in the US, where exclusion is said to mainly operate on the basis of 'race' and compounded by public neglect. Conversely, marginalisation in European cities is supposed to be arranged around the variable class, but also tempered by state intervention. In brief, while the US hyper-ghetto is depicted as an ethnically and socially homogeneous universe, characterised by extreme levels of physical and social insecurity, European urban peripheries are seen as heterogeneous urban settings where isolation is mitigated by the strong presence of public institutions.

But what is a hyper-ghetto? We may compare it with previous forms of exclusion and marginalisation. The 'communal ghetto', for example, was a 'sharply circumscribed socio-spatial formation' inhabited by black people from all classes, while the hyper-ghetto is a socio-geographical entity segregated on the basis of 'race' and class. The communal ghetto of the immediate post-war years was bounded by a unifying collective consciousness and shared values and aspirations which could be displayed in periodical moments of mobilisation. The distinction between place and space is, in this regard, very useful. While the old ghettos were *places*, therefore fixed and stable social sites, hyper-ghettos are *spaces*, namely areas of potential threat, to be feared or fled. In sum, the new ghetto is *new* because its population suffers from more severe relative deprivation, and because it lacks the organisational infrastructure and the associational networks that gave the ghetto of the 1950s its communal character and strength, making it a place of collective solidarity and potential mobilisation.

Some reference to the work of Lefebvre (1968), again, may be useful here. Collective consciousness, shared values and mobilisation are seen by Lefebvre as expressions of 'love' for the city, whereby groups elaborate a strategy aimed to re-plan the urban environment. Such 'love' coincides with the right to the city, which the authorities slowly reduce to the right to housing. The result is the habitat in its purest form, a habitat burdened with restraints. The notion of *habitat* excludes that of *inhabit*, that is, 'the plasticity of space, its modelling and the appropriation by groups and individuals of the conditions of their existence' (Lefebvre, 1968, p 79). Old ghettos, one may suggest, incorporate the concept of 'the right to urban life', namely the right to use the city as a place of encounter, where the underprivileged 'appear on all the networks and circuits of communication, information and exchange' (Lefebvre, 1968, p 80). However, while Wacquant's distinction between place and space echoes that of Lefebvre between *habitat* and *inhabit*, their explanation of the shift from the former to the latter appears to be completely opposite. In Lefebvre, such a shift results from local and national institutions responding to contestation and demands by entering the ghetto, whereas in Wacquant, it is caused by authorities abandoning it. In this way, the old ghetto, characterised by shared emotions, joint meanings and institutions of mutuality, is turned into an hyper-ghetto, characterised by mere survival.

> In the final analysis, however, it is the collapse of public institutions, resulting from state policies of urban abandonment and leading to the punitive containment of

the black sub-proletariat, that emerges as the most potent and most distinctive cause of entrenched marginality in the American metropolis. (Wacquant, 2008b, p 4)

Here, it is worth highlighting a controversial issue revolving around two contrasting ways of analysing the role of institutional agencies. On the one hand, we have a view of agencies as organisms that distil, select, distort demands, and offer surrogate 'social goods' to those requesting genuine ones (Lefebvre). On the other hand, we have views of agencies as authorities practising social absenteeism, thus totally ignoring demands.

A functioning disorganisation

From Wacquant's description it is not easy to evince whether between urban outcasts and the official society there is any meaningful relationship, or to put it in different terms, whether the values adopted by excluded groups and those embraced by dominant ones are totally extraneous to one another. It is my contention that there is an ambivalent and contradictory nature in excluded and ostracised communities. The separation of the ghetto from official society is only apparent, and there are strong ties uniting the two in a number of ways. One such tie, for example, pertains to the structural transformation of the ghetto and the changes taking place in the economy. While the ghetto, therefore, may be 'an institutional form, that is, a distinctive, spatially based, concatenation of mechanisms of ethno-racial closure and control', it is also a territory providing 'a protective buffer against the dominant institutions of the encompassing society' (Wacquant, 2008b, p 49). This formulation mainly revolves around the variables of isolation, exclusion and protective withdrawal from institutional control. In other elaborations, however, other variables could be introduced that transcend the sheer relationship between controllers and controlled.

Ghettos perform specific functions within the broader metropolitan system. Some districts may be repositories of the contemporary version of 19th-century rabble, the hordes of 'unproductive thugs' who will not and cannot be turned into labourers. Others may be containers of despicable groups segregated less for their lack of productive capacity than for the hatred their 'race' elicits. Finally, some districts may act as reservoirs of low-skill labour force. Note the ambivalence: ghettos are inhabited by disposable but usable people, rabble and labour at the same time. In my view, at this point our analysis requires more robust elaboration. It is true that the variable disorganisation has guided mainstream research on marginalisation since the early works of the Chicago School, but it is also true the Chicago sociologists themselves were very ambivalent about the concept of disorganisation. Their participant observation proved that 'disorganised' areas were very well organised indeed, based as they were on unwritten codes of conduct guiding their material and moral interactions. Similarly, one may remark that the contemporary ghetto does not suffer from social disorganisation, but is organised differently. In some studies conducted by the Chicago sociologists, it is not the sense of isolation and exclusion that the areas studied convey, but rather the opposite: in such areas the licit and the illicit intermingle, both in the economic arena and in the political sphere. Think of Landesco's (1973 [1929]) study of organised crime in Chicago, where gangsters have long-standing relations with community leaders in athletic clubs, business, the church and politics. Successful inhabitants of the ghetto develop ties of mutual interest with the police, politicians and customers for the goods and services they supply. Even their violence is the result of such ties, because it is used during electoral campaigns and functions as a clandestine, supplementary tool deployed by official political parties. The ghetto, therefore, is the strong arm of the political apparatus: institutional violence accompanying political campaigning is 'contracted out' to organised criminal groups residing in the ghetto.

Returning to the question of 'ambivalence', some Chicago scholars failed to consider the mixture of legality and illegality within urban territories, treating city areas as both morally and physically isolated. Such areas appeared to possess some sort of imaginary perimeters isolating delinquents and their delinquency. Other Chicago students of marginalised areas, instead, described the activities conducted in such areas as incorporating sections of both the official and the hidden labour market. Similarly, some contemporary researchers focus on the constant movement of individuals who simultaneously inhabit licit and illicit markets and find in both opportunities and income (Pearson and Hobbs, 2001; Friman, 2004). I have already mentioned the notion of *urban bazaars*, constituted by a network of retailers, ambulatory vendors, distributors, wholesalers, seasonal workers, casual assistants and apprentices, who are all required to possess flexibility and versatile skills. Such bazaars also act as informal employment agencies, where people hear of potential job opportunities and emerging economic sectors, be they legitimate or otherwise. In brief, the metaphor of the bazaar intends to convey an image of city areas as a marketplace, a notion of urban economic activity servicing a diffuse general store, where licit consumables, regular pleasures and illegitimate services are made available within the same context (Ruggiero, 2000).

The contemporary hyper-ghetto described by Wacquant seems more immobile: those who dwell in it may not be part of a separate group closed in itself, as the author explains; nevertheless they do not 'commute', as in many other marginalised urban areas, between legality and illegality – they just belong 'to unskilled and socially disqualified fractions of the black working class, by virtue of their unstable position at the margins of the wage-labour sphere' (Wacquant, 2008b, p 51). Again, note the ambivalence: the hyper-ghetto appears to be a fixed social aggregation, a homogeneous marginal settlement, spatially isolated and morally distinctive, but at the same time, those who dwell in it do not form a separate group.

There is an important issue in recent studies of 'urban outcasts' which begs further consideration, namely, the hypothesis of a double polarisation, from above and from below. Polarisation from above connotes the studies of the global, dual city, epitomised by the work of Sassen (1991) and Castells (1998), where technological development and advanced forms of production coexist with intensive, unskilled, low-paid work. We may hypothesise that the development of this dual socioeconomic model is not only accompanied by 'unification at the top', that is, the establishment of a transnational elite, but also by fragmentation at the bottom, what we may term 'polarisation from below'. I would interpret this type of fragmentation and polarisation as a process creating obsessive individualism, harsh competitiveness and, crucially, social and occupational barriers within the ghetto itself. Returning to the metaphor the urban bazaar, I would suggest that polarisation from below determines unequal roles and careers, so that even in marginalised or illicit economies a principal-agent model prevails. In the ghetto bazaar the principal commands a number of agents to take actions on his/her behalf in exchange for monetary reward. Fragmentation, therefore, manifests itself in the form of exploitation and inequality, in a marginal economy which reproduces some of the worst aspects of the official economy. Hence the plausible remark that there is a 'scandalous' similarity between deviance and conformity: one of the problems with illegal economies is that in so many ways they are, sadly, paradoxical reflections of legal ones.

Self-victimisation

Violence is one of the most vivid expressions of this conformity, and establishes barriers and hierarchies within the ghetto itself. Wacquant

(2008b, p 128) describes a climate of 'perpetual latent mini-guerrilla of the dispossessed among themselves', within a context in which criminality in general is inward-turning and self-destructive. Physical danger and insecurity pervade the hyper-ghetto, but far from being specific pathologies of its inhabitants, they are engendered by the 'penetration and mode of regulation of this territory by the state' (Wacquant, 2008b, p 54). Internecine violence is analysed as a response to various kinds of institutional violence, composed of three elements: mass unemployment, relegation in decaying neighbourhoods and stigmatisation for residing in such neighbourhoods.

> Youngsters raised in this environment of pandemic violence
> suffer serious emotional damage and display post-traumatic
> stress disorders similar to those endured by veterans.
> (Wacquant, 2008b, p 56)

There is, however, another aspect to this violence, which is responsive to, as well as a mimic of, the institutional violence suffered. It is a type of violence learned from the official agents who monopolise the use of force, but also an expression of failure, a devastating mark of impotence. In my view, the analysis of violence cannot be extrapolated from the general context in which 'violence as a resource' is distributed within a society. Violence producing benefits for perpetrators is normally less visible than violence harming perpetrators. In other words, the costs of violence in marginalised communities are much higher than elsewhere, and while replicating the brutality of law enforcers and other specialists of aggression (the army), violent inhabitants of the ghetto are constantly compelled to increase the use of force as a consequence of the meagre results this produces for them. It is indeed self-destructive, but it is also consistent with specific forms of law enforcement and criminal justice practices: if crime cannot be reduced, let us at least make sure that the perpetrator and the victim are one and the same. This type of self-victimisation is legible in the end result of the violent choice in marginalised settings, where violence or threat of violence may temporarily be used as a resource for discouraging competitors and establishing territorial and market control, but inevitably leads to 'early retirement' from crime in the form of imprisonment. We have returned to the notion of the *carceral social zone*, namely, an area where the violence suffered and inflicted mimics and anticipates the quintessential institutional violence of custody. It is true that young people brought up in such a *carceral zone* may develop post-traumatic stress disorders, but it is also true that all the inhabitants of the ghetto, due to the dire social conditions experienced, will learn to substantially lower their expectations. The ghetto, therefore, educates its dwellers to devalue themselves and reduce their demands, so that those fortunate enough to be employable will accept any job, at any condition. Those who find work will have assimilated the principles of insecurity and internalised their expendability and low monetary value on the labour market, while those unemployable will find even in prison a less violent environment than the one to which they are inured.

Collective action

It is not surprising that the youth inhabiting excluded communities and ghettos regard the police as an occupying, extraneous, military force. An intimidating presence in French working-class *banlieues*, the police are the main targets of street collective violence. This is also the case elsewhere:

> In the desolate districts of the LA ghetto, the forces of order act as if they were waging a trench war with the residents, treating them as an army of occupation would its enemies. (Wacquant, 2008b, p 32)

Violent responses to such military occupation seem, therefore, triggered by what Wacquant terms 'ethno-racial injustice rooted in discriminatory treatment' (2008b, p 33). Collective violence and riots, we are told, also possess a class logic and manifest a will to rebel against widening inequality and deprivation. Direct confrontation with the agents of order, lacking other tools and resources, becomes the only available form of contestation. Likened to a distorted expression of a *lumpen* protest, collective street violence is seen as a response to the unprecedented violence inflicted on marginal communities by 'the impersonal machineries of the neoliberal state and the deregulated market'.

This analysis echoes similar interpretations proposed by conflict theorists in sociology, according to whom violent outbursts are nothing but reactive rebellions staged by those constantly victimised by law enforcers: in brief, pure responses to police harassment and violence. Representatives of this school of thought, during the 1960s, coined the phrase 'police riots' to designate urban violent clashes provoked and initiated by the police themselves, who forced youths to use violence in their turn as a form of self-defence (Quinney, 1970, 1971). The first problem with this interpretation is that it depicts street violence by marginalised groups as pre-political conduct, implying that missionaries, vanguards and radical sociologists should unite their efforts to try and politicise that conduct. This subtly patronising (or paternalistic) logic, in the past, has shown that the only forms of violence with which conflict theorists are analytically comfortable are those embryonic forms of social dissent, or even those unconscious elements of contention that one could read in conventional criminal acts. In this case, at least, radical sociologists can fulfil their mandate by unveiling the 'conscious' meaning behind such acts. Their role, instead, tends to wither away when consciously organised conducts prove that, at times, actors have nothing to learn from those interpreting them. In short, radical sociologists are at ease when analysing endemic violence caused by structural inequality, institutional racism or criminalisation processes, namely, a type of violence that they would like to marshal in a political project. They become uneasy when actors, through their organised violence, delineate their political project (Ruggiero, 2006). The second problem with this approach is that it neglects the seductive nature of some forms of collective violence, the thrill and the fun that recent analyses recognise in a variety of transgressive and deviant acts (Katz, 1988; Presdee, 2000; Hayward, 2004; Young, 2007).

But does collective action by marginalised groups engender new meanings that open up a possible space for collective demands? One may suggest that contemporary exclusion (or 'advanced marginality') differs from previous forms of urban poverty, in that it reflects a broader context of class decomposition rather than class consolidation. In such context unification and homogenisation among marginalised subjects is extremely problematic, also because subjects do not hold a clear memory of past mobilisation, and nor are they familiar with the organisational tools necessary for the expression of demands. They are 'deprived of a language, a repertoire of shared images and signs through which to conceive a collective destiny and to project possible alternative futures' (Wacquant, 2008b, p 245).

This is a crucial point that echoes classical questions posed by collective action theorists. Assuming that conflicting interests are a permanent trait of social settings, why do these turn into collective action in some contexts and not in others? Behind this question lies a fundamental sociological dilemma: do groups always act in their common self-interest? Self-interested behaviour is deemed the rule, at least when material goods are at stake, and particularly if rational calculus is thought to lead choices. According to Olson (1966), unless some types of devices are used, rational self-interested individuals and groups will not act to achieve their common interests. Action is, therefore, potential, and group-oriented behaviour is latent, until separate and selective incentives will stimulate collective action and help formulate demands. In this perspective, groups do not, spontaneously and rationally, pursue their collective goals; rather, they rationally choose to 'free ride', namely, to enjoy the benefits of collective action while abstaining from participating in it. Many groups, like, for instance, consumers or migrant workers, are not organised, while others, like, for example, unionised labourers and farmers, rely on some degree of organisation. To put it a different way, collective action is not just the result of frustration and discontent, but predominantly of strength and capacity to mobilise. Groups need 'resources', that is, anything from material things such as income, savings, concrete goods and services, to non-material items such as authority, collective memory, an established repertoire of action, a symbolic patrimony, moral commitment, trust, skills or camaraderie (Ruggiero and Montagna, 2008). It is true that the hyper-ghetto is a 'composite conglomerate, made up of heterogeneous individuals and categories negatively defined by social privation, material need and symbolic deficit'. And that 'only an immense, specifically political work of aggregation and re-presentation can hope to enable this conglomerate to accede to collective existence and thus to collective action' (Ruggiero and Montagna, 2008, pp 246-7). However, if we accept that mobilisation is a process by which an aggrieved group marshals and utilises resources for the pursuit of its specific set of goals, we may well define the hyper-ghetto as a social formation which, having been denied resources (and even when producing violent outbursts), is incapacitated in producing collective mobilisation. Hyper-ghettos are such because, by definition, they cannot produce collective action. If this is a central characteristic of contemporary ghettos, the work required to fight against them is immense. Those who do not share Wacquant's pessimism, however, have another option: to re-orient their work towards the concept of social change.

Many criminologists and sociologists, by excluding possibilities for social change, end up describing society as static and social acts as facts speaking for themselves. In doing so, they omit to consider how their own emotional, cultural and political commitments create a framework in which those facts are given meaning. Scholars who re-orient their research towards social change, on the contrary, bring their subjectivity to bear on their objects of study. Examples of this re-orientation are studies of collective action carried out by victims of violence, rather than studies of violent behaviour; of initiatives set up by illicit drugs users, rather than of institutional initiatives addressed by other to them; studies of campaigns against corporate misconduct, rather than analysis of that conduct; and finally, studies of movements against the crimes of the powerful, including conventional forms of organised crime, rather than studies of those crimes (Santino, 2000). In the urban context, examples include the study of collective contentious action for the re-appropriation of space and mobility in Los Angeles (Soja, 2010), of how ordinary Americans subvert an unfair economy (Dodson, 2009), or of how citizens 'implement their values and alternatives in their experience of daily life, in local communities and in the networks and organisations of the movement' (Dodson, 2009, p 208). Finally, there are studies of the 'creation of autonomous spaces where [people] experiment with horizontal networks, alternative consumption and participatory processes' (Pleyers, 2010, p 12). This process of refocusing would fight what Pareto (1980) described as the 'instinct for the persistence of aggregates', whereby individuals, and for that matter academic disciplines, are inclined to maintain established structures of ideas and action, to continue with familiar routines. It is how we cope with the inherent unpredictability of life. Our instinct is to make the world seem familiar and therefore more manageable. Sociologically, this instinct is the basis of cultures and tradition, of social control and social order (Noble, 2000, p 110).

If we accept that by studying one phenomenon we contribute to its evolution, or even to its creation, subjective choice of the issues studied becomes paramount. Values and subjective beliefs shape reality as well as human action attempting to change it. Acknowledging the centrality of subjectivity may lead to the recognition that what is real is the mind's way of interpreting and responding to the flux of appearances. This is the conclusion reached, among others, by some historians, who claim that there is no contradiction, in their work, between the search for evidence and the use of rhetoric. Sources, in their view, are neither wide-open windows, like realists and positivists believe, nor walls blocking the gaze; rather, they are very much like deforming glasses. 'The use of desire, without which any research is impossible, is not incompatible with the refutations inflicted by the principle of reality' (Ginzburg, 2000, p 49). Similarly, sociologists may start identifying dynamics and conflicts, rather than static situations, and contribute to create the conditions for solutions and change. The subjective choice of a sociological paradigm revolving around social change may be deleterious for academic careers in the field of criminology and sociology, but may generate a perception that such change is possible and necessary.

References

Benjamin, W. (1999) *The Arcades Project*, Cambridge, MA: Harvard University Press.

Castells, M. (1998) *The age of information*, Oxford: Blackwell.

De Giorgi, A. (2010) 'Review symposium: *Punishing the poor*', *British Journal of Criminology*, vol 50, pp 596-99.

Dodson, L. (2009) *The moral underground: How ordinary Americans subvert an unfair economy*, New York: The New Press.

Durkheim, E. (1960) *The division of labour in society*, Glencoe, IL: The Free Press.

Durkheim, E. (1974) *Sociology and philosophy*, New York: The New Press.

Foucault, M. (1977) *Discipline and punish*, London: Allen Lane.

Friman, H.R. (2004) 'The great escape? Globalisation, immigrant entrepreneurship and the criminal economy', *Review of International Political Economy*, vol 11, pp 98-131.

Gaeta, G. (2008) *Le cose come sono. Etica, politica, religione*, Milan: Scheiwiller.

Garland, D. (1990) *Punishment and modern society: A study in social theory*, Oxford: Clarendon Press.

Ginzburg, C. (2000) *Rapporti di forza. Storia, retorica, prova*, Milan: Feltrinelli.

Hayward, K.J. (2004) *City limits: Crime, consumer culture and the urban experience*, London: Glasshouse Press.

Hegel, F. (1952) *Philosophy of right*, Oxford: Clarendon Press.

Kant, I. (1996) *The metaphysics of morals*, Cambridge: Cambridge University Press.

Katz, J. (1988) *The seductions of crime: Moral and sensual attractions in doing evil*, New York: Basic Books.

Landesco, J. (1973 [1929]) *Organized crime in Chicago: Part III of the Illinois Crime Survey*, Chicago, IL: University of Chicago Press.

Lefebvre, H. (1968) *Le droit à la ville*, Paris: Anthropos.

Lefebvre, H. (2003) *The urban revolution*, Minneapolis, MN: University of Minnesota Press.

Melossi, D. (2003) 'Introduction to the Transaction edition: the simple "heuristic maxim" of an "unusual" human being', in G. Rusche and O. Kirchheimer, *Punishment and social structure*, Piscataway, NJ: Transaction.

Melossi, D. and Pavarini, M. (1977) *Carcere e fabbrica. Alle origini del sistema penitenziario*, Bologna: Il Mulino. ([1981] *The prison and the factory*, London: Macmillan).

Nietzsche, F. (1968) *Twilight of the idols and the Anti-Christ*, Harmondsworth: Penguin.

Noble, T. (2000) *Social theory and social change*, London: Macmillan.

Olson, M. (1966) *The logic of collective action*, Cambridge: Harvard University Press.

Pareto, V. (1980) *Compendium of general sociology*, Minneapolis, MN: University of Minnesota Press.

Pearson, G. and Hobbs, D. (2001) *Middle market drug distribution*, London: The Stationery Office.

Pleyers, G. (2010) *Alter-globalization: Becoming actors in the global age*, Cambridge: Polity Press.

Presdee, M. (2000) *Cultural criminology and the carnival of crime*, London: Routledge.

Quinney, R. (1970) *The social reality of crime*, Boston, MA: Brown & Co.

Quinney, R. (1971) *The problem of crime*, New York: Dodd, Mead & Co.

Ruggiero, V. (2000) *Crime and markets: Essays in anti-criminology*, Oxford: Oxford University Press.

Ruggiero, V. (2003) *Crime in literature: Sociology of deviance and fiction*, London: Verso.

Ruggiero, V. (2006) *Understanding political violence*, London: Open University Press.

Ruggiero, V. (2010a) 'Social disorder and the criminalization of indolence', *CITY: Analysis of Urban Trends, Culture, Theory, Policy, Action*, vol 14, no 1-2, pp 164-9.

Ruggiero, V. (2010b) *Penal abolitionism*, Oxford: Oxford University Press.

Ruggiero, V. and Montagna, N. (eds) (2008) *Social movements: A reader*, London: Routledge.

Rusche, G. and Kirchheimer, O. (1968) *Punishment and social structure*, New York: Russell & Russell.

Sampson, R.J. (2009) 'Disparity and diversity in the contemporary city: social (dis)order revisited', *British Journal of Sociology*, vol 60, pp 1-32.

Santino, U. (2000) *Storia del movimento antimafia*, Rome: Editori Riuniti.

Sassen, S. (1991) *The global city*, New York, London, Tokyo, Princeton, NJ: Princeton University Press.

Shirlow, P. and Pain, R. (2003) 'The geographies and politics of fear', *Capital & Class*, vol 80, pp 15-26.

Soja, E. (2010) *Seeking spatial justice*, Minneapolis, MN: University of Minnesota Press.

Wacquant, L. (2001) 'Deadly symbiosis: when ghetto and prison meet and mesh', *Punishment & Society*, vol 3, pp 95-133.

Wacquant, L. (2008a) 'Ordering insecurity: social polarization and the punitive upsurge', *Radical Philosophy Review*, vol 11, pp 9-27.

Wacquant, L. (2008b) *Urban outcasts: A comparative sociology of advanced marginality*, Cambridge: Polity Press.

Wacquant, L. (2009) *Punishing the poor: The neoliberal government of social insecurity*, Durham, NC: Duke University Press.

Young, J. (2007) *The vertigo of late modernity*, London: Sage Publications.

TEN

The universal and the particular in Latin American penal state formation

Markus-Michael Müller

It took me some time to understand what the book was about. The pages were divided into columns that contained dates and names and descriptions. When he sensed that I was having difficulty, the corporal explained that this list was a list of the cells currently for sale that I could choose from. Still not believing that any of this was real, I asked the major how much a cell cost, using one of my few Spanish expressions:

"¿Cuánto cuesta?"

"Cinco mil," he responded. I thought that I knew the numbers, but I must have misheard. Five thousand was too much. I asked the translator to repeat the amount in English. He confirmed that it was five thousand.

"Dollars or bolivianos?"

"Dollars, my amigo," he said. "Cell prices in San Pedro are always in American Dollars." (quoted in Young and McFadden, 2004, p 54)

This is taken from the autobiographic account of Thomas McFadden, a British national who spent nearly five years in the San Pedro Prison in La Paz, Bolivia, for drug smuggling. With the help of another inmate, McFadden was able to set up a contract to purchase a prison cell from a Bolivian prisoner and to take over the cell for US$1,200, an amount that also included the former owner's television, refrigerator and some of the furniture he had brought into the prison (Young and McFadden, 2004, pp 107–8).

In a paradigmatic way, this episode illustrates one of many aspects of the reality of the contemporary Latin American prison system that is difficult to imagine for outside observers and analysts, but which an increasing number of people throughout the region are confronted with in their daily lives – most of all those belonging to the marginalised segments of Latin America's urban population. In fact, throughout the last two decades or so, the formation of what Loïc Wacquant described in great detail for the US and the countries of Western Europe as the emergence of a 'neoliberal Leviathan' in the guise of a 'penal state', that resorts to '*punitive containment as a government technique* for managing deepening urban marginality' (Wacquant, 2010a, p 204; emphasis in original), can also be identified for Latin America (Müller, 2012). In most countries of the region, the '"the Left Hand" of the state, that which protects and expands life chances' is dismantled and downsized, while the state's '"Right Hand," that of the police, justice, correctional administration, [is] increasingly active and intrusive in the subaltern zones of social and urban space' (Wacquant, 2009, p 6). And as elsewhere, in Latin America, part and parcel of this shift is a growing 'penalisation of poverty' (Wacquant, 2001, p 401). The latter predominantly targets the 'urban outcasts', who, as well as the urban spaces in which they live and work, are increasingly portrayed in public, political and media discourses as 'emblematic incarnations of "urban danger"' … in the sense of social decay and physical insecurity as well as in the more politically charged sense that they threaten to unravel the fabric of urban society *in toto*' (Wacquant, 2008a, p 203).

However, a closer look at the socio-political environment in which Latin American penal state formation is embedded reveals important local legacies and characteristics that differ with regards to the related experience in the global north. As Wacquant (2003, 2008b), reflecting on the case of Brazil, has pointed out, the local experience of penal state formation is decisively shaped by core features of the local context, most of all the country's subordinate position within the global economy and high levels of socioeconomic polarisation, the extremely violent nature of Brazilian policing, and the deeply embedded institutional racism of the Brazilian justice system. In such a context, Wacquant has argued, the emergence of penal state-craft 'amounts to (re-)establishing a *veritable dictatorship over the poor*' (Wacquant, 2003, p 200; emphasis in original).

Another yet largely neglected aspect of the Latin American penal state brings us back to the situation described in the cell purchase episode above: the informal dimension of the 'penalisation of poverty' in contemporary Latin America. It is this aspect that is the central focus of the present chapter. It argues that a distinctive feature of the Latin American version of penal state-craft lies in the fact that it operates in a political and institutional environment marked by the centrality of informal practices. This situation permanently exposes the objects of the neoliberal 'penalisation of poverty' to illegal, arbitrary, abusive and violent – if not lethal – practices of an expanding penal apparatus. However, this apparatus does not only consist of actors and institutions operating within the formal-institutional boundaries of the penal state (the police, courts, prisons). Being another important aspect of the Latin American penal state, its penal apparatus also incorporates a variety of actors operating beyond the formal bureaucratic field – vigilante groups, death squads, militias – into its workings of power. This incorporation further reinforces and exacerbates the exclusionary tendencies of the formal dimension of the 'penalisation of poverty'.

In order to develop this argument, this chapter is divided into two parts. It first analyses the political context that was decisive for the emergence of Latin American penal state-craft since the 1990s. After this contextualisation, the second part turns to the informal dimension of the Latin American penal state. By focusing on informal practices inside the different parts of the Latin American penal apparatus – the legal system, the police, jails and prisons – it indicates how these informal aspects further contribute to the exclusionary and polarising tendencies of the 'penalisation of poverty'. The conclusion summarises the main findings.

The crafting of Latin America's neoliberal Leviathan[1]

The unfolding of the Latin American penal state is inseparable from the mutually enforcing intersection of the following factors: (i) the 'urbanization of neoliberalism' (Brenner and Theodore, 2002), (ii) the 'metropolization of crime' (Castillo, 2008, p 181) and the related predominance of crime and (in)security issues on the local political and electoral agenda, as well as (iii) the local repercussions of the 'war on drugs'.

Penalising urban politics in Latin America

When considering the question of penal state-craft in Latin America, it should be recalled that the region was at the forefront of what can be called primitive neoliberal state formation in the early 1970s. In fact, Pinochet's coup, in 1973, against the leftist government of

Salvador Allende, was 'the first great experiment with neoliberal state formation' (Harvey, 2006, p 12). The economic reform policies prescribed by Pinochet's 'Chicago boys', favouring free market-based export-orientated economic growth strategies and a 'lean' state, were soon to be replicated throughout the region. This contributed to the dismantling of corporatist state structures, the opening of national economies and the privatisation of state enterprises and services in most Latin American countries (Boron, 2006). The urban repercussions of these processes led to the dominance of neoliberal urban development projects that adhere to the ideal of an internationally competitive 'free market city' (Portes and Roberts, 2005; Rojas et al, 2008).

For cities like Buenos Aires, Guayaquil, Mexico City, Quito or Rio de Janeiro, for example, following this, free market ideal means becoming an 'entrepreneurial city' (Harvey, 1989). A key ingredient of urban governance in the 'entrepreneurial city' is economic growth strategies that focus on urban renaissance projects to recuperate public spaces in the historic city centres and/or other urban areas, considered to be of economic interest – most of all, for so-called 'heritage tourism' and real estate development projects. This process is accompanied by the development of a variety of '[urban] crime prevention projects which are not necessarily directed at "crime" in the legal sense of the word' (van Swaaningen, 1997, p 196). Rather, their main objective is the criminalisation of certain behaviours typically associated with marginalised sectors of urban society, whose number increased significantly as a consequence of the social dislocations that accompanied the rise of neoliberalism in Latin America and which are most visible in the informalisation of local urban economies (Portes and Hoffman, 2003; Koonings and Kruijt, 2007). Within the context of 'urban renaissance', large parts of the economic and political elites perceived the presence of these 'undesired' people as a problem of 'urban (dis)order' and 'criminality'.

The criminalisation of the 'undesirables' in the 'core' areas of Latin American cities is accompanied by similar practices at the urban peripheries, where many marginal neighbourhoods are located. The latter are perceived by the well-to-do and city authorities 'as dirty and unhealthy places, dangerous, disorganized, and threatening to the established order of the greater urban area.... Residence in such a place, regardless of one's occupation or social standing, is sufficient to label one a criminal' (Goldstein, 2004, p 12).

This context confronts urban governments with the dual task of 'sanitizing the streets [in those urban spaces relevant for economic capital investment] of urban undesirables, many of whom are of indigenous descent' (Swanson, 2010, p 92) and that of exercising socio-spatial control over the 'dangerous', 'disorganized', 'unhealthy' and 'criminal' urban peripheries. Successfully fulfilling both tasks requires the deployment of the neoliberal state's capacity to function as an efficient 'street cleansing agency' (Wacquant, 2008c, p 202). And the most preferred 'detergent' for such street cleansing activities has been the import of 'zero tolerance' policing in countries throughout the region (Dammert and Malone, 2006; Davis, 2007; Swanson, 2007; Gutiérrez Rivera, 2010).

These policing models, advertised in the language of 'quality of life policing', promise the 'recuperation of public spaces' from the urban 'undesirables' as well as the control of more peripheral urban 'threats', like urban gangs roaming marginalised urban communities. The latter are most heavily targeted by such new policing practices in Central America. Here 'zero tolerance' policing merged with the local 'wars on gangs', leading to the enacting of overly repressive anti-gang legislation and militarised policing of marginalised urban communities in the urban peripheries:

> The opening salvo of this campaign was El Salvador's adoption of *mano dura* ('iron fist') policy, promulgated by the Salvadoran President Ricardo Maduro in July 2003, which advocated the immediate imprisonment of a gang member simply for having gang-related tattoos or flashing gang-signs in public, something that became punishable with two to five years in jail and applicable to gang members from the age of twelve and upwards.... Honduras implemented a comparable policy called *cero tolerancia* ('zero tolerance') almost simultaneously in August 2003, which was also inspired by Rudy Giuliani's (in)famous eponymous policy in New York. Among the measures that this package adopted was the reform of the penal code and the adaptation of legislation that established a maximum twelve-year prison sentence for gang membership, a penalty which was later stiffened to thirty years, as well as provisions for better collaboration between the police and the Honduran army in urban patrolling. Guatemala, likewise adopted its *Plan Escoba* ('Operation Broomsweep') in January 2004, which although not as draconian as the Salvadoran *mano dura* and the Honduran *cero tolerancia* still contained new provisions allowing minors to be treated as adults, and the deployment

of 4,000 reserve troops in troubled neighborhoods in Guatemala City. (Rodgers, 2009, p 967)

Whereas these examples are indicative of the new role of punitive policing and the exercise of political control over the 'criminal other' in Latin America's urban peripheries, the case of Rio de Janeiro illustrates the other end of the 'zero tolerance' policing spectrum, embedded in the local government's adaptation of 'free market city' politics. Here, as in Central America, local police forces temporarily occupy marginalised neighbourhoods (*favelas*) in so-called 'blitzes', presented to the local public as 'zero tolerance' policing (Koonings and Veenstra, 2007). Many of these operations are related to Rio's entrepreneurial urban development strategy that focuses on attracting tourism, international summits and sport events, as these policing efforts aim at pre-empting potential incidents that could damage the city image during important events such as the local carnival or international summits (Wacquant, 2008b, p 60). These 'media-friendly "quality of life" mobilizations and public-morality "blitzes"' (Amar, 2009, p 518) are accompanied by a high level of police violence, leading to the fact that the 'democratic Brazilian state has killed more people in its recent "urban security operations" than any war in Latin America since the 19th century' (Amar, 2009, p 515).

Insecurity and penal populism

Another important factor behind the growing importance of punitive urban policing in Latin America resides in the real and perceived rise of urban crime and insecurity during the last two decades (Caldeira, 2000; Rotker, 2002; Koonings and Kruijt, 2007; Arias and Goldstein, 2010). As, according to local opinions polls, questions of urban crime and insecurity rank among local residents' top priorities, the import of 'zero tolerance' policing also responds to pressure from the local electorate for local governments to confront urban insecurity. These pressures are reinforced by powerful civil society organisations, capable of mobilising hundreds of thousands of people in countries such as Mexico or Argentina under the banner of more security and harsher punishment of criminals, as well as by the influence exercised by 'pro-order coalitions' (Fuentes, 2005). These networks of conservative politicians, civil society groups and state agents, want to provide the police forces with wide-ranging legal tools for enhancing their order-maintenance and crime-fighting capacities. Therefore, 'pro-order coalitions' argue that the rights of citizens 'should be circumstantial and that authorities must restrict citizens' rights and widen police powers to maintain social peace' (Fuentes, 2005, p 42). In response to these pressures, politicians and governments throughout the region resorted to penal populism which has become a core ingredient of Latin America's electoral landscape (Chevigny, 2003; Arteaga Botello, 2004; Sozzo, 2007; Dammert and Salazar, 2009).

Although penal populism's rhetoric seems to '"run against the state", complaining that the judges, the executive, and the laws themselves are too weak in the face of crime' (Chevigny, 2003, p 79), it ultimately tends to reinforce and 'underline the authority of the state on the symbolic level (with a view toward electoral dividends)' (Wacquant, 2009, p 9). This happens at a time where Latin America's neoliberalised states and their governments 'cannot promise a large number of jobs or other relief measures to their constituents' (Chevigny, 2003, p 83). What this symbolic reinforcement of state authority offers in such a context is 'one of the foundational myths of modern societies: the myth that the sovereign state is capable of delivering "law and order" and controlling crime' (Garland, 2001, p 109). This promise is framed in the antagonising and criminalising language of penal populism, 'which poses clearcut distinctions between that which belongs and that which does not. The basis for its distinction is the opposition of evil and good; clearly, crime and the criminal are on the side of evil' (Caldeira, 2000, p 77). Thereby, penal populism denies the active complicity of Latin American states in creating the structural conditions on which violence and insecurity emerge. Moreover, as this promise operates on the basis of an exclusionary discourse, by evoking dichotomies of 'good' and 'evil', it re-frames the problem of insecurity and violence in socio-spatial terms, thereby giving them a classificatory, differentiating and exclusionary character.

However, as the populist 'law and order' commitment needs a material underpinning to be effective, it also contributes to a material reinforcement of the Latin American penal apparatus. One important element of this reinforcement consists in a growing law-making activity throughout the region, leading to a toughening of existing legislation, the lengthening of sentences as well as the enacting of new laws and the creation of other legal instruments. Most of these legal activities are targeting socioeconomic practices, in general associated with the marginalised segments of the urban population, including product piracy, informal parking attendance, street vending or, in some Central American countries, having a tattoo (Dammert and Zúñiga, 2008). In this regard, Latin American penal populism has become a decisive factor behind the growth of the local prison population throughout the last two decades (Dammert and Salazar, 2009; Müller, 2012).

When taking data provided by the World Prison Briefing[2] as a base to quantify the growth of the Latin American prison population, the following picture emerges: in Mexico, the number of inmates rose from 85,712 (1992) to 212,841 (2007). During the same period, Guatemala's prison population grew from 5,592 to 7,143, while Honduras witnessed a growth of its prison population from 5,717 (1992) to 10,809 (2007). El Salvador's inmate population nearly tripled during these 15 years, from 5,348 (1992) to 16,786 (2007), and the number of people locked up in prisons in Costa Rica more than doubled, rising from 3,346 (1992) to 8,246 (2007). Quite a similar scenario can be found in the Andean countries. Colombia's prison population rose from 27,316 (1992) to 63,603 (2007), while the number in Ecuador more than doubled, from 7,998 (1992) to 18,218 (2007). Peru's prison population increased from 15,718 (1992) to 39,684 (2007), and Bolivia's number of inmates rose from 5,412 (1996) to 7,683 (2007). In Chile the number of inmates increased from 20,989 (1992) to 46,825 (2007). Moving on to Brazil and the countries of the Southern Cone, a nearly fourfold growth of the Brazilian prison population has been documented, rising from 114,337 (1992) to 422,590 (2007). In Paraguay, the number of inmates doubled from 2,972 (1995) to 6,037 (2006), as did the prison population in Uruguay, growing from 3,037 (1992) to 7,076 (2007). Similarly, Argentina's prison population rose from 21,016 (1992) to 60,621 (2006). The only Latin American country not to follow this general trend of growing prison populations has been Venezuela, where, according to available data, the number of inmates slightly declined, from 23,200 (1993) to 19,853 (2005).

When considering the 'triple selectivity' of the incarceration pattern in Latin America, which is marked by a 'triple selective' pattern of incarceration that proceeds 'along steep gradients of class, race, and space' (Wacquant, 2010b, p 85), it is hardly surprising that prisons in general host the poorest and not the most dangerous criminals, most of all, those that have committed minor street crimes (Carrión, 2007, p 7).

Internalising the 'war on drugs'

The previously described developments received an additional impetus from the 'war on drugs' promoted by the US. After the end of the Cold War, drug enforcement became a top priority for the US and increasingly defined US military relations with most of its southern – Latin American – neighbours. In this process, the Panama-based US

Southern Command (relocated to Florida in 1997), responsible for US military activities in South and Central America, was turned into a 'de facto forward base for drug interdiction' (Andreas and Nadelmann, 2006, p 164). This contributed to a growing militarisation of Latin American law enforcement, as '[w]ith pressure, aid, and training from Washington, many Latin American countries deployed their militaries to the front lines of the drug war' (Andreas and Nadelmann, 2006, p 164). Moreover, and in response to the US certification process, which links US development aid to the active cooperation of countries in the 'war on drugs', many Latin American countries introduced new drug laws and mandatory minimum sentences in their penal codes.

This internalisation of the 'war on drugs' inscribed the prerogative of counter-narcotics law enforcement into local policing practices, which increasingly target marginalised urban communities and neighbourhoods considered breeding grounds for 'narco-crimes'. Policing these spaces in the name of the 'war on drugs' further exacerbates the above-mentioned penalising tendencies of Latin American policing, as it once more 'tends to produce excluded populations, and [depicts] the spaces they inhabit, as criminal' (Corva, 2008, p 191). The legal and policing repercussions of the 'war on drugs' are an important factor behind the growth of Latin America's prison population. As a recent publication on the impact of new drug laws on the growth of prison populations in Argentina, Bolivia, Brazil, Colombia, Ecuador, Mexico, Peru and Uruguay observed:

> In all these countries, the emphasis placed by drug control efforts on criminal sanctions has given rise to a significant increase in the number of persons incarcerated for drug offenses. The enforcement of severe laws for drug offenses has not only been ineffective in curbing the production, trafficking, and consumption of illicit substances, but has generated enormous negative consequences, including overwhelming caseloads in the courts, over crowding in the prisons, and the suffering of tens of thousands of persons behind bars for small-scale drug offenses or simple possession. The weight of the drug laws has been felt with greater force among the most disadvantaged and vulnerable sectors of society. (Metaal and Joungers, 2011, p 5)

Although the 'war on drugs' cannot account for the overall growth of incarceration rates, and its impact varies from country to country, its impact is significant, as can be seen in the case of Argentina. In 1985 only 1 per cent of the inmate population served time for drug-related offences; by 2000 their number increased to 27 per cent (Corda, 2011, p 15).And in Bolivia, to give another telling example, since the enacting of the Law on the Regime Applicable to Coca-controlled Substances (Law 1008) in 1988, about 45 per cent of the national prison population consists of people locked up for drug trafficking or related offences (Giacoman Armayo, 2011, p 22).

The informal side of the Latin American penal state

Most studies on the penal state focus on its formal institutional aspects. Such a perspective is clearly justified for most settings in the global north where states have acquired an impersonal (although not impartial) character. In such a context, the state's impersonal character, in correspondence with the rule of law, serves as guiding principles for actions taken within the bureaucratic field, and are defining features of state–society relations. However, an exclusive emphasis on the formal aspects of the state cannot account for the complexities of penal state formation in countries outside the global north. Here, state–society relations and the exercise of government control are heavily, if not predominantly, influenced by informal and paralegal practices (Chatterjee, 2004). This also holds true for Latin America. This present section offers an analysis of this informal dimension of Latin American penal state-craft by focusing once again on three interrelated, but analytically separated, aspects central to this issue: (i) the legal environment in which penal state formation takes place; (ii) the informal characteristics of Latin American policing; and (iii) the internal dynamics of custodial institutions.

Penal state formation beyond the rule of law

As could be observed above, a central element within the unfolding of the Latin American penal state, as well as elsewhere, has been deployment of the neoliberal state's law-making machinery 'to impose a sense of order upon its subordinates by means of violence rendered legible, legal, and legitimate by its own sovereign sword' (Comaroff and Comaroff, 2006, p 30). Legality in the Latin American context, however, should not be confused with impersonal, rational formal-legality, or a universal application of laws.

On the contrary, a core characteristic of contemporary Latin America is a widespread 'unrule' or 'misrule' of law that permanently subverts formal-legal state practices and state–society relations. In this context, legality has become a terrain where 'illegal practices produce law and extralegal solutions are smuggled into the judicial process. In this paradoxical situation, law itself is a means of manipulation, complication, stratagem, and violence by which all parties – public and private, dominant and dominated – further their interests' (Holston, 2008, pp 203-4). In other words, far from representing impersonal and formal means of conflict regulation and mediation of state–society relations, legal practices in Latin America are highly informal, personalised and appropriable resources. Popular sayings like the Brazilian '*Para meus amigos tudo, para meus inimigos, a lei*' ('For my friends everything, for my enemies the law') or the Mexican '*La ley se obedece pero no se cumple*' ('The law is obeyed but not applied') clearly reflect how deeply embedded everyday experiences with a highly personalised and informal legal system are in the Latin American political imagination. However, the de facto possibility of appropriating/influencing the law to further one's interests ultimately depends on the available social, economic and/or political capital at a person's disposal. When considering the fact that Latin America has the highest income inequality levels in the world (Franknema, 2009, pp 1-4), as well as the prevailing 'elite liberalism' in many countries of the region – which behind the facade of formal-legal equality in practice favours a non-universal and selective application of law according to existing social hierarchies (Pereira, 2000) – and the rapid expansion of urban exclusion and 'second-class citizenship' (Koonings and Kruijt, 2007), the 'benefits' of the 'unrule of law', that is, the capacity of influencing the law in one's favour, are highly selective. They most of all favour those on top of the social ladder: 'In such circumstances, law has little to do with notions of neutral or fair regulation. Rather, it ensures a different norm: the maintenance of privilege among those who possess extralegal powers to manage politics [and] bureaucracy' converting the 'misrule of law' into an 'effective, though perverse, means of rule' (Holston, 2008, pp 228-9).

Whereas the centrality of legal practices within the formal dimension of the unfolding of penal state-craft in Latin America already selectively targets the 'urban outcasts' in a way that qualifies as 'lawfare', that is, 'the resort to legal instruments, to the violence inherent in the law to commit acts of political coercion' (Comaroff and Comaroff, 2006, p 30), the informal legal environment in Latin America represents an additional layer of exclusion and hardship for the people most affected by the 'penalisation of poverty'. As their encounters with the representatives of the penal apparatus (judges, attorneys, police agents, etc) are frequently characterised by the de facto neglect of services and rights to which they are legally entitled, the outcome of these encounters becomes a highly unpredictable and paralegal affair, an issue that ultimately depends on the possibility of converting money and personal connections into influence. In this regard, punitive law making further marginalises the most marginalised segments of the 'urban outcasts', that is, those with little or no access to economic, social and political capital that could be used for enhancing their informal bargaining position with the 'formal' enforcers of penal state-craft.

Policing Latin American-style

Latin American policing, it is widely acknowledged, is a highly arbitrary and violent affair, marked by systematic police abuse, arbitrary detentions, torture and extralegal killings. Although the actual degree and systematic nature of police violence differs from one country to another, throughout Latin America, the principal targets of police violence and abuse are the marginalised segments of the urban population (see, for instance, Chevigny, 1995; Moser and McIlwaine, 2004). The ubiquity of police misconduct in the region, as well as the corresponding high levels of police impunity, indicate that such practices are informally institutionalised (see Brinks, 2006) – they are tolerated and accepted by bureaucratic and political elites. Facilitated by the above-mentioned 'elite liberalism' and the 'unrule of law', this informal institutionalisation generally provides impunity 'for those who commit offenses against victims considered "undesirable" or "subhuman"' (Pinheiro, 2000, p 126). However, in Latin America, violence directed towards the 'undesirables', and justified in the name of 'law and order', is not only committed by the state's formal coercive powers. Another characteristic feature of the Latin American penal state – and its policing practices – consists of the inclusion of actors that operate outside the formal boundaries of the penal apparatus proper. Nonetheless, these actors also participate in controlling and repressing the 'urban outcast'. These 'policing extensions' (van Reenen, 2004) include vigilante groups, 'justice' makers and death squads. Such actors are integrated into the practices of the penal state through officially tolerated informal networks, linking these actors to agents and institutions operating in the formal-institutional parts of the penal apparatus – most notably the police sector (Huggins, 2000).

These informal actors serve as veritable 'auxiliary forces' of the neoliberal state's function of a 'street-cleansing agency', as they actively participate in the 'identification, screening, and isolation of undesired people' (Caldeira, 2000, p 199). In other words, they 'protect an increasingly segmented, isolated, and socially "gated" population of "true citizens" from those marginalized and delegitimized as "dangerous criminals," a designation that reinforces the latter's status as "noncitizens"' (Huggins, 2000, p 118). Additionally, these actors also perform much of the 'dirty work' involved in street cleansing – including lethal violence directed at the urban 'undesirables', like street children, beggars, homosexuals or drug users. As Gay, for example, observed for the case of Brazil: 'Death squads comprising off-duty and retired police officers are often hired by local merchants to clear the streets of "undesirables" and are responsible for killing a large number of Brazilian youths each year' (Gay, 2009, p 209). As the activities of Don Berna, a dominant figure in the Medellín drug business after the death of Pablo Escobar, illustrate, such informal 'street-cleansing' activities are not unrelated to the urban renewal projects that stand at the centre of the 'urbanisation of neoliberalism' in Latin America:

> In the late 1990s, publicly sanctioned security forces incorporated into Don Berna's growing network, 'cleansed' – *limpiaron* – a large area of the city center, dominated by a red-light district and open-air market on the north side and a street of gay salons to the west. Hired thugs in the pay of Don Berna threatened, displaced, or murdered the district's 'disposable' inhabitants – drug sellers, addicts, prostitutes, street kids, petty thieves, called *desechables* – to make it safe for urban redevelopment. After 2000, this city-wide 'pacification' campaign was supported by state security forces, businessmen, politicians … and the Catholic Church. (Hylton, 201, p 356)

Cases like that of Don Berna, as well as the other aspects of informal policing mentioned in this section, point towards the implicit and explicit complicity of political and institutional actors involved in the informal and violent dimension of the 'penalisation of poverty' in Latin America. This complicity, and the related exacerbation of punitive social exclusion, can also be observed within the region's custodial institutions.

Custodial institutions

It makes sense to begin the analysis of custodial institutions in Latin America[3] with jails, the first place people end up after they have been arrested by the police. The findings of a representative study on Mexico City, based on 3,666 interviews, are telling in this regard. Any person arrested by the police in Mexico City has to be brought immediately to the *ministerió publico* (public prosecutor, MP). Indicating the local impact of the 'penalisation of poverty', 80 per cent of the people being transferred by the police to the MP come from the lowest socioeconomic segments of the local population (Naval, 2006, p 33). The transfer situation is marked by high levels of police abuse. In general, 7 out of 10 transfers involve cases of police abuse, including 10 per cent of physical abuse (Naval, 2006, p 31). However, on their way to the MP, 38 per cent of the detainees achieve some kind of 'arrangement' with the involved police officers, guaranteeing the arrested a 'drop off' in the street (Naval, 2006, p 36). Those detainees not capable of achieving an 'agreement', the report demonstrates, face a very hostile environment in the MP agencies, as 67 per cent of the encounters with the MP agents involve a kind of abuse – physical and non-physical. And physical ill treatment *exclusively* takes place in the MP jails, the so-called *separos*, converting them into the most dangerous part of the local penal apparatus (Naval, 2006, p 39).

However, jails are not only violent spaces of 'processing' and 'transfer'. Within the overall trend of rising prison populations throughout Latin America, they additionally serve as places to 'store' regular prisoners. In the province of Buenos Aires, for instance, the punitive turn in local politics contributed to such an increase of prisoners that the local prison system nearly collapsed. In response to these problems, the local authorities decided to use jails in police stations as substitutes for the lack of 'regular' prison spaces. As a result, nearly 6,000 prisoners were held in police jails – not constructed to accommodate people for a longer period of time – in 2005 about 16 per cent of the entire prison population of the Province of Buenos Aires (Asociación por los Derechos Civiles, 2005). The case of Argentina also indicates another defining feature of contemporary Latin American institutions of confinement: the growing number of prisoners under preventive detention. In the Argentine Federal Prison System, the number of people standing/awaiting trial is higher than that of convicted prisoners. In 2007, for instance, of a total of 9,024 prisoners, 5,038 were awaiting/standing trial (Dammert and Salazar, 2009, p 69). Argentina, however, is not an exception in this regard. Nor is preventive detention the only 'system-immanent' cause contributing to the growth of Latin America's prison population. Extremely slow judicial proceedings are as important as delayed processing of release papers. Alone in Colombia, in 2006, about 2,500 people were still imprisoned, although they had completed their sentences (Dammert and Salazar, 2009, p 67).

When considering the observations presented in the proceedings parts of this section, 'slow processing' is also related to arbitrary practices and corruption. As one observer, writing on Venezuelan prisons, observed: 'Because of the precarious working conditions in the prison system and the serious corruption in some instances, the system is transforming the inmate into victim.... Almost all the practices, even those most basic to their needs and rights, may carry a fee' (Hernández, 2008, p 108). So instead of describing imprisonment as 'doing time', Venezuelans refer to imprisonment as *pagando condena* (literally, 'paying [a] sentence') (Birkbeck and Pérez-Santiago, 2006, p 290). In fact, most prisons of the region provide only insufficient basic services, such as food or hygiene products (Ungar, 2003; Dammert and Salazar, 2009). Therefore, prisoners are forced to resort to internal black markets that are protected, 'taxed' and operated by the prison personnel, in collaboration with inmates, who additionally manage the illegal trafficking of weapons, cell phones, alcohol, drugs or prostitution inside the prisons as well as the systematic extortion of prisoners (Cavallaro et al, 2007; Gutiérrez Rivera, 2009).

When considering the fact that access to social, economic or political capital facilitates informal access to basic service provision, once again, those prisoners at the bottom of social hierarchies suffer additional economic hardship with respect to the possibility of gaining access to 'public' services inside the prison – not to mention the protection of their physical integrity – thereby perpetuating and aggravating the socioeconomic bias of the local penal apparatus behind bars.

Conclusion

Neoliberalism, Wacquant argues, 'is a transnational political project aiming to remake the nexus of market, state, and citizenship from above' (Wacquant, 2009, p 306), and one central component of this project is the expansion of the state's penal apparatus. In this regard, the concept of the 'penal state' provides a useful theoretical and analytical framework for assessing the contemporary re-making of the market–state–citizenship nexus and the resulting 'fabrication of social order' (Neocleous, 2000), a fabrication process that is transnational in nature and global in scope. However, the internal configurations of markets, states and citizenship regimes do not exist in the abstract. They are embedded in particular socio-political settings that produce decisively local path dependencies. Therefore, in order to offer a truly comprehensive 'contribution to the *historical anthropology of the state* and of *transformations of the field of power in the age of ascending neoliberalism*' (Wacquant, 2009, p xvii; emphasis in original), the theoretical and analytical toolbox of the 'penal state' needs to catch up with the global reach of its object of analysis – the neoliberal political project. This implies that the concept of the 'penal state' must travel beyond the empirical context of Western Europe and the US, the empirical settings that so far have attracted most attention from scholars working within this framework. It is through this 'conceptual travelling' that we are able to better assess the reach of our theoretical tools and to analyse and understand important commonalities and differences involved in the processes of penal state formation in a globalised world.

It was such an effort that formed the basis of this present chapter. From the vantage point of contemporary Latin America, it demonstrated that Latin American countries have indeed followed the path of neoliberal penal state formation and the 'penalisation of poverty' that Wacquant and others observed for many countries in the global north. This is most visible in growing incarceration rates during the last two decades as well as the importance of punitive policing within contemporary Latin American urban governance. However, this chapter also indicated that local factors, such as the political opportunity structure created by the intersection of the 'metropolisation of crime', the internalisation of the 'war on drugs' and the 'urbanisation of neoliberalism', played an important role in the unfolding of penal state-craft throughout the region. In addition to this, this chapter has pointed towards the analytical limits of assessing only the formal dimension of the Latin American penal state. It stressed the informal, and largely illegal, nature of many aspects of the 'penalisation of poverty' in Latin America and the existence of a penal apparatus that informally incorporates actors operating outside the formal-institutional boundaries of the bureaucratic field into its (penalising) workings of power.

By pointing towards these aspects, the chapter will hopefully sensitise readers to the importance of paying more (systematic and cross-regional) attention to the interaction between formal and informal structures and practices and their impact on the place-specific unfolding of the penal state and the 'penalisation of poverty' in 'most of the world' (Chatterjee, 2004). It is through the inclusion of these aspects into a cross-regional research agenda that we can offer a more nuanced analysis of the continuum of globally existing penal state-craft as an important step towards a comprehensive 'contribution to the *historical anthropology of the state* and of *transformations of the field of power in the age of ascending neoliberalism*' (Wacquant, 2009, p xvii; emphasis in original).

Notes
[1] This section draws on and further develops arguments that were originally published in the *Contemporary Justice Review* (Müller, 2012).

[2] The World Prison Briefing is available at www.prisonstudies.org/info/worldbrief/

[3] Due to the marginal role played by workfare practices, custodial institutions are the most important part of the penal apparatus in charge of warehousing the poor (Müller, 2012).

References

Amar, P. (2009) 'Operation Princess in Rio de Janeiro: policing, "sex trafficking", strengthening worker citizenship, and the urban geopolitics of security in Brazil', *Security Dialogue*, vol 40, no 4-5, pp 516-41.

Andreas, P. and Nadelmann, E. (2006) *Policing the globe. Criminalization and crime control in international relations*, Oxford: Oxford University Press.

Arias, E.D. and Goldstein, D.M. (eds) *Violent democracies in Latin America*, Durham, NC: Duke University Press.

Arteaga Botello, N. (2004) *En busca de la legitimidad: Seguridad pública y populismo punitivo en México, 1990-2000*, Alicante: Universidad de Alicante, Centro de Estudios Iberoamericanos Mario Benedetti.

Asociación por los Derechos Civiles (2005) *Informa ADC sobre el fallo 'Verbitsky'*, Horacios/Habeas Corpus (www.adccorte.org.ar/recursos/243/DOCUMENTO+CASO+HABEAS+CORPUS.pdf).

Birkbeck, C. and Pérez-Santiago, N. (2006) 'The character of penal control in Latin America: sentence remissions in a Venezuelan prison', *Criminology and Criminal Justice*, vol 6, no 3, pp 289-308.

Boron, A. (2006) *Estado, capitalismo y democracia en América Latina*, Buenos Aires: Clacso.

Brenner, N. and Theodore, N. (2002) 'Cities and the geographies of "actually existing neoliberalism"', *Antipode*, vol 34, no 3, pp 356-86.

Brinks, D. (2006) 'The rule of (non)law: prosecuting police killings in Brazil and Argentina', in G. Helmke and S. Levitsky (eds) *Informal institutions and democracy: Lessons from Latin America*, Baltimore, MD: John Hopkins University Press, pp 201-26.

Caldeira, T.P.R. (2000) *City of walls. Crime, segregation, and citizenship in São Paulo*, Berkeley, CA: University of California Press.

Carrión, F. (2007) '¿Por qué todos los caminos conducen a la miseria del panóptico?', *URVIO. Revista Latinoamericana de Seguridad Ciudadana*, vol 1, no 1, pp 5-9.

Castillo, J. (2008) 'After the explosion', in R. Burdett and D. Sudjic (eds) *The endless city*, London: Phaidon, pp 174-85.

Cavallaro, J., de Biedermann, S.V., Kopas, J., Lam, Y. and Mayhle, T. (2007) *Security in Paraguay. Analysis and response in comparative perspective*, Cambridge, MA: Harvard Law School, Human Right Program (www. law.harvard.edu/programs/hrp/documents/SecurityinParaguay.pdf).

Chatterjee, P. (2004) *The politics of the governed. Reflections on popular politics in most of the world*, New York, NY: Columbia University Press.

Chevigny, P. (1995) *Edge of the knife: Police violence in the Americas*, New York: New Press.

Chevigny, P. (2003) 'The populism of fear: politics of crime in the Americas', *Punishment & Society*, vol 5, no 1, pp 77-96.

Comaroff, J. and Comaroff, J. (2006) 'Law and order in the postcolony: an introduction', in J. Comaroff and J. Comaroff (eds) *Law and disorder in the postcolony*, Chicago, IL: University of Chicago Press, pp 1-56.

Corda, R.A. (2011) 'Imprisonment for drug-related offenses in Argentina', in J. Metaal and C. Youngers (eds) *Systems overload. Drug laws and prisons in Latin America*, Amsterdam and Washington, DC: Transnational Institute and WOLA, pp 11-20.

Corva, D. (2008) 'Neoliberal globalization and the war on drugs: transnationalizing illiberal governance in the Americas', *Political Geography*, vol 27, no 2, pp 176-93.

Dammert, L. and Malone, M.F. (2006) 'Does it take a village? Policing strategies and fear of crime in Latin America', *Latin American Politics and Society*, vol 48, no 2, pp 27-51.

Dammert, L. and Salazar, F. (2009) *¿Duros con el delito? Populismo e inseguridad en América Latina*, Santiago de Chile: Flacso.

Dammert, L. and Zúñiga, L. (2008) *Prisons: Problems and challenges for the Americas*, Santiago de Chile: Flacso.

Davis, D.E. (2007) 'El factor Giuliani: delincuencia, la "cero tolerancia" en el trabajo policiaco y la transformación de la esfera pública en el centro de la ciudad de México', *Estudios Sociológicos*, vol 25, no 75, pp 639-68.

Frankema, E. (2009) *Has Latin America always been unequal? A comparative study of asset and income inequality in the long twentieth century*, Leiden: Brill.

Fuentes, C. (2005) *Contesting the iron fist. Advocacy networks and police violence in democratic Argentina and Chile*, New York: Routledge.

Garland, D. (2001) *The culture of control: Crime and social order in contemporary society*, Oxford: Oxford University Press.

Gay, R. (2009) 'From popular movements to drug gangs to militias: an anatomy of violence in Rio de Janeiro', in K. Koonings and D. Kruijt (eds) *Mega-cities. The politics of urban exclusion and violence in the global south*, London: Zed Books, pp 29-51.

Giacoman Aramayo, D. (2011) 'Drug policy and the prison situation in Bolivia', in J. Metaal and C.Youngers (eds) *Systems overload. Drug laws and prisons in Latin America*, Amsterdam and Washington, DC: Transnational Institute and WOLA, pp 21-30.

Goldstein, D.M. (2004) *The spectacular city. Violence and performance in urban Bolivia*, Durham, NC: Duke University Press.

Gutiérrez Rivera, L. (2009) 'Enclave y territories: Estrategias territoriales del estado y de las pandillas en Honduras', PhD, Berlin: Freie Universität Berlin.

Gutiérrez Rivera, L. (2010) 'Discipline and punish? Youth gangs' response to "zero-tolerance" policies in Honduras', *Bulletin of Latin American Research*, vol 29, no 4, pp 492-504.

Harvey, D. (1989) 'From managerialism to entrepreneurialism: the transformation in urban governance in late capitalism', *Geografiska Annaler B*, vol 71, pp 3-17.

Harvey, D. (2006) *Spaces of global capitalism. Towards a theory of uneven geographical development*, London:Verso.

Hernández, I. (2008) 'TheVenezuelan prison system: violence, idleness and inequality', in L. Dammert and L. Zúñiga (eds) *Prisons: Problems and challenges for the Americas*, Santiago de Chile: Flacso, pp 106-9.

Holston, J. (2008) *Insurgent citizenship: Disjunctions of democracy and modernity in Brazil*, Princeton: Princeton University Press.

Huggins, M.K. (2000) 'Urban violence and police privatization in Brazil: blended invisibility', *Social Justice*, vol 27, no 2, pp 113-34.

Hylton, F. (2010) 'The Cold War that didn't end: paramilitary modernization in Medellín, Colombia', in G. Grandin and G.M. Joseph (eds) *A century of revolution. Insurgent and counterinsurgent violence during Latin America's long Cold War,* Durham, NC: Duke University Press, pp 338-67.

Koonings, K. and Kruijt, D. (eds) (2007) *Fractured cities. Social exclusion, urban violence and contested spaces in Latin America*, London: Zed Books.

Koonings, K. andVeenstra, S. (2007) 'Exclusión social, actores armados y violencia urbana en Río de Janeiro', *Foro Internacional*, vol 17, no 3, pp 616-36.

Metaal, J. and Youngers, C. (2011) 'Executive summary', in J. Metaal and C.Youngers (eds) *Systems overload. Drug laws and prisons in Latin America*, Amsterdam and Washington, DC: Transnational Institute and WOLA, pp 5-7.

Moser, C. and McIlwaine, C. (2004) *Encounters with violence in Latin America: Urban poor perceptions from Colombia and Guatemala*, New York: Routledge.

Müller, M.-M. (2012) 'The rise of the penal state in Latin America', *Contemporary Justice Review*, vol 15, no 1, pp 57-76.

Naval, C. (2006) *Irregularities, abuses of power, and ill-treatment in the Federal District*, Mexico City: Fundar.

Neocleous, M. (2000) *The fabrication of social order: A critical theory of police power*, London: Pluto.

Pereira, A.W. (2000) 'An ugly democracy? State violence and the rule of law in postauthoritarian Brazil', in P.R. Kingstone and T.J. Power (eds) *Democratic Brazil: Actors, institutions and processes*, Pittsburgh, PA: University of Pittsburgh Press, pp 217-35.

Pinheiro, P.S. (2000) 'Democratic governance, violence and the (un) rule of law', *Daedalus*, vol 129, no 2, pp 119-44.

Portes, A. and Hoffman, K. (2003) 'Latin American class structures: their composition and change during the neoliberal era', *Latin American Research Review*, vol 38, no 1, pp 41-82.

Portes, A. and Roberts, B.R. (2005) 'The free-market city: Latin American urbanization in the years of the neoliberal experiment', *Studies in Comparative International Development*, vol 40, no 1, pp 43-82.

Rojas, E., Cuadrado-Roura, J.R. and Fernández Güell, J.M. (eds) (2008) *Governing the metropolis. Principles and cases*, Cambridge: David Rockefeller Center for Latin American Studies.

Rodgers, D. (2009) 'Slum wars of the 21st century: gangs, mano dura and the new urban geography of conflict in Central America', *Development and Change*, vol 40, no 5, pp 949-76.

Rotker, S. (ed) (2002) *Citizens of fear: Urban violence in Latin America*, Piscataway, NJ: Rutgers University Press.

Sozzo, M. (2007) '¿Metamorfosis de la prisión? Proyecto normalizador, populismo punitivo y "prison-warehouse" in Argentina', *URVIO. Revista Latinoamericana de Seguridad Ciudadana*, vol 1, no 1, pp 88-116.

Swanson, K. (2007) 'Revanchist urbanism heads south: the regulation of indigenous beggars and street vendors in Ecuador', *Antipode*, vol 39, no 4, pp 708-28.

Swanson, K. (2010) *Begging as a path to progress. Indigenous women and children and the struggle for Ecuador's urban spaces*, Athens, GA: University of Georgia Press.

Ungar, M. (2003) 'Prisons and politics in Latin America', *Human Rights Quarterly*, vol 25, no 4, November, pp 909-34.

van Reenen, P. (2004) 'Policing extensions in Latin America', in K. Koonings and D. Kruijt (eds) *Armed actors. Organised violence and state failure in Latin America*, London: Zed Books, pp 33-51.

van Swaaningen, R. (1997) *Critical criminology. Visions from Europe*, London: Sage Publications.

Wacquant, L. (2001) 'The penalisation of poverty and the rise of neo-liberalism', *European Journal on Criminal Policy and Research*, vol 9, no 4, pp 401-12.

Wacquant, L. (2003) 'Toward a dictatorship over the poor? Notes on the penalization of poverty in Brazil', *Punishment & Society*, vol 5, no 2, pp 197-205.

Wacquant, L. (2008a) *Urban outcasts: A comparative sociology of advanced marginality*, Cambridge: Polity Press.

Wacquant, L. (2008b) 'The militarization of urban marginality: lessons from the Brazilian metropolis', *International Political Sociology*, vol 2, no 1, pp 56-64.

Wacquant, L. (2008c) 'Relocating gentrification: the working class, science and the state in recent urban research', *International Journal of Urban and Regional Research*, vol 31, no 1, pp 198-205.

Wacquant, L. (2009) *Punishing the poor. The neoliberal government of social insecurity*, Durham, NC: Duke University Press.

Wacquant, L. (2010a) 'Crafting the neoliberal state: workfare, prisonfare, and social insecurity', *Sociological Forum*, vol 25, no 2, pp 197-220.

Wacquant, L. (2010b) 'Class, race and hyperincarceration in revanchist America', *Daedalus*, vol 139, no 3, pp 74-90.

Young, R. and McFadden, T. (2004) *Marching powder. A true story of friendship, cocaine and South America's strangest jail*, New York: St Martin's Griffin.

ELEVEN

Neoliberal, brutish and short? Cities, inequalities and violences

Peter Squires

Introduction

The aim of this chapter is to critically reflect on the analytical themes and issues reflected in two of Loïc Wacquant's major works (*Urban outcasts*, 2008a, and *Punishing the poor*, 2009). Despite the essential similarities of their respective subject matters, the books are quite different in content, style, tone and methodological orientation. The former, by far the most conventionally research-led, explores, on the basis of survey data and area-based indicators, comparisons and contrasts between life and living conditions in the deteriorating ghettos of Chicago's South Side and conditions in the *banlieue* estates on the outskirts of Paris. Differences of scale, the extent of inequality and racial polarisation aside, there is still much that these areas, and their residents, have in common and might find recognisable.

The concept 'advanced marginality' perhaps best describes the precarious conditions of these increasingly disadvantaged, economically marginal and socially toxic areas. Tim Hope's concept for similar areas (albeit in a British context), 'communities of despair' (Hope, 2001), captures something of the issue, except that, the aim here is not necessarily to chronicle despair. On the contrary 'despair' implies far too passive a notion to describe the (often desperate) survival practices of the urban outcasts themselves. Accordingly, one theme of the chapter is to develop some reflections on Frances Fox Piven's observation regarding Wacquant's work in *Punishing the poor*: 'We should also wonder about the role of the people who were the objects of penal control. Were they merely the witless objects of social control, or were they also actors in the drama?' (Piven, 2010, p 114). With that idea in mind, a related concern involves what we might term 'neoliberalism beyond the state'.

The two themes are intended to connect; the argument will be that neoliberalism corrodes the conditions of social order and that while states certainly contribute to these processes they typically have far wider ramifications. Violence and resistance, in particular, are often a direct consequence of these de-civilising processes although states often further imperil the conditions of civilised coexistence by the ways in which they, often selectively, seek to re-impose forms of order and authority. A key question for Wacquant concerns the extent to which he devotes sufficient attention to these wider 'non-statutory' questions of violence and resistance.

Neoliberalism beyond the state?

The second of Wacquant's two books forming the springboard for this chapter is subtitled *The neoliberal government of social insecurity*. This book is at once more ideological and critical, explicitly focused on the US and offering a powerful polemic against the neoliberal governance which has transformed an incomplete US 'welfare state' into a 'workfare state' and, now, Wacquant contends, into a 'prisonfare' state. Unlike *Urban outcasts*, rooted in empirical research and centred on the *condition* of the ghetto or *banlieue*, *Punishing the poor* is developed via a structural and theoretical analysis exploring the manufactured insecurity of working-class life, the racialisation of poverty and inequality and the criminalisation and penalisation of deprivation. These processes, in Wacquant's eloquent phrasing, are overseen by a *centaur state*: 'a liberal head mounted upon an authoritarian body, applying the doctrine of laissez faire and laissez passer upstream ... [but] brutally paternalistic and punitive downstream', when dealing with the victims of neoliberalism (Wacquant, 2009, p 43).

This rolling back of welfare and the rolling forth of discipline evokes many of the discussions of the first 'great moving right show' (Hall, 1977), authoritarian populism (Hall et al, 1978) and not least, Gamble's neoliberal formula of the 'free economy and the strong state' (Gamble, 1988) intended to describe the post-Thatcherite, post-Reaganomics new world order. More recently, these more general analyses have become linked intellectually with another generic argument about the supposed creeping punitiveness ('penal populism') of Western liberal cultures and their penal systems (Garland, 2001; Pratt et al, 2005; Simon, 2007). The point is often made that while the US may serve Wacquant reasonably well as a laboratory of punitive exceptionalism, the case is not always so easily made elsewhere (Lacey, 2008), which is not to say that a variety of commentators have not tried to do so, citing a range of evidence – rates of incarceration, sentencing trends, increased criminal penalties, criminal justice expansionism, discipline dispersal, legislative hyperactivity (new criminal laws) and the tone and content of law and order rhetorics (Steinert, 2004; Squires and Stephen, 2005; Tonry, 2010).

Nonetheless, it is clearly Wacquant's argument that US neoliberalism is influencing other societies and jurisdictions around the world, and that the forms of analysis developed for exploring US punitiveness *can* be applied elsewhere. The final sections of *Punishing the poor* are given over to what he calls the *European declinations* of the new 'law and order reason' as the '*Carceral Aberration comes to France*'. Along with a number of other commentators, for Wacquant this 'aberration', itself the product of a deviant neoliberal imagination (p 273), has entailed a more exacting redefinition of deviant incivility, a marked intensification of intolerance and the 'defining up' (Rodger, 2008) of routine and petty criminalities and nuisance (Squires, 2008). So it has been rather less crime itself that has changed in recent years 'than the gaze that politicians and journalists, as spokespersons for dominant interests, train upon street delinquency and the populations that are supposed to feed it' (Wacquant, 2009, p 274).

Discipline and security: 'safe European homes' and beyond

Sheltered by this comforting myth of the 'criminal other', the punitive policy transfer is driven by two mutually reinforcing arms of a pincer movement. On the one hand there is a shift at the level of social security that Wacquant loosely equates with a shift from a security *of the poor* rooted in a progressive politics of social citizenship to a security provided *against the poor*. Entailed in these transitions are changes in the form and character of social inclusion in respective societies. As he puts it: 'the misery of American welfare and the grandeur of American prisonfare at century's turn are the two sides of the same political coin' (Wacquant, 2009, p 292). Contrasts are often typically drawn here with the UK although public policy commentators have often overlooked (until more recently) parallel developments in the much heralded British welfare state. Principles of class control and work discipline were no strangers to the British social security system (Dean, 1990; Squires, 1990). After the 1970s, driven by concerns about cost, dependency and 'abuse', social security benefits and pensions targeted towards the poorest and unemployed became subject to increasingly restrictive entitlement testing which, under the guise of modernising welfare and 'need', cumulatively limited the scope, value, duration and coverage of the benefits (Andrews and Jacobs, 1990; Bryson and Jacobs, 1992; Taylor-Gooby and Dean, 1992; Jones and Novak, 1999). These changes were complemented by an increasingly restrictive supply of public housing, effectively residualising the sector as 'welfare housing' for problem populations such that, by the 1990s, public housing became the 'test bed' for the anti-social behaviour project. Increasing conditionality in welfare and probationary tenancies (Burney, 2005) were the means by which social policy turned further into anti-social behaviour management and public policy became a form of criminalising pest control (Squires, 2008).

While the shifts described by Wacquant in the US may have been dramatic, politically blatant and racially coded, aided by the relatively limited purchase that an idea of 'welfare' had attained in US public policy, in Britain the transformations have been, perhaps, more subtle, incremental and contested. As neoliberal principles began increasingly to shape economic policy, the management of the labour market and the welfare sector, so the criminal justice system, especially its leading edges, policing, surveillance and anti-social behaviour management, began to play an increasing part in the lives of the most disadvantaged, the least well-educated and the most economically marginal. With the exception of the anti-social behaviour management processes affecting youth and the 'new youth justice' (Goldson, 2000; Squires and Stephen, 2005), there was no wholesale transfer from 'workfare' to 'prisonfare' as Wacquant describes in the US. In any event, the strangely resilient British class system had seen to it that the most disadvantaged, the least well-educated and the most economically marginal always had been the groups of greatest interest to the police and local authorities. Slowly but surely, principles of police, surveillance and security management began to shape the design and experience of advanced marginality in the urban environment (Graham, 2010), recycling a power to judge and exclude. As Hempel and Topfer argue, the *ban-opticon* (Bigo, 2006) allows Western societies a 'comfortable illusion' of social inclusion even as 'the power of exception and the production of normative imperatives amalgamate into a "governmentality" of uncertainty, unease, fear and (in)security ... [whereby] liberal societies can approve their own self-image' (Hempel and Topfer, 2009, p 161) even as they exclude those who cannot cope, conform or consume within socially approved limits.

Inequality and security

It hardly matters that the 'demand for law and order' emerged, at least in part, from the very areas (inner cities, sink estates) subjected to the most crime and violence or (in what might well be left realist criminology's Achilles' heel) those most thoroughly acquainted with and least satisfied by the enforcement arms of the state. What the criminal justice system could deliver was not safety but a selective kind of order for some. Pushed to be more efficient and effective and to climb league tables or meet performance standards, criminal justice agencies, and in the front line, the police, went for the easiest results (the 'low hanging fruit'), targeting offenders, offences and hotspots. And behind them, the rest of the criminal justice system risk-assessed, fast-tracked, registered and processed, hoping that hyperactivity might be mistaken for effectiveness. Overall crime fell, but generally not in the areas where poverty and violence were most entrenched.

Acknowledging the differentiated impacts of public policy, the idea that public policy is not experienced as uniform and that in matters of (re-)distributional justice (the social division of welfare) there are always 'winners' and 'losers', is an idea with which, for perhaps obvious reasons, critical social policy has long been relatively comfortable. The parallel notion that some people's safety might be achieved at the cost of others' freedom is not an idea that has always penetrated as far as it should into criminology (Squires, 2006). Nevertheless, the idea of differentiated policy regimes and experiences was developed, first with Richard Titmuss's concept of the 'three welfare states' (Titmuss, 1963) then subsequently extended to five by commentators such as Frank Field (1981). Field described the following welfare state regimes: the benefits welfare state, the tax allowance welfare state, the company welfare state, the inheritance welfare state and the private market welfare state.

An important point regarding these various layers to the welfare state was that, while, over time they did (for some people) entail transitions from one welfare form to another, they also existed *simultaneously* and were related to one another. They defined the means by which segments of the population derived their welfare and well-being, but they were not all part of what is generally regarded as the conventional Beveridgean welfare state. Nor are these 'regimes' all so obviously functions of the state, even though they operate to some extent within (and to some extent beyond) the state itself. In a similar fashion for the US, Wacquant has outlined three formal layers of the state, the welfare state, the workfare state and prisonfare state, each exercising different controls over different populations. His further point is that these three regimes reflect a process of punitive transition in the governance of the poorest. Likewise, in the UK, just as we can describe the affluence-enhancing welfare regimes for the rich and powerful operating, in part, outwith the state, so there are welfare/discipline regimes in the lower reaches of the state – and beneath it – reinforcing poverty and social exclusion.

First, as suggested already, we might describe the social and spatially differentiated 'social housing welfare state', beyond that the casual labour welfare state, the 'off the books' informal economy welfare state and the criminal welfare state (contraband, dealing and protection). At each remove, the states of well-being may become ever more precarious and survival oriented and in each layer the nature and risk of exposure to law enforcement or criminal victimisation will differ. The point is, just as the lifestyles of the affluent may not be directly governed through daily interactions with the state, so it may not be the state itself which looms largest in the lives of the poorest. A variety of non-state actors, from the 'dark side' of civil society (Koonings and Kruijt, 2004), including perhaps, the local loan shark, resident drug dealers, the neighbourhood gang or criminal network, may well be supplying the most pressing and unavoidable forms of 'sub-political' governance from below (Beck, 1996, quoted in Rodgers, 2009, p 39). As we will see later, a range of commentators, discussing order maintenance especially in weak or failed states, have pointed to the role of these agents: perhaps 'armed actors', 'policing extensions', 'violence entrepreneurs' and gangs, in establishing order in the community (Koonings and Kruijt, 2004; Savenije and van der Borgh, 2004; van Reenen, 2004; Arias, 2006; Rodgers, 2009; Sonnevelt, 2009).

Developing these points, while Wacquant's *Punishing the poor* explains the predicament of the US racialised underclass in terms of neoliberal state governance, his *Urban outcasts* gives us important glimpses of a rather different range of actors also playing their part in structuring and both sustaining and imperilling (governing through crime, violence and fear) the lives of the poorest. It is to this that we now turn.

Governance and outcasts

The opening section of *Urban outcasts* provides what Wacquant refers to as the 'tools for rethinking urban marginality'. This is spatially located in ghettos, *banlieues, favelas,* 'stigmatised neighbourhoods situated at the very bottom of the hierarchical system of places that constitute the metropolis' (2008, p1). They are the 'lawless zones', 'problem estates', 'no-go areas' or 'wild districts' – 'badlands of the republic' or 'outlaw areas' in Dikeç's phrases (2007), 'hotbeds of vice, violence and social dissolution' (Dikeç, 2007), places (and peoples) to be feared, fled from or shunned, although from the outside, such areas are typically represented as essentially similar, 'barren, chaotic and brutish' (Wacquant, 2008, p 1).

Wacquant's first key point is that 'urban marginality is not everywhere woven of the same cloth' (2008, p 1).

Central to this conception of marginality entailed by Wacquant are notions of the 'collapse' of public institutions, 'state policies of urban abandonment,' and of failure and retreat, leading to the 'punitive containment' of the resident poor (2008, pp 3-4). Yet state policies and controls have been reconfigured rather than relinquished, for 'state structures and policies play a decisive role in the differential stitching together of inequalities of class place and origin ... on both sides of the Atlantic' (Wacquant, 2008, p 6). Ghettos, *banlieues* and *favelas* are, above all, 'effects of state projected on the city' (p 6). Even Paulo Lins' celebrated portrait of *Cidade de Deus*, the infamous favela on the outskirts of Rio de Janeiro (Lins, 1997), in which the complex tapestry of daily life, comprising constant negotiation of peer and familial obligations, the demands of love, respect and survival, among the fluctuating street jurisdictions of drug dealers, gangsters and corrupt police – even this complex melting pot of dangerous and weaponised passions, where state authority seems at best quite remote, began life as an ambitious and idealistic municipal housing project to re-house (at a distance) the stigmatised inhabitants of the city's slums. And it is precisely the absence of accountable state authority which exposed the inhabitants to these other, more erratic (if no less brutal), influences. State interventions, typically police raids, have predominantly taken the form of abrupt militarised interventions that, from the perspective of the residents, typically lack legitimacy, accountability or precision. And to that extent they are often ineffective and/or unsustainable while often 'only aggravate[ing] the very ills [they are] supposed to treat' (Wacquant, 2008, p 7).

For example, as was reported in November 2010 by ABC News International:

Rio police, troops preparing invasion of drug gang stronghold

Soldiers and police crouching behind armored vehicles trained their rifles on dozens of entrances to a sprawling slum on Saturday, preparing to invade and try to push drug gangs out of an area long considered the most dangerous in Rio de Janeiro, a city set to host the 2014 World Cup and the 2016 Olympics....A delicate calm held after a night that saw intense exchanges of gunfire, filling the dark sky with bright streaks as bullets whizzed into and out of the Alemao

slum. Soldiers in camouflage, black-clad police from elite
units and regular police held their ground at the entrances to
the complex, a grouping of a dozen slums where more than
85,000 people live. (http://abcnews.go.com/International/
wireStory?id=12254023)

The backdrop to this 'invasion' had been the resistance activities
perpetrated by Alemao drug gangs to recent police crackdowns.
Attempting to 'clean up' Rio and making it safe to capitalise on
the economic opportunities presented by major sports tourism, the
police had been moving against the gangs in their neighbourhoods.
In retaliation the gangs had been venturing beyond their favela
strongholds, robbing scores of motorists, buses and lorries, then burning
the vehicles, blocking the roads and 'holding the city to ransom'. Ed
Vulliamy describes similar practices adopted by drug cartels and gangs
in a number of Mexican cities, provoking the Mexican authorities into
similar military adventures (Vulliamy, 2010). In consequence, the Rio
authorities drew in the military to drive the gangs out of the slums in
a demonstration of overwhelming force.

  Speaking specifically of Brazil, Wacquant has noted how 'criminal
insecurity ... is not attenuated but clearly *aggravated* by the intervention
of the law enforcement forces' (2003, p 199). Here we can describe
a state as *retreating* (from international norms of civilisation and the
protection of human rights) even as its armoured troop carriers bulldoze
the ghettos and shanty towns in pursuit of investment opportunities,
economic development, a dubious 'cultural renaissance' and the all-
important sports tourism dollar (Goldstone, 2001), and as *failing* even
as it represses more harshly (Wacquant, 2008b).

In the shadows and the ruins

As Wacquant notes in *Punishing the poor*, a central aspect of such
failures and retreats has been the adoption of police-led solutions for
law and order, drawing on a 'prefabricated discourse on the efficacy
of police repression, disinterred as the sole remedy for the congenital
wantonness of the dangerous classes' (2009, p 259). Here there is perfect
consistency with *Urban outcasts* as he describes the '"police fetishism" –
the ideological illusion that make[s] policing the solution to the crime
problem' (p 12). Thus, 'putting working class districts left economically
and socially fallow under police restraint has recently become popular
amongst rulers because it enables the high state nobility to give itself the
comforting feeling that it is responding to the demands of the "people"

while at the same time exculpating its own historic responsibility in the making of the urban outcasts of the new century' (p 12).

By the same token, in the liberal West, anti-social behaviour and crime and disorder management strategies, from the New York 'miracle' to the Parisian suburbs and the sink estates of South London, were not primarily about alleviating the condition of the poorest (they had so little impact here in any event) but rather were about shifting responsibility and exploiting the opportunity of disorder to discipline the marginal into acceptance of their condition, position and function. In Foucault's (1977) terms they reproduce 'useful delinquency' and the profoundly crimogenic consequences of intensive policing and mass incarceration strongly suggest that it is political authority which is at issue rather than any given level of crime or victimisation. As Wacquant argues, it is this fact that explains the persistence of the continuing spectacle, the addictive allure, of law and order.

But if criminalisation and a voracious, expanding, penal establishment are most effective in perpetuating the social insecurities of outcast life in the ghettos and slums, what does this mean for those condemned to live these lives? Moreover, what other processes, including those somewhat external to the state itself, either beyond its reach or beneath its radar, including the practices of the marginal themselves, contribute to the predicament of marginality? As was noted earlier, Wacquant's *Punishing the poor* says very little about the agency and activism of the marginalised whereas, in fact, from around the world a wide range of research evidence is now filling in some of these silences. The picture received is far from pretty and certainly far from clear but if one perspective sees nothing more than a brutal Hobbesian war of all against all fought out in the shadows and among the ruins of neoliberal state failure, another sees the situated urban activism of the poorest – even in the form of gangs – as loaded with social potential. That is 'potential', rather than 'promise', for there is much that can prevent positive development here (not least the heavy-handed and counter-productive response of state authorities themselves), trapping gang members and their communities in vicious cycles of conflict and destructive violence. As an entire tradition of gang researchers have reminded us (Thrasher, 1927; Hagedorn, 1988; Klein, 1995), gangs thrive on conflict, but conflict, violence and a ready supply of weapons also limit and reverse social development and what the gang might become.

As noted, despite acknowledging that the dramas of urban survival have to be understood in context – 'urban marginality is not everywhere woven of the same cloth' (Wacquant, 2008a, p 1) – it is nonetheless true that the dilemmas of life in the world's murder capitals are reflected and refracted across the zones of urban marginality from first world cultures, to the global south and what Castells (2000) has termed the 'fourth world'. Yet before turning to consider how Wacquant himself describes the politics and adjustments associated with marginality in these various urban contexts, it is worth briefly reflecting on some of the common denominators serving to reproduce chronic under-development and de-civilisation.

Conflict traps and violence

Paul Collier's recent and challenging book, *The bottom billion* (Collier, 2008), describes the factors that he considers are not just holding back the social and economic development of the 50-odd poorest countries in the world (and thereby the well-being of the billion or so people living within such failed states) but rather, the circumstances which are actively eroding their capacity to progress, widening inequalities and exacerbating their social, economic and political problems. Collier employs four explanations (he calls them 'four traps') to account for the economic under-development of certain societies. These are what he refers to as: the '*conflict trap*', the '*bad neighbours trap*', the '*resources trap*' and the '*bad governance trap*'. The aim here is to take the principles from his analysis and adapt them to the situations of deprived and marginalised communities *within* existing societies, to extend the analysis of impoverishing contexts beyond the simple realm of the state, even though the state is often implicated.

The conflict trap serves as an acknowledgement that problems of violence, weaponisation and rates of gang membership are typically highest in the poorest and most marginal urban communities (Currie, 1997; Morenoff et al, 2001; Jutersonke et al, 2007; Dorling, 2008; Hagedorn, 2008). States are certainly implicated in these violence processes, not least because (as we saw in the Rio illustration earlier) it is often the reactions of states and 'officialdom' in the form of the police (or paramilitaries) that provide the critical catalysts for gang formation, resistance and conflict. Violence is chronic, recurring and endemic, analogous to the destructive 'ecologies of violence' depicted in the US ghetto as described by Fagan and Wilkinson (2002). And a point we will return to, this persistent violence is typically sustained by an, often illegal, weapon supply. According to Collier, such violence and chronic, persisting conflict represent 'economic development in reverse' (2008, p xx).

In similar fashion, here referring specifically to the US 'post-industrial' context, Elliot Currie has itemised seven dimensions of post-industrial violence: the progressive destruction of livelihood; the growth of extremes of inequality and material deprivation; the withdrawal of public services and supports; the erosion of informal networks of mutual support; the spread of a materialistic and neglectful culture; the deregulation of the technology of violence; and the weakening of social and political alternatives (Currie, 1997). Contrary to Wacquant's prioritisation of state action, only one of Currie's seven dimensions of violence and decline (the withdrawal of public services and supports) relates directly to the political decision making of state agents. Nor is it self-evident that this is a necessarily prior consideration; rampant inequality, diminishing mutuality and community neglect may well undermine mainstream political activity *leading to* the rolling back of welfare and the rolling out of tough law and order. A particular issue, drawn from Currie's list, which assumes an especial significance in the sustaining of the conflict trap concerns the degregulation of the technology of violence – or, specifically, the proliferation of firearms, the weaponisation of communities and the 'gangsterisation' that this often entails.

A second Latin American example, here concerning the Mexican border city Juárez, provides another useful illustration. Ed Vulliamy (2010) describes the fascinating and deeply conflicted social relations of the borderline in his book *Amexica*. Unfortunately Juárez embodies some of the worst of all the traps outlined by Collier. To the north it has one of the most unforgiving neighbours possible, the US, for which Juárez serves as little more than a workshop and depot on one of the world's major land trade and transportation routes. The huge volume of trade passing through the city provides plentiful and lucrative opportunities for cocaine trafficking to the insatiable market in the north, thereby explaining the bitter, violent struggles between rival drug cartels seeking to control these key trade routes. Paralleling the northern flow of cocaine is a southern flow of high grade automatic and semi-automatic arms and ammunition, from the gun stores and rather less well regulated gun-shows of Texas, Arizona and New Mexico, augmenting the firepower of the cartels. This illegal trade in firearms, known locally as the *trafico de la hormiga* ('trail of ants'), entails routine and regular smuggling of firearms across the Mexican border from the US. Over 8,000 firearms sold in the US during 2009-10 have been subsequently traced to Mexico, and around 90 per cent of surveyed illegal firearms recovered in Mexico originate within the US (Chu and Krause, 2009). At the same time the proximity to the US border accounts for the large number of would-be (illegal) transients and emigrants frustrated and piled up at the border in their quest for the American Dream. Instead they find themselves ensnared by its opposite, as the cheap dispensable labour of the sweatshop *maquiladora* factory system. These factories and assembly plants are the direct result of the North American Free Trade Agreement (NAFTA) established in 1994, by which the US capitalism was given free access to the cheap non-unionised labour of its southern neighbour, and northern Mexico gained the promise of some much needed economic investment. Unfortunately the benefits of this arrangement were far from equally distributed – for Vulliamy, the *maquiladoras* perfectly symbolise Mexico's 'subjugated but dependent relationship to the US economy' (2010, p 200).

The *maquiladoras* offer gruelling and highly exploitative working conditions for a female-dominated, apparently expendable, labour force. For many commentators, this very dispensability of the largely female labour force is reflected in another of the cruel realities of Juárez: the *femicido* murders of over 500 young women, and the hundreds more missing or lost since 1994. According to Alba and Guzman (2010) and Staudt (2008), the Juárez border area establishes a worst-case scenario of weaponised, hyper-violent misogynistic masculinity in crisis. On the one hand, the drug cartel conflicts, like many gang cultures around the world (Totten, 2000; Batchelor, 2009), have cultivated a culture of violent masculine impunity further sustained by police corruption and ineptitude. At the same time the predominantly female employment opportunities in the new factory system have allowed the resentments of displaced males to fester even as the social needs and human rights of this vast, nameless, transient and abused female workforce are ground down to the minimum on US assembly lines.

As Arriola explains, the missing element in many of the official discussions of the Juárez murders 'is the multi-national corporations' complicity with Mexican officials in disregarding the health, safety and security needs of the Mexican women and girls who work in the *maquiladoras* ... the factories run twenty-four hours a day, [but] pay no taxes, and do very little to ensure that their workers will have a roof over their heads, beds to sleep in and enough money to feed their families ... such employment has not enhanced peace and prosperity amongst the working class, instead hostility against the poor working women has increased' (Arriola, 2010, pp 27-8). Or, as Vulliamy's interviewees put it, somewhat more forcefully, 'The *maquilas* see women who work much as they see our city, as something expendable. So what if a woman is murdered? Ten or a hundred? There are always plenty more.... If you want to beat, rape or kill a woman, there is no better place than Juárez, there are thousands to choose from, plenty of opportunities and, thirdly, you can get away with it. The lives of women, especially poor women, have no value' (2010, p 164). The final irony is that Juárez – the neoliberal trap where the American Dream turns nightmare – marks not the breakdown of the late capitalist social order, or some failed state, but rather, Vulliamy suggests, it *is* the neoliberal order of the future (2010, p 106).

In such urban traps the world over, bad governance, bad neighbours, scarce resources and chronic conflict offer the poorest rather limited opportunities. As Wacquant puts it, 'for those who are repeatedly rejected from the labour market or balk [sic] at taking dead-end "slave jobs" in the deregulated service sectors that strip them of their dignity by requiring that they execute menial tasks paid at poverty wages with no benefits ... underground activities offer a bounty of full time employment opportunities' (Wacquant, 2008a, p 66). For such people, he continues, 'predatory crime constitutes a form of petty entrepreneurialism in which they put to use the only valuable assets they possess: physical prowess and a working knowledge ... of the streets' (Wacquant, 2008a, p 66). So it is not difficult to appreciate 'the main attraction of gangs for subproletarian young men in the hyper-ghetto' for they represent 'queer business concerns that can increase [one's] chances of securing income in cash and a modicum of financial security ... besides, the drug trade is often the only form of business known to adolescents, and one which has the immense virtue of being a genuine 'equal opportunity employer' (p 67). And rather than imposing alien and external (statist) categories such as 'crime' (or law and justice and right and wrong) on these behaviours, Wacquant, like Venkatesh, understands them as part of normal urban life, 'the perpetual negotiation, collusion and compromise, of the constant struggle to survive – to find a purpose for your life, to fulfil your desires, to feed your family' (Venkatesh, 2006, p xix).

Drawing on the work of Bourgois (1989, 2003), Wacquant details the 'explosive growth of the criminal economy' that 'crystallizes as a culture of terror' (Bourgois, 1989), a 'grisly lottery of homicides' (Wacquant, 2008a, pp 126-7) or, in Fagan and Wilkinson's terms, an 'ecology of violence' (Fagan and Wilkinson, 1998, 2000). In the illegal economy regular displays of violence are a 'business requirement' which serve to establish both personal and commercial credibility. It is, he contends, following Collier, an environment populated by bad and predatory neighbours, scarce resources and bad governance represented most immediately by corrupt and violent police, and where people 'must protect themselves from violence by being ready to wield it at any time' (Wacquant, 2008a, pp 66-7). Indeed Wacquant himself adopts the language of Hobbesian brutalism to describe the bitter 'economy of predation' which pits 'gangs, rival factions of a gang ("crews" and "posses") which fight … [in] a sort of free for all, a perpetual mini-guerilla war of the dispossessed' (Wacquant, 2008a, p 128).

Such conditions produce a range of responses. In the *banlieues* of Paris Wacquant describes a widely shared perception (also reported elsewhere, see Goldsmith, 2006) that young people especially are 'subjected to a generalised pattern of anti-youth discrimination that obtains both inside and outsides their estates', and that they are subject to constant 'unwarranted suspicion and surveillance' (p 189). Elsewhere, Wacquant describes the urban street life of the ghetto as a 'grotesque theatre of aggressive masculinity' (p 211), where violent confrontation, fuelled by the ready supply of handguns and drugs, establishes fragile (and often highly contested) hierarchies of honour and respect which subjects must be ready to defend (Short, 1997; Bourgois, 2003; Stewart et al, 2006; Squires, 2010b). One final consequence of these chronic relations of violence concerns the capacity or will of the criminal justice system – and especially of the police – to confront these problems effectively. In Collier's terms, this aspect of 'bad governance', which can oscillate between corrupt neglect and full-scale military intervention, can lead communities, or groups within these communities, to seek their own forms of justice (Wacquant, 2008a, p 219). Here we encounter another dimension of gang sociology.

Gangs, conflict and peace-making

One side of the gang story emerging from a police-led criminology will always be about the role of gangs as criminal parasites holding communities to ransom, corrupting and accelerating the violent delinquency of youth, defining themselves as implacably against mainstream values while engaging in all manner of criminal enterprise. But this is only part of the story. Implicit in Wacquant's acknowledgement that communities (or groups within communities) might seek their own justice when it is denied or frustrated by the agencies of the state is anticipation of a different interpretation. It is an issue he scarcely develops, especially in *Punishing the poor*, where any community capacity appears rather overwhelmed by a rather more structuralist interpretation. It was precisely this which provoked Frances Fox Piven's question, referred to earlier (Piven, 2010, p 114), for now there is plenty of evidence emerging from the work of a newer generation of sociologists and more critical criminologists of the *active* roles played by gangs – as collective actors – although, it has to be said, these are not always *positive* roles.

The argument about the gang's constructive potential (certainly recognised in Thrasher's sociology [1927]) is sketched in Elijah Anderson's critical engagement with Wacquant in the *American Journal of Sociology* in 2002. Anderson noted how:

> In some of the most economically distressed and drug and crime ridden pockets of the city, the rules of civil law have been severely weakened and in their stead a code of the street often holds sway ... the *code of the street* emerges where the influence of the police ends and personal responsibility for one's safety is felt to begin, resulting in a kind of people's law based upon street justice. (Anderson, 2002, pp 1546-7; emphasis added)

The debate surrounding this so-called 'code of the street', however, is deeply contested. A number of commentators, Anderson (1999) prominent among them, have argued that a knowledge of the street and its relations of hierarchy, deference and respect, equips the 'streetwise' with the means to negotiate their way relatively safely around potentially dangerous neighbourhoods, able to avoid either provoking or attracting status challenges. Yet these issues are seldom so clear cut. Stewart et al, in an article revealingly titled 'I ain't gonna let no-one disrespect me' (2006), and intended to test the Anderson argument, revealed how their research on street behaviour codes found that they were just as likely to *provoke* violent challenges and altercations as they were to forestall them. One issue was that the very attitudes, demeanours and behaviours which were intended to convey that a person was to be taken seriously were just as likely to be perceived by others as a *challenge*. Respect, in other words, was not something fixed and constant but a relation that needed to be renewed and forcefully reinvested constantly (Zubillaga, 2009).

Further complicating the picture, Mullins (2004) found that the masculine behaviour codes to which his interview subjects (repeat violent offenders) claimed to subscribe were only rather loosely followed in practice. At times they may have been almost entirely aspirational (never hit females, never 'grass' to the cops, never attack someone from behind) or, on other occasions, followed for purely instrumental reasons, but were largely disregarded when they conflicted with other priorities. The overwhelming masculine preoccupation with 'respect' is traced to the 'profound alienation from mainstream US society felt by many inner-city blacks, particularly the poorest' (Anderson, 1994, cited in Short, 1997, p 65). As Short has concluded, 'out of concern for being disrespected, respect is easily violated. Because status problems are mixed with extreme resource limitations, people – especially young people – exaggerate the importance of symbols, often with life-threatening consequences' (Short, 1997, p 65). Yet, respect is one currency young men can command even although it is highly contested, easily lost and constantly imperilled by the (seemingly almost random) violence that sustains it. While respect and street knowledge might form the basis for the establishment of forms of street capital (Sandberg, 2008), this too can be jeopardised when violence problems escalate. As Rodgers has argued: 'the means through which gangs … attempted to maintain and accumulate both collective and individual social capital stocks can be said to have failed at least partly due to the unsustainable nature of the violent social practices upon which they were based – which in fact is Thomas Hobbes' central point in his classic *Leviathan*' (Rodgers, 2006, p 9).

Finally, the analysis of the violent de-civilising environment of inner-urban street life has been further extended by Fagan and Wilkinson (1998, 2000) in their New York study. Their data revealed that obtaining and then using a gun had become part of a 'rite of passage' into manhood and a respected street identity. Interviewees had seemingly internalised a number of rules of behaviour, including ideas of a shortened life expectancy, which the researchers collectively referred to as 'processes of *anticipatory socialisation*', reflecting the perceived likelihood of threats, risks and victimisation from lethal violence (Fagan and Wilkinson, 1998). Here, experiences (direct or indirect) of violence fuelled future expectations of violence, leading young people to both anticipate and prepare for violent encounters. Such preparation entailed acquiring and carrying their own weapons, and being prepared to use them as occasion demanded. Preparedness also entailed the need to react quickly and a willingness to 'shoot first' as necessary. Just as we might consider the double-sided character of street codes, respect and street capital, so too there is a developing debate about gangs as community assets, as *non-state actors* providing positive forms of governance and regulation from below where few other forms of authority exist. Davis extends the point to include the wider social relations of spatial and ethno-racial governance in poor areas. 'Gangs frequently act as neighbourhood militias to police public space, enforce (or resist) ethnic and racial borders and thereby control access to jobs and housing … [providing] some measure of entrepreneurial opportunity…. If some gangs are vampire-like parasites on their own neighbours, others play Robin Hood or employer of the last resort; most combine elements of both predation and welfare' (Davis, 2008, p xi). The empirical question involves assessing where, how and why (and maybe for whom) the gang plays positive roles and can be seen as a developmental asset and where, how, why and for whom it might be seen as negative, decivilising and contrary to social development.

Varieties of violence

In the developed economies of the capitalist West, much as the phenomenon of 'gangsterisation' is largely *understood* as an outgrowth of inequality, racism, social exclusion, unequal social development and, most recently the neoliberal innovations of mass unemployment, the retrenchment of welfare regimes and the emergence of alternative illegal economies (usually based around drugs); the gang itself is invariably seen in negative terms as almost feral, violence accelerating and community destroying. The same is manifestly not so true in other parts of the world where distinctions between gangs, armed groups, citizen militias, vigilante associations, warlords, drug cartels, terrorist cells, freedom fighters and revolutionary movements can often become quite blurred (Koonings and Kruijt, 2004; Hagedorn, 2008, pp 22-4; Hazen, 2010). While the developed West, from Thrasher and the Chicago School of Sociology to the present day, understands gang development as a facet of *social disorganisation*, in the global south and 'fourth world', gangsterisation, weaponisation and militarisation are often associated with parallel notions of state *deligitimation, failure* and *retreat*. The spaces created by these state withdrawals are then filled by the activities of armed and angry young men (Hagedorn, 2008, p 31). It is in precisely such contexts, Rodgers contends, and here he is writing about the post-conflict societies of Central America, that gangs can be engaged in both financial capital asset accumulation (drug-trafficking profits) and both individual and collective social capital accumulation and neighbourhood defence (Rodgers, 2006).

There are many forms that can be taken by the violence of the urban dispossessed. Collier's four traps have already given us a sense of the ways in which bad governance, bad neighbours, poor resources and weapon-led conflict facilitation can shape the nature of the violence, either prolonging it and institutionalising its pernicious effects or fostering its social and transformational potential. However, focusing only on one aspect or dimension of these processes will never give us the whole of the story, and the socially dysfunctional neoliberalism described by Wacquant in *Punishing the poor*, while it paints a picture for us of underclass formation, tells us relatively little about how this underclass might react. For this we have to look at other processes, cultures, environments and neighbours and the behaviours of other non-state actors. Hagedorn (2008) has gone some way to explore the 'globalisation' of forms of 'gangsta' culture and there exists a growing literature on the contribution of illicit small arms transfers and how illegal weapon trafficking can contribute to the perpetuation of chronic violence in the world's most troubled societies and regions (Small Arms Survey, 2001, 2002, 2003, 2007, 2010; Cukier and Sidel, 2006; Carr, 2008). According to the Small Arms Survey 2002, firearm supplies must now be seen as 'independent variables' in conflict zones, 'situational facilitators' of violence – including chronic levels of gender-based violence and abuse. Conflicts are perpetuated by weapon supply, so durable solutions to these must focus on the tools of violence as well as the underlying causes.

Take, for example, the case of Mexico's borderland *Amexica* described earlier, and specifically the predicament of its 'murder city' – or Juárez (Bowden, 2010) so eloquently described by Vulliamy (2010). This demonstrates not only the profound consequences of having the worst neighbour in the world, to the north, but also the worst of all resources, dirt-cheapened labour and plentiful cocaine, deeply ineffectual governance largely handed over to the multinational *maquiladora* sweatshop factory system and the drug cartels, each pursuing a variant of their own 'scorched earth' social development strategy. Into this context the US's own free market in firearms pours a 'river of steel' (Vulliamy, 2010, p 248) comprising high-grade auto- and semi-automatic weapons to keep the wheels of conflict turning.

Likewise our other illustrations of, first, the situated violence in Rio's *favelas*, deemed worthy of invasion by Brazil's military after years of corruption and neglect and, second, the difficulties of escape or redemption in the *City of God*, together demonstrate the compounding consequences of bad governance, neglectful neighbours, scarce resources and excess weaponry. Yet each case is different, and the social relations of urban violence merit an understanding at a level that gives meaning to the actions of those living the most dangerous of 21st-century lives, and understands the choices they make in the light of the opportunities, constraints and fears facing them. It is in these meanest of streets, slums and ghettos that the most profoundly damaging and decivilising consequences of neoliberalism are to be found and the foundations for the most potent criticisms of neoliberalism developed.

References

Alba, A.G. and Guzman, G. (ed) (2010) *Making a killing: Femicide, free trade and La frontera*, Austin, TX: University of Texas Press.

Anderson, E. (1994) 'Violence and the inner city poor', *Atlantic Monthly* (May), pp 81-94.

Anderson, E. (1999) *Code of the street: Decency, violence and the moral life of the inner city*, New York: Norton & Co.

Anderson, E. (2002) 'The ideologically drawn critique', *American Journal of Sociology*, vol 107, pp 1546-7.

Andrews, K. and Jacobs, J. (1990) *Punishing the poor: Poverty under Thatcher*, London: Macmillan.

Arias, E.D. (2006) *Drugs and democracy in Rio de Janeiro: Trafficking, social networks and public security*, Chapel Hill, NC: University of North Carolina Press.

Arriola, E.R. (2010) 'Accountability for murder in the Maquiladoras: linking corporate indifference to gender violence at the US-Mexico border', in A.G. Alba and G. Guzman (ed) *Making a killing: Femicide, free trade and La frontera*, Austin, TX: University of Texas Press, pp 25-62.

Batchelor, S. (2009) 'Girls, gangs and violence: assessing the evidence', *Probation Journal*, December, vol 56, pp 399-414.

Beck, U. (1996) 'World risk society as cosmopolitan society? Ecological questions in a framework of manufactured uncertainties', *Theory, Culture and Society*, vol 13, no 4, pp 1-32.

Bigo, D. (2006) 'Security, exception, ban and surveillance', in D. Lyon (ed) *Theorizing surveillance: The panopticon and beyond*, Cullompton: Willan Publishing, pp 46-68.

Bourgois, P. (1989) 'In search of Horatio Alger: culture and ideology in the crack economy', *Contemporary Drug Problems*, vol 13, Winter, pp 619-49.

Bourgois, P. (2003) *In search of respect: Selling crack in El Barrio* (2nd edn), Cambridge: Cambridge University Press.

Bowden, C. (2010) *Murder city: Ciudad Juárez and the global economy's new killing fields*, New York: Nation Books.

Bryson, A. and Jacobs, J. (1992) *Policing the workshy*, Aldershot: Avebury.

Burney, E. (2005) *Making people behave: Anti-social behaviour, politics and policy*, Cullompton: Willan Publishing

Carr, C. (2008) *Kalashnikov culture: Small arms proliferation and irregular warfare*, Westport CT: Praeger Security International

Castells, M. (2000) *End of Millennium (The Information Age, Volume 3)*, Oxford: Wiley-Blackwell.

Chu, V.S. and Krause, W.J. (2009) *Gun trafficking and the South West border*, Report for Congress, 7-5700, Congressional Research Service, 21 September (www.crs.gov).

Collier, P. (2008) *The bottom billion*, Oxford: Oxford University Press.

Cukier, W. and Seidel, V. (2006) *The global gun epidemic: From Saturday night specials to AK47s*, Westport, CT: Praeger Security international.

Currie, E. (1997) 'Market, crime and community: toward a mid-range theory of post-industrial violence', *Theoretical Criminology*, May, vol 1, no 2, pp 147-72.

Davis, M. (2008) Foreword to J. Hagedorn *A world of gangs: Armed young men and gangsta culture*, Minneapolis, MN: University of Minnesota Press.

Dean, H. (1990) *Social security and social control*, London: Routledge.

Dikeç, M. (2007) *Badlands of the republic: Space, politics and urban policy*, Oxford: Blackwell.

Dorling, D. (2008) 'Prime suspect: murder in Britain', in P. Hillyard et al (eds) *Criminal obsessions: Harm matters more than crime* (2nd edn), London: Centre for Crime and Justice Studies, pp 28-40.

Fagan, J. and Wilkinson, D. (1998) 'Guns, youth violence and social identity in inner cities', *Youth Violence*, vol 24, pp 105-88.

Fagan, J. and Wilkinson, D. (2000) *Situational contexts of gun use by young males in inner cities*, Washington, DC: US Department of Justice, National Criminal Justice Reference Service (NCJRS).

Field, F. (1981) *Inequality in Britain: Freedom, welfare and the state*, London: Fontana.

Foucault, M. (1977) *Discipline and punish: The birth of the prison*, Harmondsworth: Penguin.

Gamble, A. (1988) *The free economy and the strong state*, Basingstoke: Macmillan.

Garland, D. (2001) *The culture of control: Crime and social order in contemporary society*, Oxford: Oxford University Press.

Goldsmith, C. (2006) '"You just know you're being watched everywhere": young people custodial experiences and community safety', in P. Squires (ed) *Community safety: Critical perspectives on policy and practice*, Bristol: The Policy Press, pp 13-34.

Goldson, B. (ed) (2000) *The new youth justice*, Lyme Regis: Russell House Publishing.

Goldstone, P. (2001) *Making the world safe for tourism*, New Haven, CT: Yale University Press.

Graham, S. (2010) *Cities under siege: The new military urbanism*, London: Verso.

Hagedorn, J. (1988) *People and folks: Gangs, crime and the underclass in a rustbelt city*, Chicago, IL: Lakeview Press.

Hagedorn, J. (2008) *A world of gangs: Armed young men and gangsta culture*, Minneapolis, MN: University of Minnesota Press.

Hall, S. (1977) 'The great moving right show', *Marxism Today*.

Hall, S. et al (1978) *Policing the crisis: Mugging, the state and law and order*, London: Hutchinson University Press.

Hazen, J.M. (2010) 'Gangs, groups and guns: an overview', in Small Arms Survey 2010, *Gangs, guns and groups*, Geneva and Oxford: Graduate Institute of International Studies and Oxford University Press.

Hempel, L. and Topfer, E. (2009) 'The surveillance consensus: reviewing the politics of CCTV in three European countries', *European Journal of Criminology*, vol 6, no 2, pp 157-77.

Hope, T. (2001) 'Crime victimisation and inequality in risk society', in R. Matthews and J. Pitts (ed) *Crime, disorder and community safety*, London: Routledge, pp 193-218.

Jones, C. and Novak, T. (1999) *Poverty, welfare and the disciplinary state*, London: Routledge.

Jutersonke, O., Krause, K. and Muggah, R. (2007) 'Guns in the city: urban landscapes of armed violence', in Small Arms Survey 2007, *Guns and the city*, Cambridge: Cambridge University Press, pp 161-95.

Klein, M. (1995) *The American street gang: Its nature, prevalence and control*, New York, Oxford: Oxford University Press.

Koonings, K. and Kruijt, D. (2004) 'Armed actors, organised violence and state failure in Latin America: a survey of issues and arguments', in K. Koonings and D. Kruijt (eds) *Armed actors: Organised violence and state failure in Latin America*, London: Zed Books, pp 5-15.

Lacey, N. (2008) *The prisoners' dilemma: Political economy and punishment in contemporary democracies*, Cambridge: Cambridge University Press.

Lins, P. (1997) *City of God*, London: Bloomsbury.

Morenoff, J.D., Sampson, R.J. and Raudenbush, S.W. et al (2001) 'Neighbourhood inequality, collective efficacy and the spatial dynamics of urban violence', *Criminology*, vol 39, no 3, pp 517-60.

Mullins, C. (2004) *Holding your square: Masculinities, streetlife and violence*, Cullompton: Willan.

Piven, F.F. (2010) 'A response to Wacquant', *Theoretical Criminology*, vol 14, pp 111-16.

Pratt, J., Brown, D., Brown, M., Hallsworth, S. and Morrison, W. (2005) *The new punitiveness: Trends, theories, perspectives*, London: Taylor & Francis.

Rodger, J. (2008) *Criminalising social policy: Anti-social behaviour and welfare in a de-civilised society*, Cullompton: Willan Publishing.

Rodgers, D. (2009) 'Living in the shadow of death: gangs, violence and social order in urban Nicaragua: 1996-2002', in G. Jones and D. Rodgers (eds) *Youth violence in Latin America*, New York, Palgrave Macmillan. pp 25-44.

Rodgers, G. (2006) 'Gangs, violence, and asset building in post-conflict Central America', Brookings/Ford Workshop on Asset-based Approaches to Development, 27/28 June (www.brookings.edu/global/assets06/14rodgers.pdf).

Sandberg, S. (2008) 'Street capital: ethnicity and violence on the streets of Oslo', *Theoretical Criminology*, vol 12, no 2, pp 153-71.

Savenije, W. and van der Borgh, C. (2004) 'Youth gangs, social exclusion and the transformation of violence in El Salvador', in K. Koonings and D. Kruijt (eds) *Armed actors: Organised violence and state failure in Latin America*, London: Zed Books, pp 155-71.

Short, J.R.F. (1997) *Poverty, ethnicity and violent crime*, Boulder, CO: Westview Press/HarperCollns.

Simon, J. (2007) *Governing through crime*, Oxford: Oxford University Press.

Small Arms Survey 2001 'After the smoke clears', Chapter 6, *Profiling the problem*, Geneva and Oxford: Graduate Institute of International Studies and Oxford University Press.

Small Arms Survey 2002 *Counting the human cost*, Geneva and Oxford: Graduate institute of International Studies and Oxford University Press.

Small Arms Survey 2003 *Development denied*, Geneva and Oxford: Graduate institute of International Studies and Oxford University Press.

Small Arms Survey 2007 *Guns and the city*, Geneva and Oxford: Graduate institute of International Studies and Oxford University Press.

Small Arms Survey 2010 *Gangs, groups and guns*, Geneva and Oxford: Graduate institute of International Studies and Oxford University Press.

Sonnevelt, M. (2009) 'Dealing with violence and public (in)security in a popular neighbourhood in Guadalajara, Mexico', in G. Jones and D. Rodgers (eds) *Youth violence in Latin America*, New York: Palgrave Macmillan, pp 45-62.

Squires, P. (1990) *Anti-social policy: Welfare, ideology and the disciplinary state*, Hemel Hempstead: Harvester/Wheatsheaf Books.

Squires, P. (ed) (2006) *Community safety: Critical perspectives on policy and practice*, Bristol: The Policy Press.

Squires, P. (ed) (2008) *ASBO nation: The criminalisation of nuisance*, Bristol: The Policy Press.

Squires, P. (2010) 'Young people and "weaponisation"', in B. Goldson (ed) *Youth in crisis? Gangs, territoriality and violence*, London: Routledge, pp 144-60.

Squires, P. and Stephen, D.E. (2005) *Rougher justice: Anti-social behaviour and young people*, Cullompton: Willan Publishing.

Staudt, K. (2008) *Violence and activism at the border: Gender, fear and everyday life in ciudad Juárez*, Austin, TX: University of Texas Press.

Steinert, H. (2004) 'The indispensable metaphor of war: on populist politics and the contradictions of the state's monopoly of force', *Theoretical Criminology*, vol 8, no 7, pp 265-91.

Stewart, E.A., Schreck, C.J. and Simons, R.L. (2006) '"I ain't gonna let no-one disrespect me": does the code of the street reduce or increase violent victimisation among African American adolescents?', *Journal of Research in Crime and Delinquency*, vol 43, no 4, pp 427-58.

Taylor-Gooby, P. and Dean, M. (1992) *Dependency culture: The explosion of a myth*, Upper Saddle River, NJ: Prentice-Hall.

Thrasher, F. (1927) *The gang: A study of 1,313 gangs in Chicago*, Chicago: University of Chicago Press.

Titmuss, R.M. (1963) 'The social division of welfare', in *Essays on the welfare state*, London: Heinemann.

Tonry, M. (2010) 'The costly consequences of populist posturing: ASBOs, victims, "rebalancing" and diminution in support for civil liberties', *Punishment & Society*, October, vol 12, pp 387-413.

Totten, M. (1999) *Guys, gangs and girlfriend abuse*, Peterborough, ON: Broadview Press.

van Reenen, P. (2004) 'Policing extensions in Latin America', in K. Koonings and D. Kruijt (eds) *Armed actors: Organised violence and state failure in Latin America*, London: Zed Books, pp 33-51.

Venkatesh, S.A. (2006) *Off the books: The underground economy of the urban poor*, Cambridge, MA: Harvard University Press.

Vulliamy, E. (2010) *Amexica: War along the borderline*, London: Bodley Head Publishers.

Wacquant, L. (2003) 'Toward a dictatorship over the poor? Notes on the penalization of poverty in Brazil', *Punishment & Society*, vol 5, no 2, pp 197-205.

Wacquant, L. (2008a) *Urban outcasts: A comparative sociology of advanced marginality*, Cambridge: Polity Press.

Wacquant, L. (2008b) 'The militarization of urban marginality: lessons from the Brazilian metropolis', *International Political Sociology*, vol 2, pp 56-74.

Wacquant, L. (2009) *Punishing the poor: The neoliberal government of social insecurity*, Durham, NC: Duke University Press.

Zubillaga, V. (2009) '"Gaining respect": the logic of violence among young men in the barrios of Caracas, Venezuela', in G. Jones and D. Rodgers (eds) *Youth violence in Latin America*, New York: Palgrave Macmillan, pp 83-104.

Response

TWELVE

The wedding of workfare and prisonfare in the 21st century: responses to critics and commentators[1]

Loïc Wacquant

In this chapter, I explain how and why 'the prison' has returned to the institutional forefront of advanced societies, when four decades ago analysts of the penal scene were convinced it was on the decline, if not on the path towards extinction. I draw on my book *Punishing the poor* (Wacquant, 2009a, p 315) to argue that the expansion and glorification of the police, the courts and the penitentiary are a response not to crime trends but to the diffusion of social insecurities; that we need to reconnect social and penal policies and treat them as two variants of poverty policy to grasp the new politics of marginality; and that the simultaneous and converging deployment of restrictive 'workfare' and expansive 'prisonfare' are contributing to to the forging of the neoliberal Leviathan. By way of introduction, let me indicate how I moved from the study of urban inequality to that of the penal state on my way to adapting Bourdieu's concept of 'bureaucratic field' to capture the revamping of poor discipline at this century's dawn.

Punishing the poor is the second volume in a trilogy that unravels the triangular nexus between class transformation, ethno-racial division and the revamping of the state in the era of neoliberal hegemony. Think of a triangle with the two-way relationship between class and 'race' forming the base and the state providing the top. The first book in the trilogy, *Urban outcasts* (Wacquant, 2008), explores the base: it takes up the class/'race' nexus in the dualising metropolis through a comparison of the sudden collapse of the black US ghetto with the slow disintegration of working-class territories in the Western European city after deindustrialisation. I make three main arguments: I challenge the fashionable thesis of a transatlantic convergence of 'districts of dispossession' on the model of the dark ghetto; I trace the making of the African American 'hyper-ghetto' and of the 'anti-ghettos' of

Europe in the post-Fordist age to shifts in public policy, arguing that both formations are economically underdetermined and politically overdetermined; and I diagnose the onset of a new regime of urban marginality fuelled by the fragmentation of wage labour, the curtailment of the social state and territorial stigmatisation.

The next two books mine the two sides of the triangle. *Punishing the poor* takes up the class/state nexus on both the social and penal fronts. It charts how public officials have responded to this emerging marginality through punitive containment. It also reveals that the new politics and policy of poverty, coupling disciplinary workfare and the neutralising prison, invented in the US over the past three decades, partake of the crafting of the neoliberal state, properly reconceptualised. The third volume, *Deadly symbiosis* (Wacquant, 2011), dissects the 'race'/state nexus: it shows how ethno-racial division intensifies class decomposition at the bottom, facilitates the shift to workfare and escalates the rolling out of the penal state; and, conversely, how penalisation refurbishes the meaning and workings of 'race'. It sketches a historical and theoretical model of the meshing of the bare hyper-ghetto, in which lower-class blacks become trapped after the 1960s, with the overgrown prison system in the US; it moves across the Atlantic to cover the over-incarceration of postcolonial immigrants in the European Union (EU); and it concludes by exploring the militarisation of marginality in the Brazilian metropolis, understood as a revelator of the deep logic of penalisation. A central argument is that the prison and 'race' are tied together by permutations of dishonour.

A fourth book, *Prisons of poverty*, which I wrote first a decade ago as an exercise in 'civic sociology' (Wacquant, 2009b), tracks the international travels and travails of 'zero tolerance' policing and other 'made-in-the-US' penal notions and nostrums (the 'broken windows' theory, youth curfews, mandatory minimum sentences, plea bargaining, etc), as part of the worldwide spread of neoliberalism. I demonstrate how the 'Washington Consensus' on economic deregulation and welfare retrenchment was extended to punitive crime control through the agency of think-tanks, politicians seduced by the new religion of the market, a new globe-trotting breed of 'consultants' in 'urban security' and local academics eager to smuggle US techniques of penalisation into their countries by dressing them up in scholarly garb. Now that the backdrop is set, let me move to my three theses.

Ramping up the penal state in response to social insecurity

My first thesis is that the ramping up of the penal wing of the state is a response to social insecurity, and not a reaction to crime trends. In the three decades after the peaking of the civil rights movement, the US went from being a leader in progressive justice poised to show humanity the way to 'a nation without prisons' – to recall the title of a book by US penal experts published in 1975 (Dodge, 1975) – through the development of alternatives to confinement, to apostle of 'zero tolerance' policing, architect of 'three strikes and you're out' and world champion in incarceration with 2.3 million behind bars and over 7 million under justice supervision. Why? The conventional answer is that this stupendous expansion of punishment was driven by the rise in crime. And yet, victimisation first stagnated and then decreased during this entire period. Consider this simple statistic: the US held 21 prisoners for every 10,000 'index crimes' in 1975; 30 years later, it locked up 125 prisoners for every 10,000 crimes. This means that the country has become six times more punitive, holding crime constant.

To explain this unforeseen and unprecedented upsurge, we need to *break out of the crime-and-punishment box* and pay attention to the extra-penological functions of penal institutions. Then we discover that, in the wake of the 'race' riots of the 1960s, the police, courts and prison have been deployed to contain the urban dislocations wrought by economic deregulation and the implosion of the ghetto as ethno-racial container, and impose the discipline of insecure employment at the bottom of the polarising class structure. The punitive turn in penal policy responds not to *criminal* insecurity but to the *social* insecurity caused by the casualisation of wage labour and the disruption of ethno-racial hierarchy, and not the 'diffuse anxieties' generated by the coming of 'the risk society' or the age of 'late modernity' (Ericson and Haggerty, 1997; Garland, 2001).

The ascent of the penal state was especially swift and abrupt in the US because advanced marginality is particularly prevalent, entrenched and concentrated in that country (Wacquant, 2008, pp 3-7, 89-91, 119-32). This, in turn, is due to the uniquely rigid ethno-racial cleavage that isolates African Americans in physical, social and symbolic space, and a host of related features of the national institutions: the generalised degradation of labour and the depth of social inequality, the bureaucratic splintering and rampant commodification of public goods, the unusually high levels of both class and ethnic segregation in the metropolis, the hold of a religiously inflected moral individualism and the categorical and castigating character of state programmes aimed at the poor, suspected by definition of being 'undeserving' (Katz, 1989). All these factors, which fostered the organised atrophy of welfare in reaction to the racial crisis of the 1960s and the economic turmoil of the 1970s, also facilitated the runaway hypertrophy of punishment aimed at the same precarious and stigmatised population.

Let us now cross the Atlantic to diagnose developments in Western Europe. Some analysts of the European penal scene, such as Nicola Lacey (2008), are impressed by the chasm between the Old and the New World and underscore that, with 750 inmates per 100,000, the US are in a class by themselves (with Russia and Rwanda right behind them, it is rather inglorious company indeed). It is true that Western European countries sport comparatively modest rates of confinement, ranging from one sixth to one tenth that of the US (in the 70s per 100,000 across Scandinavia to just over 150 per 100,000 for England, Scotland and Spain). But this must not hide two crucial facts. First, *penalisation takes many different forms and is not reducible to incarceration.* Second, *incarceration has shown steady and sturdy growth across Western Europe* since the early 1980s: it has increased by more than one half in France, Italy and Belgium; it has nearly doubled in England and Wales, Sweden, Portugal and Greece; and it has quadrupled in Spain and the Netherlands, long held up as models of humane penality for the other countries to follow (Downes, 1993).

In reality, a drift toward the penalisation of urban marginality has swept through Western Europe with a lag of two decades, albeit on a smaller scale (commensurate with the make-up of the state and social space in these societies) and with three distinctive twists. First, the embrace of law and order by European governments has been more virulent at the level of rhetoric than policy delivery: the new penal laws typically 'bark' louder than they 'bite' because the texture of social and economic citizenship is more robust, human rights standards thwart excessive criminalisation and judicial professionals have been able to resist penal extension from within the state apparatus (Snacken, 2010). But hyping 'insecurity' and promoting crime fighting in and around districts of dereliction to the rank of government priority, ahead of fighting unemployment in these same 'sink estates', has definitely shifted government priorities in favour of penal posturing and action.

Second, European societies endowed with a strong statist tradition are using the front end of the penal chain, the police, rather than the back end, the prison, to curb social disorders and despair in low-income districts. For example, in France, the inmate population has risen by one third over the past decade, from 51,000 in 2000 to 67,000 in

2010, but during that same period the number of people arrested and held overnight *en garde à vue* (in police custody) in a police lock-up (a procedure deemed in violation of European law and recently declared unconstitutional by the French courts) nearly tripled to approach the extravagant figure of one million. And the vast majority of these arrestees are residents of the neighbourhoods of relegation where the insecure fractions of the emerging urban proletariat concentrate, both native and immigrant (Jobard, 2006).

Third, instead of a brutal swing from the social to the penal management of poverty as in the US, continental countries have intensified both, expanding welfare protection and police intervention simultaneously in a contradictory thrust that has both stimulated and limited the extension of the punitive mesh. The recent evolution of Belgium offers an exemplary illustration of this joint stretching of the social safety-net and of the penal dragnet. Van Campenhoudt et al (2001) trace how the formation of this 'social law-and-order compromise' has fostered the development of a large third sector of state-sponsored interventions aimed at 'pacifying' derelict urban zones where poverty and postcolonial migrants cluster.

These three features define a 'Western European road' to the penalisation of poverty (which differentiates further into distinct national paths in accordance with each country's state structure and conception of citizenship) that is not that of the US. Joining the 'Washington Consensus' on proactive penality definitely does *not* imply the slavish imitation or mechanical replication of US policies and patterns. But, from a longer macro-political perspective, the dominant trend is similar: a punitive revamping of public policy that weds the 'invisible hand' of the market to the 'iron fist' of the penal state. As a result, the resurging prison has come to serve three missions that have little to do with crime control: to bend the fractions of the post-industrial working class to precarious wage work; to warehouse their most disruptive or superfluous elements; and to patrol the boundaries of the deserving citizenry while reasserting the authority of the state in the restricted domain it now assigns itself. What is notable about these three functions is that they correspond closely to the role shouldered by the prison at its historical inception in the late 16th century, as shown by the Dutch historian Pieter Spierenburg (1991): to act as a 'street sweeper' and disciplining device for the mounting wave of the urban poor as well as to project the fortitude of the ruler.

Relinking social and penal policy

My second thesis is that we must relink shifts in penal and social policy, instead of isolating shifts in criminal justice from correlative changes on the various policy fronts that interface with the same dispossessed populations and districts, for the sudden growth and glorification of punishment partakes of a broader re-engineering of the state that also entails the replacement of the right to welfare by the obligation of workfare (that is, forced participation in subpar employment as a condition of public support). The downsizing of public aid and the upsizing of the prison are two sides of the same coin of political restructuring at the foot of the social and urban order. Better yet, the same resentful and racialised vision of the poor has informed the punitive turn in both welfare and justice policy: after the revolts of the 1960s, public aid recipients and criminals were 'painted black', which activated racial animus, and came to be seen not as *deprived* but as *depraved*, social parasites in need of stern tutelage instead of support.

In 1971, Frances Fox Piven and Richard Cloward (1993 [1971]) published a classic of social science entitled *Regulating the poor* in which they proposed that poor relief expands and contracts along with the cycles of the labour market. That model worked for the half-century opened by the New Deal. But, in the age of hypermobile capital and flexible work, this cyclical alternation has been replaced by the continual contraction of welfare, leading to its replacement by supervisory programmes aimed at pushing recipients into the low-wage labour slots (Peck, 2001), and the unleashing of a diligent and belligerent penal bureaucracy. The single oversight of the poor by the maternalist arm of the social state has been superseded by the *double regulation of poverty* through the paternalist action of restrictive 'workfare' and expansive 'prisonfare'.

I use Pierre Bourdieu's (1998 [1994], pp 35-63) concept of *bureaucratic field* (that is, the set of organisations that define and distribute public goods) to bring these developments in social policy and penal policy into a single analytic framework. This concept proposes that the very shape, perimeter and priorities of the state are at once an outcome, a terrain, and a stake of struggles; and it invites us to reconnect the many 'hands' of the state involved in the political production of inequality and marginality. It allows me to reveal that welfare revamped as workfare and the prison stripped of its rehabilitative pretension now form a single organisational mesh flung at the poor according to a gendered division of control: workfare handles the women and the children, and prisonfare handles their men – that is, the husbands, brothers and sons of these same women.

My contention here is that *welfare and criminal justice are two modalities of public policy towards the poor*, and so they must imperatively be analysed – and reformed – together. Recall, first, that poor relief and the penal prison have a shared historical origin: both were invented in the 'long 16th century' to corral vagrants detached from their social moorings by the passage from feudalism to capitalism and to teach them the ethics of wage work (Gieremek, 1991). Second, the social profile of public aid recipients and inmates (in terms of class, ethnicity, education, housing, family and medical history, exposure to violence, etc) is nearly identical, save for the gender inversion, as both are recruited from the same marginalised sectors of the unskilled working class – indeed, they belong to the same households trapped in the self-same urban neighbourhoods that are the primary targets of the new policy of 'double disciplining'.

Third, supervisory workfare and the neutralising prison are guided by the same philosophy of moral behaviourism and employ the same techniques of control, including stigma, surveillance, punitive restrictions and graduated sanctions to 'correct' the conduct of their clients. Workfare is run like a labour probation programme in which recipients must fulfil certain behavioural mandates to prove their will to work, even if there are no jobs or the jobs available do not allow them to support their families (Collins and Mayer, 2010). In some states, TANF (Temporary Assistance for Needy Families) recipients stand in line together with parolees to undergo their monthly drug tests to maintain eligibility for support. In others, parolees who fall into homelessness because they cannot find a job are returned to prison for failure to maintain a stable residence.

It is important to stress that, as the bureaucratic arm of the nation, the state can seek to remedy undesirable conditions and behaviours in three ways. It can 'socialise' them by tackling their roots in the collective organisation of society. It can 'medicalise' them by treating them as individual pathologies. Or it can 'penalise' them by ramping up its law enforcement agencies and directing them at problem populations. Think of the three ways of responding to homelessness: build low-income housing, offer mental health services or throw street derelicts in jail. Over the past three decades, as the homeless have become a fixture of big cities across the advanced societies, we have witnessed everywhere a drift from the social to the penal treatment of that question, with low-grade medicalisation and 'authoritarian therapeutism' acting as a buffer or way-station between the two (Bourgois and Schoenberg, 2009; Gowan, 2010).

I developed the concept of *prisonfare* by analogy with welfare, to designate the policy stream – encompassing categories, programmes and discourses – that confronts urban ills by rolling out the police, the courts, jails and prisons, and their extensions. These include probation and parole, which today supervise five million individuals in the US, in addition to the two million-plus under lock, but also the computerised diffusion of criminal databases, which cover some 30 million, and the schemes for profiling and surveillance they undergird (such as 'background checks' by employers and realtors, which have become prevalent and extend judicial sanctions far beyond prison walls and long after sentences have been served). Prisonfare also encompasses the tropes of justification and the whirling images of criminals diffused by scholars and politicians as by the cultural industries that trade on the fear of crime and feed a public culture of vituperation of felons (the urban crime segment on the nightly news, 'reality shows' like *Cops* and *America's Most Wanted*, and the round-the-clock ranting of Nancy Grace on CNN).

Note that, just as penalisation is not limited to incarceration, it similarly extends beyond prisonfare proper to include the deployment of social, educational, medical and other agencies of the welfare state, to the extent that they operate in both panoptic and punitive modes, with the goal of exerting disciplinary supervision over troubled categories and territories, rather than serving their needs. This is the case, for instance, when inner-city public schools are turned into fortresses that prioritise enforcing behavioural standards, fighting truancy and curbing youth delinquency, at the expense of their educational mission (Lyons and Drew, 2006).

Why have researchers of criminal justice, on the one hand, and welfare policy, on the other, paid no attention to each other's work? This mutual ignorance reflects the fact that most scholars accept their object of study as it is preconstructed in reality and prescribed by the concerns of state officials. But it is also an effect of institutional inertia and intellectual lag. The late 19th century witnessed the disjunction of the social question from the penal question, with the rise of trades unions and social work, on the one side, and the development of criminal courts and the correctional prison, on the other. As these two problems came to be treated by separate institutions, they were also studied by different academic disciplines, represented at the two technical poles by social service administration and criminology. But, with the break-up of the Fordist-Keynesian compact anchored by stable factory work and protective welfare, the end of the 20th century saw the renewed fusion and confusion of the social and the penal questions.

In short, the established definitions of 'social welfare' and 'criminal justice' are the products of a political and scholarly common sense that has been overtaken by historical reality. Nowadays, you cannot track penal policy without reckoning with social policy, and vice versa. You cannot understand trends in offending without factoring in the sea-changes in welfare provision, public housing, foster care and related state programmes, including the oversight of irregular migration (Brion et al, 2003), that set the life options of the populations most susceptible to street crime (as both perpetrators and victims). One illustration: on release, drug convicts are barred from living with their family if the latter rents an apartment in public housing or through 'Section 8' vouchers due to changes in welfare laws; interestingly, the same restriction does not apply to upper-class drug criminals returning to mansions subsidised by federal tax deductions for mortgage interest payments. Conversely, you cannot chart the peregrinations of welfare recipients if you ignore the fact that they are embedded in households and neighbourhoods involved by necessity in illicit activities and destabilised by the continual intrusion of the police and the prison (Black, 2010). How can inner-city residents achieve a modicum of social stability when one half of the local young men are exiled behind bars and the other half cannot find jobs because of the prevalence of criminal background checks (Clear, 2007)?

So much to say that the penal state has become a major engine of stratification, a continuing fount of social instability and a powerful cultural machine that has a decisive impact on the shape of the city and the fate of the poor. It truncates the options and twists the system of strategies of sustenance and mobility of the marginal fractions of the post-industrial working class like never before. No serious scholar of poverty and inequality can afford to overlook it. So I say, students of welfare and criminal justice unite, you have nothing to lose but your conceptual chains!

Crafting the neoliberal state

My third thesis is that the meshing of workfare and prisonfare contributes to the making of the neoliberal state. Economists have propounded a conception of neoliberalism that equates it with the rule of the 'free market' and the coming of 'small government' and, by and large, other social scientists have adopted that conception (Steger and Roy, 2010). The problem is that this conception captures the ideology of neoliberalism, not its reality. The comparative sociology of actually existing neoliberalism reveals that it involves everywhere the building of a *centaur state*, liberal at the top and paternalistic at the bottom. The neoliberal Leviathan practises *laissez faire et laissez passer* towards corporations and the upper class, at the level of the causes of inequality. But it is fiercely interventionist and authoritarian when it comes to dealing with the destructive consequences of economic deregulation for those at the lower end of the class and status spectrum. This is because the imposition of market discipline is not a smooth, self-propelling process: it meets with recalcitrance and triggers resistance; it translates into diffusing social instability and turbulence among the lower class; and it practically undermines the authority of the state. So it requires institutional contraptions that will anchor and support it, among them an enlarged and energetic penal institution (Wacquant, 2010a).

Against the 'thin' conception of neoliberalism deployed by economists, I propose a 'thick' sociological characterisation of neoliberalism that adds three components to market rule: supervisory workfare, an invasive police and prison apparatus and the cultural trope of 'personal responsibility' to glue them all together. *Punishing the poor* shows that, like supervisory workfare, the hypertrophic and hyperactive penal state erected by the US to contain the reverberations of social insecurity and project sovereignty is not a deviation from neoliberalism but one of its constituent ingredients. Moreover, the causal link between economic neoliberalisation and penal expansion is obvious as soon as you go international (Cavadino and Dignan, 2006; Wacquant, 2009b): it is not by chance that England vaulted to the rank of incarceration leader in Western Europe under Blair, while Chile, the initial real-life 'laboratory' of neoliberalism, claimed the title for South America.

The question that typically gets asked at this juncture is, are the policy changes that have produced this centaur state deliberate? This is a tricky question that would demand a long response: the short one is that all public policies result from a mix of leadership intention, bureaucratic groping, organisational slippage, practical trial-and-error and electoral profiteering. So there is political intent operating at multiple levels, but the overall shape of the neoliberal state is not subject to rational design – least of all in the US, due to the extreme fragmentation of its bureaucratic field. I emphatically reject the conspiratorial view of history that assigns the punitive turn to a deliberate 'plan' pursued by omniscient rulers, or derives it from the systemic necessities of some grand structure, whether it be capitalism, racism or panopticism. Against the demonic myth of the 'prison-industrial complex' (Davis, 2001), I demonstrate that the prison boom is not driven by the search for profit (private interests are a sideshow to punishment) and even less so by the exploitation of convict labour (how could that be with under 0.5 per cent of inmates employed by firms?), but contributes instead to a political project of state-crafting. Against the tentacular vision of punishment inspired by Foucault (1977 [1975]), I show that the deployment of the penal state is not ramifying throughout the social body capillary-style but is instead finely targeted on the stigmatised populations ensnared at the foot of the hierarchy of classes and places. Today, America's urban subproletariat lives in a 'punitive society', but its middle and upper classes certainly do not – and that applies to the black bourgeoisie, which, remarkably, has *benefited* from penal expansion (Wacquant, 2010b).

One of the great virtues of Bourdieu's concept of bureaucratic field here is that it forces us to drop the lazy notion that 'the state' is a coherent entity that acts as such to construe it as a splintered space of struggles over the selection, definition and treatment of 'social problems'. It is there to stress that the meshing of workfare and prisonfare is not the spawn of a malevolent design, but the result of the gradual and partial convergence of battles, waged toward as well as within the bureaucratic field, over three streams of government action relating to the low-wage labour market, public aid and criminal justice. Each of these arenas of contest has its own protagonists and stakes, but after the mid-1970s they have become interlinked by the facts that they concern the same despised clientele; that they are viewed through the same prism of moral behaviourism and racial stigma; and that the political institutions and civic culture of the country offer immense rewards for adopting similarly punitive attitudes towards welfare recipients and criminals, who are also prime recruits for degraded labour as well as living antonyms of the good citizen. But, like neoliberalism, the voracious penal Moloch grown by the US is not a preordained necessity. Other historical paths out of the turmoil of the 1960s were open, and remain open, but to locate them we must first elucidate the overall architecture of the institutional maze that contains them.

Another virtue of Bourdieu's (1998 [1994]) rethinking of the state is that it stresses its function as the 'central bank of symbolic power' and helps us grasp the ongoing campaign for law and order as a symbolic exhibition. Indeed, one of the challenges of *Punishing the poor* is to overcome the ritual opposition between materialist approaches, descended from Karl Marx (and Friedrich Engels, who never gets his rightful due as a social analyst of marginality and the law), and symbolic approaches, inspired by Émile Durkheim. The former, exemplified by Rusche and Kirchheimer's (2003 [1939]) *Punishment and social structure*, see welfare and criminal justice as instruments for class control, while the latter, well represented by Kai Erikson's (1966) *Wayward puritans,* construe them as vehicles for sending messages, communicating norms and binding communities. In fact, the penal state is multilayered and complex enough an institution to operate in both registers simultaneously or sequentially, so we must put an end to the hereditary hostility between these two visions and combine them as needed. The *forte* of Bourdieu's theories (1990 [1980]) on this front is precisely that they compel us to weave material and symbolic factors into an integrated analysis.

It is essential to heed the symbolic dimensions of punishment at a time when penal policy is increasingly driven by expressive considerations running amok and biased toward the lurid display of punitive action. Here I draw on the work of Linda Williams (1999) on 'the frenzy of the visible' in hard-core pornography to point out how policing and punishment have been recast into ritualised, repetitive and predictable figures arranged into a titillating *spectacle.* Crime fighting has mutated everywhere into a grotesque theatre of civic morality which elected officials use to stage their masculine fortitude and vituperate the 'undeserving' poor so as to shore up the deficit of legitimacy they suffer when they abandon the protective mission of the state on the social and economic front. Politicians advocate measures – like youth curfews, automatic life sentences for recidivists or chain gangs in striped uniforms – that are utterly worthless from the practical standpoint of crime reduction, so long as they are well-suited to venting vengeful sentiments and to dramatising the boundary between 'us', the law-abiding working families, and 'them', the loathsome underclass.

The feverish campaign to blacklist and banish sex offenders that I dissect in Chapter 7 of *Punishing the poor* is a sort of test case in that regard. It is incomprehensible from the standpoint of rational crime control adopted by mainstream criminology or in a logic of class control emphasised by the political economy of punishment. The diffusion of statutes like 'Megan's Law' (requiring the registration and public notification of the whereabouts of former sex offenders), just when the incidence of sexual crimes is dropping, makes no sense in terms of instrumental rationality: it wastes the scarce resources of criminal justice and it subjects ex-sex offenders to repeated humiliation, pushes them into clandestinity, and thus increases their likelihood of reoffending. But it makes good sense if you consider the emotional and cultural dimensions of such measures: treating sexual criminals like social trash to be incinerated displaces collective anxiety from jobs, the family and sexuality towards heinous law breakers, and it figuratively cements the moral unity of those who define themselves by contraposition to them. So there is a material underpinning to the symbolic game of sex offender castigation; but this semiotic safari, in turn, has concrete material consequences for government action, and both are interlaced into the remaking of the state.

It is important to stress that the rhetoric and policy of law and order are not a matter of 'repression' but, on the contrary, a question of 'production'. The pornographic theatre of law and order partakes of what Kenneth Burke (1966) calls a 'terministic screen': a ritualised cultural performance that deflects attention from the new social question of the early 21st century, namely, the generalisation of precarious labour and its manifold impacts on the life chances and life strategies of the post-industrial proletariat – what we might call the everyday predicament of the *precariat* in the polarising city.

To say that we must forsake the idiom of 'repression' to elucidate the contemporary permutations of penality is not a rhetorical turn of phrase. The tale of repression is part of the discursive fog that enshrouds the makeover of the means, ends and justifications of government action. The building of the penal apparatus is not about suppressing something that is already there; it is about producing new realities: new social types like the ghetto 'gang banger' and the roaming 'paedophile'; new bodies of knowledge as with the legend of 'broken windows theory' and the consultants in urban security that peddle it around the world; new government programmes, bureaucracies and rhetorics targeted on certain zones of the city and their inhabitants; and ultimately a different kind of state. The leftist militants who vituperate the 'punishment machine' on both sides of the Atlantic – denouncing the chimera of the 'prison-industrial complex' in the US and castigating a diabolical *programme sécuritaire* in France – sometimes appear to forget that crime fighting is but a convenient pretext and propitious platform for a broader redrawing of the perimeter of responsibility of the state operating simultaneously on the economic, social welfare and penal fronts.

Note

[1] This chapter presents the main arguments of my keynote address to the centennial meeting of the Deutsche Gesellschaft für Soziologie, Goethe Universität, Frankfurt am Main, Germany, 14 October.

References

Black, T. (2010) *When a heart turns rock solid: The lives of three Puerto Rican brothers on and off the streets*, New York: Vintage.

Bourdieu, P. (1990 [1980]) *The logic of practice*, Stanford, CA: Stanford University Press.

Bourdieu, P. (1998 [1994]) *Practical reasons: On the theory of action*, Stanford, CA: Stanford University Press.

Bourgois, P. and Schoenberg, J. (2009) *Righteous dopefiend*, Berkeley, CA: University of California Press.

Brion, F., Réa, A., Schaut, C. and Tixhon, A. (eds) *Mon délit? Mon origine. Criminalité et criminalisation de l'immigration*, Brussels: Éditions de Boeck-Université.

Burke, K. (1966) *Language as symbolic action: Essays on life, literature, and method*, Berkeley, CA: University of California Press.

Cavadino, M. and Dignan, J. (2006) *Penal systems: A comparative approach*, London: Sage Publications.

Clear, T.R. (2007) *Imprisoning communities: How mass incarceration makes disadvantaged neighborhoods worse*, New York: Oxford University Press.

Collins, J.L. and Mayer, V. (2010) *Both hands tied: Welfare reform and the race to the bottom in the low-wage labor market*, Chicago, IL: University of Chicago Press.

Davis, A. (2001) *The prison industrial complex*, Oakland, CA: AK Press.

Dodge, C.R. (ed) (1975) *A nation without prisons: Alternatives to incarceration*, Lexington, MA: Lexington Books.

Downes, D. (1993) *Contrasts in tolerance: Post-war penal policy in the Netherlands and England and Wales*, Oxford: Clarendon Press.

Erikson, K. (1966) *Wayward puritans: A study in the sociology of deviance*, New York: Wiley.

Ericson, R.V. and Haggerty, K.D. (1997) *Policing the risk society*, Toronto: University of Toronto Press.

Foucault, M. (1977 [1975]) *Discipline and punish: The birth of the prison*, New York: Random House.

Garland, D. (2001) *The culture of control: Crime and social order in contemporary society*, Oxford: Oxford University Press.

Gieremek, B. (1991) *Poverty: A history*, Cambridge: Basil Blackwell.

Gowan, T. (2010) *Hustlers, hobos, and backsliders: Homeless in San Francisco*, Minneapolis, MN: University of Minnesota Press.

Jobard, F. (2006) 'Sociologie politique de la "racaille"', in H. Lagrange and M. Oberti (eds) *Émeutes urbaines et protestations, une singularité française*, Paris: Presses de la FNSP.

Katz, M.B. (1989) *The undeserving poor: From the war on poverty to the war on welfare*, New York: Random.

Lacey, N. (2008) *The prisoners' dilemma: Political economy and punishment in contemporary democracies*, Cambridge: Cambridge University Press.

Lyons, W. and Drew. J. (2006) *Punishing schools: Fear and citizenship in American public education*, Ann Arbor, MI: University of Michigan Press.

Peck, J. (2001) *Workfare states*, New York: The Guilford Press.

Piven, F.F. and Cloward, R.A. (1993 [1971]) *Regulating the poor: The functions of public welfare*, New York: Vintage (expanded edition).

Rusche, G. and Kirchheimer, O. (2003 [1939]) *Punishment and social structure*, Piscataway, NJ: Transaction Press.

Snacken, S. (2010) 'Resisting punitiveness in Europe?', *Theoretical Criminology*, vol 14, no 3, pp 273-92.

Spierenburg, P. (1991) *The prison experience: Disciplinary institutions and their inmates in early modern Europe*, New Brunswick, NJ: Rutgers University Press.

Steger, M.B. and Roy, R.K. (2010) *Neoliberalism: A very short introduction*, New York: Oxford University Press.

van Campenhoudt, L. et al (eds) (2001) *Réponses à l'insécurité. Des discours aux pratiques*, Brussels: Éditions Labor.

Wacquant, L. (2008) *Urban outcasts: A comparative sociology of advanced marginality*, Cambridge: Polity Press.

Wacquant, L. (2009a) *Punishing the poor: The neoliberal government of social insecurity*, Durham, NC and London: Duke University Press. [German translation *Bestrafen der Armen. Zur neoliberalen Regierung der sozialen Unsicherheit*, Leverkusen: Barbara Budrich Verlag.]

Wacquant, L. (2009b) *Prisons of poverty*, Minneapolis, MN: University of Minnesota Press. [German translation of shorter version: *Elend hinter Gittern*, Konstanz: UVK Universitätsverlag Konstanz, 2000.]

Wacquant, L. (2010a) 'Crafting the neoliberal state: workfare, prisonfare and social insecurity', *Sociological Forum*, vol 25, no 2, pp 197–220. [German translation: 'Die neoliberale Staatskunst: "Workfare", "Prisonfare" und soziale Unsicherheit', *Das Argument* (Berlin), vol 281, Summer 2009, pp 479-92.]

Wacquant, L. (2010b) 'Class, race and hyperincarceration in revanchist America', *Daedalus*, vol 140, no 3, pp 74–90. [German translation forthcoming in R. Voigt (ed) *Staatsräson: Steht die Herrschaft über dem Recht?*, Stuttgard: Franz Steiner Verlag, 2011.]

Wacquant, L. (2011) *Deadly symbiosis: Race and the rise of the penal state*, Cambridge: Polity Press.

Williams, L. (1999) *Hard core: Power, pleasure, and the 'frenzy of the visible'*, Berkeley, CA: University of California Press (extended edition).

Index

Brighton and Hove Inspire project
161-6
'Broken Society'/'Broken Britain'
113-14
'broken windows' theory 26, 244
Brown, Gordon 114
Bruer, S. 91-2
bureaucracy 19, 90, 208-9
bureaucratic field 10, 53, 243, 248-51,
252-3
Burke, Kenneth 254
business 28, 32-3, 50, 228, 234

C

Caldeira, T.P.R. 201, 206
Cameron, David 114, 115
Campbell, John 3-4, 6, 11, 134, 146-7
Campenhoudt, L. van 247
capitalism
cycles of accumulation 89, 92-4, 133
and social relations 91-2
carceral social zones 180-1, 186-7
care system and welfare regimes 67
Carlen, Pat 154, 159
Castells, Manuel 185, 226
CCTV 26, 28, 220
'centaur state' 2, 6, 24, 31, 218, 252
Centre for Social Justice (CSJ) 113-14
Cheliotis, L.K. 5
Chesney-Lind, M. 5-6
Chevigny, P. 201
cities *see* urban space
citizenship and control 23-4, 200-1
civil society 200-1, 254-5
civilising and de-civilising processes 87-
8, 89-100, 218
and amoralism of capitalism 91-2
civilising offensives 89-91, 94-6, 98,
112, 119, 123-4, 247
and cycle of accumulation 89, 92-4
de-civilising process in ghetto and
banlieues 87, 95, 96-100, 103-4
gangs in violent context 229-34
moral panics and de-civilisation 95
Clarke, Kenneth 61
class *see* social classes
Clinton, Bill 43, 78
Cloward, Richard 248
Coalition government in UK 77, 78-9,
166
benefits reduction 115-17, 121-2, 153
cuts to urban programmes 121
Cobb, J. 88
coercion *see* control and coercion
Cohen, Stan 6-7
Coleman, R. 28, 32
collective action 187-90, 230-1

collective conscience and punishment
179
collective consciousness and ghetto 182
collective representation 123, 124,
175-6
weakening of 29, 109
Collier, Paul 226, 227, 229, 230, 233
colonialism and state-crafting 33
Comaroff, J. and J. 204, 205
community cohesion 26, 34
loss of attachment 102, 108-9, 182
see also social solidarity
community sentencing of women 160-
1, 166
conditional welfare 2, 24, 122, 123-4
'compassion' as justification 116-17
and prison system 23, 219, 248
see also workfare
conflict traps and violence 226-30, 234
Conservatives 61, 70-2, 75, 110, 113-14
see also Coalition government in UK
consumption 174-5, 184-5, 231-2
control and coercion
cities and social order 175
disorder and discipline 225
distribution in social spaces 31-3
expansion in Europe 247, 252
expansion to middle classes 31
fear of poor and carceral social zones
173-81, 223
and housing policy 26, 27, 110, 112,
116-17, 122, 222
and informal penal state-craft in Latin
America 196-7, 204-9, 210, 223-4
neoliberalism and role of state 1, 20,
42, 217-18
non-punitive liberalism 51-2, 245
and non-state actors 206-7, 222, 232,
233-4
panoptic control 23, 24-31, 220, 250
penal system and 'warehousing' 23
and phases of capitalism 93-4
social policy beyond the penal state
119-23, 124
violent conflict and excluded
communities 187-8, 226-30
police violence in Latin America
199-200, 206-7, 208, 223-4
women as recipients 151-2, 152-3
see also 'centaur state'; penal policy;
penal state; 'warehousing' approach
Corston Report (2007) 160-1, 166
council housing *see* social housing
'counter-publics' 132, 135, 147
Crawford, A. 27, 119-20
crime
control in schools 25-6, 32, 250
gangs and economy of ghetto 229-30

indolence *see* uselessness and punishment
inequality
  and gender relations 137-8
  increase and polarisation 20, 24, 177
    and persistence of poverty 226-7
    polarisation from below 185
  and paralegal practices in Latin America 205
  and sense of self 102-3
  and women offenders 161
  see also advanced marginality; social equality
informal economy *see* illegal economic networks
informal practices
  in Latin America 195-6, 196-7, 204-9, 210, 223-4
  non-state actors 206-7, 222, 232, 233-4
insecurity *see* uncertainty and insecurity
Inspire project (UK) 161-6
institutions
  institutional anomie and monetarisation 91
  and penal state thesis 66, 182-3
  and social sciences 53, 54
internment camps for migrants 23-4
interventionist state 19, 21, 63, 252
  civilising offensives 89-91, 94-6, 98, 112, 119, 123-4, 247
  historical context 75-6
  New Labour's policies 75, 76
  social equality in Finland 67, 68
  'Islamisation' perception in UK 109

J

Jessop, Bob 32
Jones, Martin 10
Juárez, Mexico 227-9, 234

K

Kant, Immanuel 177-8
Kelling, G.F. 26
Keynesianism 19, 20-1, 34, 51-2, 109-10
Kirchheimer, O. 179, 180, 253-4
knowledge *see* academic knowledge
Koskela, H. 28
Krieken, R. van 90

L

labour movements 25, 28, 29, 109
Lacey, Nicola 3, 4, 246
'laissez-faire' capitalism 34, 46, 218, 252
Landesco, J. 184
Lansley, S. 24
Latin America

neoliberal historical context 197-8, 252
penal state formation 195-211, 223-4, 244
  informal aspects 196-7, 204-9, 210, 223-4
  policy transfer 3, 4, 199-202, 202-4, 244
  political context 197-204
Law, A. 64
'law-and-order' approach in US
  demand and enforcement 220-1, 224-5
  policy transfer 3-4, 45, 78, 219, 244, 247
    Latin America 199-202, 202-4, 223-4
  urban policy and security state 26-7, 27-9, 32, 224
Lefebvre, Henri 175-6, 182, 183
'left hand'/'right hand' analogy 7, 68, 196
legislation in Latin America 201-2, 203-4
Lemke, T. 32
Liberal Democrats *see* Coalition government in UK
liberalism 47-8, 51-2, 63-4, 245
Linebaugh, Peter 9, 131, 133, 134
Lins, Paulo 223
Loader, Ian 11
local context
  and neoliberal punitiveness 4-5, 10-11, 62, 218-19
  women offenders 161-6
  and penal state formation in Latin America 196
  and welfare regimes 67-70
Local Housing Allowance (UK) 116, 122
location
  loss of attachment 102, 108-9, 182
  see also 'ghettos' and *banlieues*;
    territorial stigmatisation; urban space
lone mothers *see* single mothers
low-wage labour
  and hyper-ghettos 185
  and illicit economic activity 180, 184
  and Mexican *maquiladoras* 227-8
  disposable female labour 228-9, 234
  new panopticon 25, 26-7
  and 'precariat' 1-2, 255
  habituation 27, 31, 62, 99, 180, 187, 247, 248
  migrants as constituent part 23-4
  psycho-social effects 103

Williams, Linda 254
Wilson, J.Q. 26
women
 increases in prison population 5–6, 161
 as *maquiladora* labour 228–9, 234
 welfare and the penal state 151–67, 248–9
  complexity of issues 156–60, 166
  policy and reducing offending 160–1
  support programmes 161–6
 see also gender; mothers; teenage mothers
workfare 2, 20, 42
 and Coalition government in UK 122
 and 'compassion' 116–17
 historical basis in US 46, 109, 244
 link with penal system 22–3, 43, 99, 173, 220, 243–55, 248–51
 women as recipients 151–2, 152–3, 248–9
working classes
 exclusion from urban space 175
 habituation to low-wage labour 27, 31, 62, 99, 180, 187, 247, 248
 increase in 'precariat' 20
 lack of protection under neoliberalism 1–2
 loss of attachment 102, 108–9
 'poverty porn' representations 111–12, 117–18, 118–19, 124
 and racial history in US 44–5, 181, 244
 see also 'ghettos' and *banlieues*; low-wage labour
World Prison Briefing 202
Wouters, C. 102

X

Xenakis, S. 5

Y

Young, Iris Marion 139–40
Young, Jock 101, 103
young people
 and care systems in Europe 67
 as compliant labour 26–7
 discrimination and criminalisation 230
 expansion of policing and management of 27–8
 gender and denunciation of teenage mothers 136–8
 historical policy context in UK 75–6
 New Labour's social investment 73, 74
 and penal state thesis 76–9
 violent conflict with state forces 187–8

youth justice and penal state in UK 70, 71, 74–9, 220
 see also teenage mothers
Youngers, C. 203
youth services: expansion in UK 73

Z

Zedner, L. 158
'zero tolerance' policing agenda 244
 adoption and adaptation in UK 4, 43
 in Latin America 199–200, 206–7, 224
'zombie neoliberalism' 7